TWENTY-FIRST-CENTURY
ACCESS
SERVICES

On the Front Line of Academic Librarianship

Edited by

Michael J. Krasulski and Trevor A. Dawes

D1232476

Association of College and Research Libraries · 2013

The paper used in this publication meets the minimum requirements of American National Standard for information Sciences - Permanence of Paper for Printed Library Materials, ANSI Z39.48 - 1992

LIBRARY OF CONGRESS CATALOGING-IN-PUBLICATION DATA

21st century access services : on the frontline of academic librarianship / edited by Michael J. Krasulski and Trevor A. Dawes.

   pages   cm

  Includes bibliographical references and index.

  ISBN 978-0-8389-8666-0 (pbk. : alk. paper) 1. Academic libraries—Circulation and loans—United States. 2. Public services (Libraries)—United States. I. Krasulski, Michael J., Jr., editor of compilation. II. Dawes, Trevor A., editor of compilation. III. Title: Twenty-first century access services.

  Z675.U5A135 2013

  025.6—dc23

2013021583

Printed in the United States of America.

17 16 15 14 13   5 4 3 2

Cover design based on concept by Timothy Davidson

CONTENTS

FOREWORD

James G. Neal
**Vice President for Information Services and
University Librarian, Columbia University**

IN THE mid-1980s, serving as an assistant university librarian at Penn State, I recognized the need to bring together the essential but disparate services that enabled our students and faculty to obtain collections, make use of technologies and spaces or take advantage of services provided by the libraries. This early deployment of an access services department, in a largely predigital period, addressed the persistent and pressing importance of core user support. The "usability" of the academic library had entered the professional vocabulary, and a focus on "human" objectives, like user success, happiness, productivity, and impact, had become more fundamental to library mission.

And here we are thirty years later, still celebrating the centrality and critical importance of access services in an increasingly postdigital environment. This volume of essays captures so effectively the evolution and adaptability of access services. It defines the hybrid qualities that characterize the suite of services that have bridged analog and electronic content, physical and virtual space, and self-sufficient and radically collaborative and collective relationships among libraries. Scientists tell us that there are two types of extinction: *terminal extinction* is defined as the termination of a species with no descendants, while *phyletic extinction* is defined as one species evolving into another. Surely, the experience of the last three decades would posit access services as a remarkable example of organizational relevance and survival.

Access services reflects many of the strategic trends stimulating the advancement of the academic library. Rapidly shifting user behaviors and expectations indicate the importance of creating a customized and personal library experience. The persistence of redundant and inefficient library operations emphasize the value no of automating traditional workflows, but of creating new combinations among libraries to enable "discovery to delivery" success for users. The often aging and ineffective library service paradigms are competing with a range of alternative information providers, thus encouraging a heightened commitment to mutability, experimentation, and maverick approaches. The economic context means a renewed focus on productivity and assessment in the face of smaller budgets, less political support, and fierce vying for resources.

Access services helps us to see the potential for the positive scale and network effects of aggregation. Academic libraries are finally confronting the potential of the collective collection and a systemic approach to managing legacy print holdings. The spirit of openness allows for innovative support for the new majority learner, who brings an episodic, distant, and career-directed expectation to the academy. It enables responsive support for scholars working on multidisciplinary and multi-institutional teams and coping with the deformalism and destructuring of scholarship.

Access services interacts with all of our users: the students, where diversity abounds; the faculty, with expectations galore; the researchers and their tribal differences; the administration and the bottom line; the off-campus communities and their local politics; working professionals and visitors and their immediate and practical needs; alumni and donors who cannot be ignored; special populations with distinctive needs; and the world on the web that now wants to be connected and served.

Access services knows how to respond to user expectations and how to enhance the student and faculty experience. Users want more and better content, high-quality access, services that are convenient, new capabilities, the ability to be productive, to participate and interact, and to control their individual information environments. They want technology ubiquity, point-of-need information, no limitations of time, no lines, spaces for privacy, spaces to play and experiment, and a library that, on the one hand, is predictable and dependable and safe but, on the other hand, is flexible and adaptable.

It might be a testimonial to access services that, in the rhetoric of success for academic libraries, it often is not part of the presentation. New and innovative digital projects, major acquisitions of special collections, issues of copyright and information policy, newly renovated or constructed spaces, budget reductions—these are the topics that dominate the conversation. But as a library director over the last twenty-five years, I understand what really makes the library work.

Access services opens the library in the morning and secures it at night. It serves as our essential link to campus operations, like building maintenance, security, and food services. It oversees the quality and usability of library space. It manages our physical collections and connects us with often our largest library facility, which is in an offsite location. It circulates materials and technologies and supports the special facilities for distinctive formats, for group and class use, and for accessibility by print-disabled users. It supports teaching and learning through traditional and electronic reserves, enabling a strong presence for libraries in course management systems and online education. It is the front line of our consortial relationships, managing an expanding array of regional, national, and global interlibrary loan and document delivery services that support quality scholarship. It is the early warning system for building environmental issues and collection preservation and damage problems. It is the gatekeeper for the authorization and authentication of library users to the vast array of electronic resources we have leased and acquired. Access services is essential, fundamental, and pervasive. This timely volume, describing its evolution, affirming its present, and projecting its future roles and responsibilities, is a ratification of the continuity of the academic library and a validation of the centrality of access services to its success.

INTRODUCTION

Michael J. Krasulski

Assistant Professor of Information Science and Coordinator of Access Services, University of the Sciences, Philadelphia, PA

Trevor A. Dawes

Associate University Librarian, Washington University in St. Louis

ACCESS SERVICES is the administrative umbrella found in academic libraries where the circulation, reserves, interlibrary loan, stacks maintenance, and related functions typically reside. Access services functions are central to the daily operations of the academic library. Those unfamiliar with the development of access services may assume that access services departments have always been a part of the academic library. It is not an erroneous assumption, of course, since the functions that comprise access services have been a part of the academic library, in some instances, since at least the late nineteenth century. However, the first combined access services departments began to appear in academic libraries in the 1970s. Although the origins of access services as a concept are unclear, the creation of access services departments signaled an important shift in thinking about our interactions with our users. Users can come to the access services staff for assistance at any part of the access and retrieval process, from locating misshelved books to acquiring articles from international libraries.

Access services is a sum of many disparate parts, and its encompassed operations impact every user of the academic library. Several access services functions are unseen and often go unnoticed. This volume will explore how access services staff contribute vital functions within the academic library and the roles access services plays in the ever-evolving academic library. The services provided by access services departments in academic libraries to users (students, faculty, staff, and other members of the academic community) have continued to increase over the last few decades. In this monograph, the contributors will highlight the expanded roles of access services departments and discuss the role these services will continue to play in the success of the library, as well as the relevant knowledge, skills, and abilities needed for one to be successful in managing these areas. And in the process, we hope to fill a major void in the professional literature. Further, this work is geared toward access services practitioners as well as those curious about access services, including library and information science graduate students and faculty. This monograph may also be viewed as an independent study taught by a group of dedicated and experienced access services professionals.

The most significant contemporary look at access services was produced in 2005 by the Association of Research Libraries (ARL). In its second SPEC Kit on access services (the first was produced in 1991), ARL revealed a number of significant themes in libraries as they have moved from a circulation model of service to access services.[1] One theme that emerged from the SPEC Kit survey was that libraries are doing more with less. Library services are expanding, while staffing may not have kept pace with this expansion. Another trend is the flattening of library organizations. As academic libraries have reduced departmental organizational levels, the visibility of access services in the libraries' organizational scheme has been raised. Furthermore, many access services departments have taken on services that were traditionally in other departments. Examples include the staffing of general information desks, copyright clearance, computer labs, and group study room support, as well expanding opportunities for customer self-service functions. In turn, these changes have significantly influenced the staffing and reporting requirements of access services departments.

Another theme that emerged from the SPEC Kit survey was the increasing need of libraries to evaluate their services. This trend has led to increased assessment and benchmarking of all services, including those within the access services units. In addition to measuring traditional circulation and access services effectiveness, more recent assessment tools to measure the impact of access services are the ARL LibQual+ instrument and locally developed variants of this instrument.

There is no single definition of an access services department. Each library has organized and will continue to organize itself and evolve to meet local needs. However, many share a similar background, having been organized around traditional circulation services. Access services builds on this core set of services by adding combinations of related functions. The SPEC Kit themes were used as the building blocks for the development of this volume. As demonstrated by this volume, the roles of access services in academic libraries have expanded since 2005. In some ways, this volume can be seen as continuing the work begun in the 2005 SPEC Kit.

The editors also took a long look back through the historical literature on access services and its antecedents. We were immediately drawn to Harvey Brown and Humphrey Gambler Bousfield's 1933 work titled *Circulation Work in College and University Libraries*. *Circulation Work* was the first ever monograph on the topic. (About ten years earlier, a volume was written on circulation work in public libraries.) Brown and Bousfield were the first to consider the importance of circulation and its related activities to the success of the academic library. They predicted a glorious future for circulation. The administrative unit that oversaw circulation work, which they called the *loan department,* "should be the center of the activities of the library."[2] The terrific future envisioned by Brown and Bousfield never transpired, as evidenced by the summer 1957 issue of *Library Trends* titled "Current Trends in Circulation Services."[3] This issue attempted to explain the key roles of the circulation area in its broadest form, including reserves, interlibrary loan, and stacks management, to other academic library colleagues who had little interest, knowledge, or regard for these service areas.

This volume will not only demonstrate access services' value but also go beyond by defining access services' responsibilities and providing perspectives on how access services departments are evolving to provide additional services and place these services in the context of supporting the academic mission of the institutions of which the libraries are a part. Some of these new and expanding services include electronic reserves (e-reserves), increased cooperative and shared services, facilities management, assessment initiatives, e-book lending initiatives, and copyright management.

The book is organized into three parts. Part 1 examines circulation and stacks management, which are traditionally access services' core functions. Part 2 charts the new and sometimes unexplored territory toward which access services departments are moving. Part 3 looks at five special topics in access services. Chapter 7 examines the relationship between the library and access services, as well as the relationship between the academic institution and access services. Chapter 8 examines the structure of access services departments and utilizes a recent reorganization at Yale University as a case study. Chapter 9 demonstrates how the access services department contributes to the continued success of the academic library. Chapter 10 explains the importance of assessment and benchmarking access services functions. Chapter 11 discusses the resources necessary to remain current with access services and, to some extent, general academic library developments.

These sections are written by a group of contributors who bring a breadth of access services experience in a variety of academic libraries—from small liberal arts colleges to large research institutions. Each contributor was invited to contribute based upon his or her unique perspective on the latest developments and trends in access services. Our contributors are

- **Michael J. Krasulski,** co-editor, is Assistant Professor of Information Science and Coordinator of Access Services at University of the Sciences, Philadelphia. He was previously the Coordinator of Public Services at Philadelphia University. Michael is currently working on various research projects that he hopes will improve the status of access services librarians in the profession. Further, he has a variety of interests beyond academic librarianship, including genealogy, urban history, and Episcopal Church affairs. He earned his MSLIS from Drexel University and has an additional master's degree from Temple University. Michael is also an adjunct instructor in the MSLIS program at the iSchool at Drexel University.

- **Trevor A. Dawes,** co-editor, is an Associate University Librarian at Washington University in St. Louis. He was previously the Circulation Services Director at the Princeton University Library, and prior to that held several positions at the Columbia University Libraries in New York City. He has worked with staff in developing and providing training for various services, has written widely on access services topics in libraries, and has either planned or presented at various local, national, and international conferences on a variety of topics. Since 2006, Dawes has been an instructor in the MSLIS program at the iSchool at Drexel University. Dawes earned his MLS from Rutgers University, and has two additional master's degrees from Teachers College, Columbia University. He is an active member of the American Library Association and is the 2013–2014 president of the Association of College and Research Libraries.

- **Brice Austin** is Director of Circulation at the University of Colorado, Boulder, Libraries. He received his MLIS from the University of Denver in 2003, and also holds an MA in English literature from the University of Colorado, Boulder. He is the author of *Reserves, Electronic Reserves, and Copyright: The Past and the Future* (Haworth Information Press, 2005) and various articles dealing with access services–related topics. He is also the author of a collection of short stories, *The Afterlife Road* (Owl Canyon Press, 2012).

- **David W. Bottorff** is the Head of Collection Management for Regenstein Library at the University of Chicago Library. David has a master's degree in the humanities from the University of Chicago, as well as a master's degree in English literature from Brandeis University, and will be completing his master's degree in library and information science from the University of Illinois at Urbana-Champaign in the fall of 2013. David recently planned and oversaw a year-long reorganization of Regenstein Library's 4.5 million volumes and is happy to report that both the books and his sanity survived the process. He is interested in the impact of electronic monographs on the research practices and service needs of scholars in the humanities and social sciences and in bringing together physical and virtual services and spaces in ways that improve the user experience in academic libraries.

- **Thomas Bruno** is the Associate Director for Resource Sharing and Reserves at the Sterling Memorial and Bass Libraries at Yale University. He received his master's degree in library and information science from Simmons College and has a BA in ancient Greek and Latin from Boston University. In another life, Tom wanted to be an astronaut, and he eagerly looks forward to filling his first interplanetary interlibrary loan request.

- **Nora Dethloff** is Assistant Head of Information and Access Services, University of Houston. She received her MLIS from Kent State University and also holds an MFA in English and creative writing from the University of Notre Dame. Nora's research interests include process improvement, management, and user experience design. She has presented on trends and technology in access services and electronic interlibrary loan, and her work has appeared in the *Journal of Access Services* and *New Library World.*

- **Katherine Furlong** is Director, Access and Technical Services at Lafayette College, where she also served as project manager for Lafayette's $22 million expansion and renovation of Skillman Library. Previous professional positions include Instruction Coordinator and Reference Librarian at Gettysburg College and User Education/Electronic Resources Librarian at the University of Maine at Farmington. Katherine holds an MLIS from the University of Pittsburgh and has participated in the Frye Leadership Institute (2011), the ACRL/Harvard Leadership Institute (2006), and the Institute for Information Literacy.

- **Karen Glover** is the Access Services Librarian, Assistant Department Head, and Library Service Desk Manager at the Georgia Tech Library. She earned her MLIS at Florida State University in 2004. She is a strong supporter of the circulation and access services field, in which she has worked for over twenty years, and is the creator and coordinator of the Access Services Conference, an annual event started in 2009. She also presents and publishes on the topic of libraries and popular culture and is the author of the *Pez Librarian* blog.[4]

- **David K. Larsen** is Head of Access Services and Assessment at the University of Chicago Library. He received his master's degree in library and information science from the University of Illinois, and he also holds a PhD in American religious history from the University of Chicago Divinity School. His responsibilities include oversight of library assessment, document delivery services, library privileges, campus ID carding, circulation at Regenstein Library, and access services at the Mansueto Library (an automated storage and retrieval library).

- **David McCaslin** is Head of Access and Fulfillment Services at California Institute of Technology. He received his MLIS from the University of Pittsburgh. Previously he worked at Yale University and the Pennsylvania State University libraries. David enjoys academic librarianship and believes at the heart of any successful university is an excellent university library. In David's spare time, he enjoys traveling with his wife and golf.

- **Paul Sharpe** is Head of Access Services at the University of Missouri–St. Louis. He earned his master's degree in library and information science from the University of Denver in 2003.

Previously he worked at the University of Houston and the University of Denver. In 2012 he was named editor-in-chief of the *Journal of Access Services.*

- **Stephanie Atkins Sharpe** earned her master's degree in library and information science from the University of Illinois at Urbana-Champaign in 1999. She worked at Ball State University and the University of Illinois at Urbana-Champaign before becoming the Head of Access at Washington University in St. Louis in 2007. Stephanie is the "stereotypical" librarian in that she loves books and cats, but she has also completed nine marathons and will probably continue the insanity until her legs fall off.

- **Brad Warren** is Director of Access Services at Yale University's Sterling Memorial and Bass Libraries, Yale's main research and undergraduate libraries. He also has responsibilities for the development of access services programs across the Yale University library system. He has been at Yale University since 2009, with previous positions at North Carolina State University and UNC Charlotte. He earned his master's degree in library and information science from Indiana University.

Finally the editors would like to thank those who played a part in making this monograph possible. First we would like to thank Kathryn Deiss at ACRL, our publisher, for all her support and her flexibility. Without her patience and guiding hand, this project would never have been completed. Second, we would like to thank James Neal for taking the time to write the foreword. Third, we thank our respective partners who have endured long hours of hearing about libraries and access services. Fourth, we thank our respective access services staffs for their patience and understanding throughout this project. Fifth we would like to acknowledge specifically those who have directly shaped our views on librarianship and specifically on access services. For Trevor, these include Dr. Tyrone Cannon, Curtis Kendrick, Mayra Melendez, Shawn Calhoun, Kimberly Sweetman, Cathy Von Elm, and all my Ivies+ access services colleagues (you know who you are, and I apologize for not listing all your names here); and for Mike, these include Steven Bell, Ken Garson, Dee Linke, Charles Myers, Penelope Myers, John Wiggins, and Ellen Wolk.

NOTES

1. Trevor Dawes, Kimberly Burke Sweetman, and Catherine Von Elm, *Access Services: SPEC Kit 290* (Washington DC.: ARL, 2005); Virginia Steel, *Access Services: Organization and Management: SPEC Kit 179* (Washington, DC: ARL, 1991), 5.
2. Charles Harvey Brown and Humphrey Gambler Bousfield, *Circulation Work in College and University Libraries* (Chicago: ALA, 1933), 11.
3. Wayne S. Yenawine, ed., "Current Trends in Circulation Services," special issue, *Library Trends* 6, no. 1 (Summer 1957).
4. Karen Glover, "Home," Pez Librarian, http://pezlibrarian.com/ (accessed 11 Jan 2013).

BIBLIOGRAPHY

Brown, Charles Harvey, and H. G. Bousfield. *Circulation Work in College and University Libraries.* Chicago: American Library Association, 1933.

Dawes, Trevor A., Kimberly Burke Sweetman, and Catherine Von Elm. *Access Services: SPEC Kit 290.* Washington DC: Association of Research Libraries, 2005.

Glover, Karen. "Home." *Pez Librarian,* accessed 11 Jan 2013, http://pezlibrarian.com/.

Yenawine, Wayne S., ed. "Current Trends in Circulation Services." Special issue, *Library Trends* 6, no. 1 (1957).

PART 1

CORE ACCESS SERVICES

Circulation

Karen Glover

Access Services Librarian, Assistant Department Head, and Library Service Desk Manager, Georgia Tech Library

THE WORD *circulation*, in its most basic definition, means "passage or transmission from person to person or place to place."[1] Libraries generally define circulation as both passage of and access to materials. Determining who will receive access and how they will receive it is one of the core functions of any access services or circulation department. While the terms *circulation* and *access services* are somewhat interchangeable,[2] for this chapter, we consider circulation as just one function of an access services department. Within this chapter, *circulation* will refer merely to the loaning of materials both in person and remotely, as well as patron access and accountability. Figure 1.1 shows the average life cycle of the circulation of any item. This chapter will focus on only half of that life cycle, since stacks maintenance is deserving of its own unique chapter. As you can see from the figure, stacks maintenance plays a very important role in circulation services.

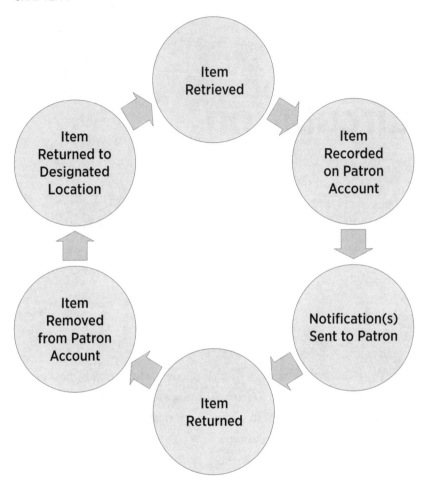

Figure 1.1
Circulation life cycle

One could argue that this life cycle is too simplistic a view for the modern academic library. However, there is nothing simple about holding individuals accountable for the items we are giving access to. Nor is it simple determining who you will allow access to those materials and what the parameters of that access will consist of. It's quite complicated and messy and is a source of continual discussion among access services and circulation professionals. The purpose of this chapter is to highlight different patron management policies and procedures that are common among academic libraries and the different service points that are used not only to physically circulate materials, but also for communication purposes as well.

Circulation, as a singular function of access services, is the passing of physical items between the library and the patron. As good stewards of the library, the circulation staff are responsible for recording to whom they are loaning items and for making sure the items return in a timely fashion—*timely* being relative to the policies of the particular institution. Because we need to connect a person with an item, management of our information is imperative for operating effectively. Circulation is heavily reliant on cataloging for the integrity of item records while also relying on whatever method is used to record patron information. Without adequate record keeping, our mission is a failure. Consistency and quality control are essential. Since access services staff generally have very little, if any, control over cataloging, our focus should be on the quality of our patron records and the consistency of our policies.

The primary function of any circulation department is to know where the physical collection is at all times. If an item is on the shelf, staff should know exactly where, and if it is loaned out, they should know to whom and when it is expected to be returned. In the past, these records were kept by hand and were prone to errors. Luckily, these circulation record-keeping functions are now automated, making the work of a circulation clerk or access services professional much easier.

The implementation of integrated library systems (ILS) has allowed access services the ability to move beyond simply recording circulation transactions to managing fines and providing e-mail notifications as well. It is easy to assume that, since the computer allows us to work more efficiently and does not have the element of human error; our records would have very few inaccuracies. However, most functions are still recorded by a human, and errors are inevitable. The ILS gives us automation but also allows for more complex policies. At present, most libraries are circulating materials in formats other than books—such as electronic reading devices and audiovisual materials—and the sophisticated library systems give us the flexibility to offer a myriad of policies depending on the type of patron as well as the type of item. The possibilities seem almost limitless, but this makes for more challenges when hiring and training individuals to work in circulation.

The complexity that these systems brought to circulation departments has created a need for the individuals working the front lines of a circulation operation both to be very tech-savvy and to know and understand all of the complex circulation policies. While those individuals might not set the policies, they represent the institution and sometimes must defend policies with which patrons may not agree. Individuals who represent the library must conduct themselves in a way that balances good service to the community and good service to the library. That balance is not always easy to achieve.

One could argue that circulation is the heart of access services, or even of the library. Just as the heart pumps the blood to all of the organs of the human body, the circulation area moves materials between the library and the patron in a circular pattern. If you cut off blood circulation, a limb will die. If you stop circulating to a certain group or groups, those connections die, so the art of policy making is imperative to the success of the library and an access services operation. Often, policies created in circulation must be thus followed in other areas, such as interlibrary loan, reserves, and stacks maintenance. You can have circulation without access services, but you would be hard-pressed to find access services without circulation. For this reason, we speculate that many institutions will use the term *circulation* when referring to access services. Whether the library uses the term *circulation* or *access services*, two primary functions exist: patron management and patron interaction.

PATRON MANAGEMENT

What Ann Catherine Paietta refers to, in *Access Services: a Handbook,* as "circulation control," or the management of circulation records, many academic libraries refer to as "patron management" since all circulation records have a patron record attached to them in some manner. Paietta stated that "the function of circulation control is to locate materials that are borrowed or are not in their proper location within the library through use of either a manual or an automated record keeping system" and thus "allows equal and efficient use of the materials."[3] We argue that this is more of an ideal than a reality for many circulation operations. In an academic environment, equality is not always important, nor encouraged, but equity is. Many faculty members reap the benefits of much more flexible and lenient policies than most other campus community members.

Patron management involves the policy making and record keeping so that circulation knows where items in the physical collection are at all times, when items are expected to be returned, and how to impose sanctions against those who do not return items in a timely fashion. For a library to successfully manage patron records, at least three considerations must be taken into account:

- Who are your borrowers?
- What are the policies for those borrowers?
- How are your borrower records created and maintained?

Borrowers

In academic libraries the terms *borrower* and *patron* are used interchangeably to describe those who use library services. This is particularly true in the access services since any patron borrowing materials from the library is a borrower. The concept of borrower is a bit nuanced in that the borrower is a patron who assumes the responsibility for a particular library item with the understanding that the item must be returned. Determining who a library's borrowers are is probably the most important function of patron management.

Primary Borrowers

In academic libraries, the primary group of borrowers is faculty, students, and staff. These are the very people who are at the core of any college or university. Primary borrowers can be further organized into subgroups, such as undergraduate or graduate students, visiting scholars, emeritus faculty, alumni, affiliates, or family members, among others. Institutions may have inclusive policies that lump all persons working for the institution into the same group or a tiered policy based on each borrower's need of library services: for example, faculty have longer borrowing privileges than undergraduate students. In either scenario, whether a person is, or qualifies as, a borrower depends on that person's current status at the institution. A borrower might be a former member of one of those groups, such as alumni or emeritus faculty. Those groups are usually given privileges that are markedly reduced from their privileges when they were current members of the institution.

Secondary Borrowers

Anyone not a primary borrower is a secondary borrower. Depending upon the institution, they could be referred to as "community borrowers, external users, guest borrowers, nonaffiliated users, permit patrons, secondary users, unaffiliated users, and visitors."[4] Whatever the terminology used, each institution and library must determine who is allowed to borrow materials and what type of verification or (in some cases) fee is required. Some institutions serve a large community and allow public borrowers, while others allow only patrons from peer academic communities outside of the primary patron groups to borrow. Over thirty years ago, an ARL study on secondary borrowers found that "because increased costs and declining budgets challenge libraries' abilities to meet institutional needs, any diversion of resources to services and materials for the outside community has become more difficult to justify."[5] The statement is still true today. Determining who outside the primary clientele to loan materials to is not an easy task, and some justification might be required by the institution.

Many academic institutions now have consortial agreements with peer institutions. There might be a combined catalog function and even a shared ILS. Consortial agreements allow users to borrow from another institution without needing to have direct ties to that institution, and they often receive a greater level of privileges than a community or guest borrower. Tight budgets and vast access to information have increased the desire to share our resources statewide and sometimes across state lines. A 2004 ALA study on reciprocal borrowing found that 50 percent of respondents "reported statewide reciprocal borrowing between all library types."[6] Anecdotal evidence suggests that this number has grown since 2004 and will likely continue to grow for the foreseeable future. This wide scope of potential users adds a level of complication when determining who should be borrowers: other institutions and their definitions of borrower.

Policies

Each borrowing group within the academic library will have its own associated borrowing policies. The policies can be simple or quite complex. There is no general rule as to what the policies should be, but libraries will often follow an unwritten standard by looking at the policies of peer institutions when creating their own policies.

Circulating Items

The most important policy is determining what can be borrowed from the library. Many institutions have collections that do not leave the building or are noncirculating. Circulation staff are often not responsible for developing these policies, but they are responsible for implementing them. It could be that certain borrower groups are not allowed to borrow certain types of items. For example, a faculty member might be allowed to borrow from a film collection, while a student would have to view the film in the library. Often, secondary borrowers, such as consortial borrowers, are limited to just general materials, and special items such as "digital cameras, laptops, and other AV equipment [are] restricted to faculty and/or student use."[7]

Loan Periods

Different borrower groups are given different lengths of time to use an item. Practices are far from universal. For example, at the Georgia Institute of Technology, an undergraduate student may borrow an item for twenty-eight days, while a graduate student utilizing the same item would have an entire semester.[8] Each institution sets loan periods based upon local need. The twenty-eight-day loan period is fairly common for undergraduate users, as are semester- or term-based loans for faculty. In some cases, faculty have indefinite loans. The type of item is also a consideration in determining loan periods. Shorter periods are used for formats such as film, maps, and e-readers and for restricted collections such as course reserves or reference. The policy for any user group can become quite complicated when adding different loan periods for different item types. The ILS is able to manage these various types of policies. For example Ex Libris's ILS product Voyager, which is used by many academic libraries including Georgia Institute of Technology, uses a "matrix" to create and maintain these complicated policies. While it is somewhat tedious, it is important to keep track (either on paper or electronically) of the policies for all of your borrowers and associated item types. Having that "matrix" will help answer many questions as well as inform the ILS. Some schools offer a matrix-like chart on their websites listing policies for patron groups. It is helpful information for the borrowers as well as circulation staff. Although different patrons have different needs and the nature of some materials may warrant shorter or longer circulation periods, every library should attempt to simplify circulation policies as much as possible in order to reduce patron—and staff—confusion.

Overdue Materials

In an ideal situation, patrons will return material on time without incident. In reality, circulation areas have to deal with overdue materials.

Libraries have a long history of using the threat of overdue fines to ensure that materials are returned in a timely manner. The rationale for fines is that if the borrower faces a monetary penalty, that is enough incentive to return the borrowed item on time. Fines may have developed as an incentive, but they have become punitive in many academic libraries. Many academic libraries began asking themselves "to fine or not to fine"[9] and began implementing very lenient policies regarding fines. A fine structure can get complicated if added to the policy matrix. Different borrowing groups and different item types have different associated fines. Some institutions have chosen to eliminate fines for primary borrowers, but still charge fines to secondary borrowers. Again, this policy is not universal and can differ dramatically across academic libraries. Mosley believed that when considering a fine policy change, the library should "consult with library, or even university level, financial officers" since it could be a "fiscal policy change."[10] This is another instance where policies are determined by a collaborative effort between circulation and other groups within the library and institution. Mosley also stated "library administrators and appropriate managers should work together to maintain some type of system that will encourage responsible use of materials."[11]

There may be a fear that if fines are eliminated, items will not be returned. Those libraries that have eliminated fines have developed administrative ways to ensure items are returned. For example, some academic libraries have instituted a lost-item charge as soon as the item becomes overdue. Whether this fee is waived upon return of the item varies by library. Others may prevent patrons from using library services, and still others have the ability to withhold grades or prevent registration for classes until overdue items are returned. Whatever method is used, when attempting to change "the role of the circulation staff from 'policy enforcer' to 'service provider'"[12] by creating more lenient fine policies, there must be a consequence for the failure to return materials, even if that consequence is merely inconvenience to the patron.

The primary function of the library is to provide information to the community it serves, not collections and billing. This is why it is not unusual for academic libraries to seek outside help when it comes to fines and billing. Some libraries will transfer all of the billing to the registrar or bursar of the institution while others will contract with collection agencies. The act of billing and collections is time-consuming and labor-intensive, and the library must determine if the return on investment is worth the drain on one of the library's most valuable resources: staff time.

Borrower Records

In the ILS environment, a patron record or account is created automatically utilizing the data from the campus's "people data management" system such as Blackboard, PeopleSoft, or Datatel. Records for primary borrowers are created and stored in the library patron database (within the ILS) and accessed upon checkout. Records for secondary users are generally created manually. Whichever method is used, the library needs to have a few very important pieces of information in order to create a patron record.

Patron Identification

Identification is the most important piece of information you will need to create a patron record. In academic libraries, the borrower's library card is usually the school-issued ID card. The school-issued ID card also serves as the primary form of identification when transacting library business. Institution-issued IDs will have identification numbers used for institutional record keeping, and the libraries often use that same ID number for patron records. These numbers are usually embedded in the ID cards as a barcode. These cards will also often give patron status information as well. If a school ID is not available, then another form of photo identification, such as a driver's license, is often acceptable. Some type of photo identification is usually required to borrow materials from libraries, though there are exceptions.

Patron Status

Determining the borrower group (often referred to as patron status) is not always an easy task. While automated records eliminate some of the confusion, it is a good idea to ask the patron his or her current status information—based on his or her affiliation with the institution—and have some way to verify that information. For example, if a student comes to the desk to check out an item and the circulation desk attendant needs to create a record, one might go into a registration system to verify that the student is currently enrolled. No system is flawless, so having a good understanding of who can borrow and how to verify a borrower's status is important to keeping accurate patron records. With the increase in electronic resource subscriptions and the licensing requirements of vendors, patron status verification is becoming even more important outside of circulation and access services. This information is shared in departments where access to journals and databases is granted. Some patrons may request a borrowing account merely to have access to electronic resources; therefore, having an accurate record of who is eligible to use the library's various resources is increasingly fundamental to library services as a whole.

Patron Contact Information

Contact information could include the patron's home address, campus address, e-mail, and telephone number, or any combination of the above. Today, e-mail has become the primary method of contact between the library and a borrower, although some libraries are increasingly contacting patrons regarding some matters via text or SMS messaging. A patron record must have current and accurate contact information in order to send notices and information about accounts to patrons.

Borrower Fees

For secondary borrowers, a fee might be required in order to obtain library access or borrowing privileges. For instance, an alumnus might need to pay an association fee, or a community borrower might need to pay an annual borrower fee. In some extreme cases, an external borrower might be asked to put a credit card on file in order to assure "the return of materials or collecting the outstanding debt if materials were not returned."[13]

All borrowers, whether primary or secondary, should be assured of the accuracy of the library's patron records. While errors will occasionally occur, circulation staff should strive to maintain records that are accurate and complete. Circulation staff can attempt to keep patron records sound by using quality control measures; having a second person check the patron record for accuracy is one example.

Proxy Borrowers

In academic libraries, it is not uncommon for faculty members to empower a graduate student, teaching assistant, or administrative assistant to borrow library materials on their behalf. Many libraries have developed a system for a faculty loan "by proxy," meaning a student or other designated person may borrow items for the faculty member, and the faculty member assumes responsibility for the materials borrowed. Many ILS offer proxy-borrowing capabilities that streamline this process. Written approval from the faculty member is usually required when requesting this service. Proxy service is often restricted to faculty members because this practice goes against a primary rule of most circulation operations: that loans are not transferrable. Privacy and confidentiality concerns when using this type of service make it important to restrict the information given to a proxy borrower, even if that person has permission from the faculty member.

Patron Confidentiality and Privacy

In addition to the accuracy of records, the library has a responsibility to maintain the privacy and confidentiality of patron records. The *American Library Association Guidelines for Developing a Library Privacy Policy* suggests that "the right to privacy is the right to open inquiry without having the subject of one's interest examined or scrutinized by others. Confidentiality exists when a library is in possession of personally identifiable information about users and keeps that information private on their behalf."[14] Essentially, the library must keep any piece of patron information or data, such as address, library activity, and other private information, confidential. Often circulation has the most access to private information and has a higher level of commitment to patron confidentiality than other areas of the library. However, it is the responsibility of the library as a whole to honor confidentiality policies.

It is not just a courtesy; in many cases it's the law to keep library records confidential. Forty-eight out of the fifty states have confidentiality laws on the books according to the American Library Association.[15] Academic libraries also have a responsibility to abide by the Family Educational Rights and Privacy Act (FERPA), which grants only parents the right to access confidential student records "until the child turns 18 years old or attends a school beyond the high school level."[16] Parents no longer have permission to access their children's library records once the children are enrolled in a college or university, and it is our responsibility to abide by this rule.

It is important to understand the confidentiality laws of your state or geographic region, but also the confidentiality policies of your institution. Remaining compliant and following institutional procedures for dealing with subpoenas or warrants is a necessity. It is also necessary to determine who has access to patron information and to limit access to those who have a direct need for that information.[17] This can be implemented by giving staff different levels of authorization such as, for example, not allowing student assistants to create or edit records. Many libraries choose to limit the information they store that can potentially cause a confidentiality issue. They do this by purging certain information from their databases on a regular basis. This information could be personal patron information as well as borrowing or transaction histories.

Whatever methods your library is using to secure patron information, a clearly written and distributed policy is a necessity. This is both to assure your patrons that you are protecting their privacy and to inform your staff of the policies they must follow. Having written procedures on what to do if served with a warrant or if dealing with a breach of policy will help guide staff during those, hopefully rare, situations.

PATRON INTERACTION

Patron interaction in circulation and access services can fall into one of two categories: in person or remote. Traditionally, in person has been the primary means of interacting between access services and patrons. However, with increased reliance on technology, access services staff no longer need to have a face-to-face conversation in order to provide a great—or (hopefully not) a poor—patron experience. While circulation has offered phone service for many, many years, the circulation desk and the US Postal Service were our primary methods of communication. Today, we offer a myriad of service points, including online records and instant messaging services. Some libraries are even introducing alternate reality games as a way to connect with their patrons. Whether you are offering the traditional at-desk service or an online remote service, it is important to maintain a service consistency that transfers to all methods of interactions. This book will go into further details about some of the service points mentioned here, but in this chapter we will highlight some of the most common points of patron interaction seen in circulation today.

In Person

Our in-person interactions can be seen as the most important interactions that you will have with patrons. Face-to-face service has always been a library's primary service point and where most efforts for customer service and availability lie. In addition to checking materials in and out, the traditional circulation desk is where you might find help looking for an item, help setting up a library account, help finding an item in the stacks, or just a referral for a good book. While all of these services still apply, the look and feel of the circulation desk has been changing quite dramatically in academic libraries. Electronic resources and the decline in circulation statistics are creating a shift in services offered at the circulation desk. Computer clusters offering sophisticated software packages and printing functionality have created a need for technical services that did not previously exist in circulation. In addition, the drive towards one-stop shopping in many academic libraries, in conjunction with library-as-place renovations, has opened the gates for combined service desks to eliminate patron confusion and streamline services offered. Combining reference and circulation is a current trend, and what was once the Circulation Desk is now the Library Service Desk, or ASK, or any of a variety of other titles.[18] What has remained the same is the expectation of service during normal hours of operation or being "staffed whenever the library is available to patrons for the circulation of materials."[19] This has changed pretty rapidly over the years. In academic libraries everywhere, 24/7 operations are popping up, and keeping up with the demands of service over a twenty-four-hour period is very labor-intensive. Some libraries will employ student assistants to work the overnight hours, while others offer full-time staff during every hour of operation. Either way, the expectation is there for service in person when the building is open to patrons.

Telecommunications

Offering telephone service at a circulation desk is standard in libraries. What is not standard is the array of services now offered via telephone, or how the telephone patron is triaged for service. Some operations see the in-person patron as the primary service point and will move the telephone patron to the back of the line. Other libraries will schedule a telephone operator to answer phone calls during a certain period of time in lieu of answering phone calls at the desk. Irrespective of the method, one thing is universal: the checking in and out of materials is not a service available via telephone. You cannot get 100 percent of the same service on the phone as you would in person. Most libraries will offer renewals, account information, and even bill paying over the phone, but compliance with patron privacy and confidentiality and solid record keeping prevent most libraries from offering checkout and checkin over the phone.

The proliferation of cellular phones and smartphone technologies is changing the way we look at service in the library. We are now focusing less on in-person interactions and more on applications and convenience to the patron. Circulation operations are no different, and we are implementing ways to communicate with our patrons without the need for face-to-face or even voice-to-voice moments. Many libraries are now offering a wide variety of types of self-service via the telephone. Patrons may now receive text messages for courtesy notices, overdue notices, and hold/pickup notices; the libraries at Virginia Tech provide us with one example.[20] While this type of service is not standard at this time, it is very possible that it will be soon. Most ILSs now offers SMS options within the software to enable such text messaging services to patrons.

Online Services

Most circulation operations now offer online services. These services are varied and somewhat limited in scope. The very basic service a circulation department can offer is account access via the web. Libraries now offer book renewals and bill paying online via the web. There are still many limitations to what some circulation departments feel comfortable allowing over the web. Bill paying is far from universal, as financial transactions are often complicated and controlled on an institutional level. Some renewals, such as reserves or audiovisual equipment, are not allowable online. Often, once an item is overdue, it is no longer eligible for online renewals. These limitations can force users into having in-person interactions, making online services just a supplementary service.

It is important that, although you may not offer all services online, your online presence represent your library and your department in a positive light. Negative experiences online are just as bad for business as negative experiences in person.

Libraries are now using their online presence to house and display circulation policies and procedures. For most libraries, their website is now the primary location and communication vehicle for this type of information, and keeping it updated and accurate is an added essential function of a circulation department.

E-mail

E-mail has become the primary means for communication with patrons, outside of in-person interactions. E-mail is not used just for circulation notifications such as overdue notes and billing notices, but also for primary communication with patrons. Some patrons prefer to e-mail a complaint or comment to the appropriate person instead of coming in person or even calling on the telephone. We now have an electronic "paper trail" that we can use when dealing with patrons' concerns that we did not have previously. We also have the ability to bring multiple individuals into conversations with ease, where it would be a great inconvenience using other methods of communication. Additionally, it's virtually free. We no longer need to pay postage fees or copy supplies to correspond with our patrons. And automation means that our e-mails can be sent with the click of a button, where traditional mail required more staff time to process.

Self-Check

As libraries are combining service points and reducing workforce, the desire for more automated services are common in academic libraries. Many are now offering self-check machines to allow patrons to check out books, as well as videos and other specialized types of items, without staff involvement. Ideally, the patron uses self-check without the need to speak to circulation staff. However, many libraries that implement these machines find that staff interaction is often still necessary, and it is recommended that these machines be located near the circulation desk or in proximity to some other point of service.[21]

Other Interactions

The service points mentioned above are in no way exhaustive. There are many opportunities to interact with our patrons not listed here. Each circulation or access services department will find communication and service points that serve its community best. However, it is important to understand the changing nature of communications and to keep up with the needs and desires of your community by implementing services that they have requested—and sometimes, innovative services that they didn't even know they wanted, but love.

CONCLUSION

While technologies have drastically changed how a circulation department operates, what has remained the same is the need for outstanding patron management and patron interactions. As long as we know where everything is located, our records are accurate, and we are providing a good customer experience, no matter the service point, we can have a successful circulation operation.

NOTES

1. *Merriam-Webster Online*, s.v. "circulation," accessed February 1, 2013, http://www.merriam-webster.com/dictionary/circulation.
2. Trevor Dawes, Kimberly Burke Sweetman, and Catherine Von Elm, *Access Services: SPEC Kit 290* (Washington DC.: ARL, 2005), 11–14.

3. Ann Catherine Paietta, *Access Services: A Handbook* (Jefferson, NC: McFarland, 1991), 8.

4. William H. Weare and Matthew Stevenson, "Circulation Policies for External Users: A Comparative Study of Public Urban Research Institutions," *Journal of Access Services* 9, no. 3 (2012): 112.

5. *External User Services: SPEC Kit 73* (Washington, DC: ARL, 1981), [1].

6. Dennis Davis, "Reciprocal Borrowing Arrangements Widespread," *American Libraries* 36, no. 1 (January 2005): 26.

7. Weare and Stevenson, "Circulation Policies for External Users," 123.

8. "Graduate and Undergraduate Borrowing Privileges," Georgia Tech Library, accessed February 1, 2013, http://www.library.gatech.edu/services/borrow/students.php.

9. Pixey Anne Mosley, "Moving Away from Overdue Fines: One Academic Library's New Direction," *Journal of Access Services* 2, no. 1 (2004): 11–21.

10. Ibid., 13.

11. Ibid., 14.

12. Eric Rupp, Kimberly Sweetman, and David Perry, "Updating Circulation Policy for the 21st Century," *Journal of Access Services* 7, no. 3 (2010): 162.

13. Metta Nicewarner and Matthew Simon, "Achieving Community Borrower Compliance with an Urban University Library's Circulation Policies: One University's Solution," *Journal of Academic Librarianship* 22, no. 6 (November 1996): 437.

14. ALA Intellectual Freedom Committee, *American Library Association Guidelines for Developing a Library Privacy Policy* (Chicago: ALA, August 2003), http://www.ala.org/offices/oif/iftoolkits/toolkitsprivacy/libraryprivacy.

15. "State Privacy Laws regarding Library Records," ALA, accessed February 1, 2013, http://www.ala.org/offices/oif/ifgroups/stateifcchairs/stateifcinaction/stateprivacy.

16. "Federal Privacy Laws and Policies," in *Privacy Tool Kit*, ALA, accessed May 1, 2013, http://www.ala.org/offices/oif/iftoolkits/toolkitsprivacy/privacypolicy/privacypolicy.

17. Kathleen Fouty, "Online Patron Records and Privacy: Service vs. Security," *Journal of Academic Librarianship* 19, no. 5 (November 1993): 289–293.

18. Pamela S. Bradigan and Ruey L. Rodman, "Changing Services and Space at an Academic Library," *Journal of Access Services* 4, no. 3–4 (2006): 107–117.

19. Paietta, *Access Services,* 10.

20. "Circulation Notices via Text Message," Virginia Tech University Libraries, accessed February 1, 2013, http://www.lib.vt.edu/circ-reserve/notice-texting.html.

21. Pamela Soren Smith, "Self-Check: A Lesson in Mistaken Assumptions," *Computers in Libraries* 28, no. 2 (February 2008): 14–18.

BIBLIOGRAPHY

ALA Intellectual Freedom Committee. *American Library Association Guidelines for Developing a Library Privacy Policy.* Chicago: American Library Association, August 2003, http://www.ala.org/offices/oif/iftoolkits/toolkitsprivacy/libraryprivacy.

American Library Association. "Federal Privacy Laws and Policies," in *Privacy Tool Kit.* American Library Association, accessed May 1, 2013, http://www.ala.org/offices/oif/iftoolkits/toolkitsprivacy/privacypolicy/privacypolicy.

———. "State Privacy Laws Regarding Library Records." American Library Association, accessed February 1, 2013, http://www.ala.org/offices/oif/ifgroups/stateifcchairs/stateifcinaction/stateprivacy.

Association of Research Libraries. *External User Services: SPEC Kit 73.* Washington, DC: Association of Research Libraries, 1981.

Bradigan, Pamela S., and Ruey L. Rodman. "Changing Services and Space at an Academic Library." *Journal of Access Services* 4, no. 3–4 (2006): 107–117.

Davis, Dennis. "Reciprocal Borrowing Arrangements Widespread." *American Libraries* 36, no. 1 (January 2005): 26.

Dawes, Trevor A., Kimberly Burke Sweetman, and Catherine Von Elm. *Access Services: SPEC Kit 290.* Washington DC: Association of Research Libraries, 2005.

Fouty, Kathleen. "Online Patron Records and Privacy: Service vs. Security." *Journal of Academic Librarianship* 19, no. 5 (November 1993): 289–293.

Georgia Tech Library. "Graduate and Undergraduate Borrowing Privileges." Georgia Tech Library, accessed February 1, 2013, http://www.library.gatech.edu/services/borrow/students.php.

Mosley, Pixey Anne. "Moving Away from Overdue Fines: One Academic Library's New Direction." *Journal of Access Services* 2, no. 1 (2004): 11–21.

Nicewarner, Metta, and Matthew Simon. "Achieving Community Borrower Compliance with an Urban University Library's Circulation Policies: One University's Solution." *Journal of Academic Librarianship* 22, no. 6 (November 1996): 435–439.

Paietta, Ann Catherine. *Access Services: A Handbook.* Jefferson, NC: McFarland, 1991.

Rupp, Eric, Kimberly Sweetman, and David Perry. "Updating Circulation Policy for the 21st Century." *Journal of Access Services* 7, no. 3 (2010): 159–175.

Soren Smith, Pamela. "Self-Check: A Lesson in Mistaken Assumptions." *Computers in Libraries* 28, no. 2 (February 2008): 14–18.

Virginia Tech University Libraries. "Circulation Notices via Text Message." Virginia Tech University Libraries, accessed February 1, 2013, http://www.lib.vt.edu/circ-reserve/notice-texting.html.

Weare, William H., and Matthew Stevenson. "Circulation Policies for External Users: A Comparative Study of Public Urban Research Institutions." *Journal of Access Services* 9, no. 3 (July 2012): 111–133.

Stacks Management

David W. Bottorff

Head of Collection Management, Regenstein Library, University of Chicago

STACKS MANAGEMENT encompasses a wide range of tasks associated with storing, retrieving, and maintaining the physical collections of a library. Above all else, the mission of stacks management is to connect users with library materials and services as seamlessly as possible. Little has been written about stacks management in a formal sense, although much has been written over the years about various functions that fall under it.[1] This chapter will attempt to provide a broad overview of those functions, as well as a more holistic understanding of stacks management operations.

Shelving books and other library material, shelf reading to maintain call number order, searching for missing items, and shifting collections in order to create space for collection growth are all core elements of stacks management. Stacks management may also include paging items from library bookstacks or high-density storage and routing library materials between locations, as well as responsibility for signage and wayfinding tools that assist users in finding library materials. Stacks management staff need to draw on disciplines such as project management, process improvement, and inventory management in addition to traditional library skill sets to successfully address the diverse challenges of managing library collections.

Increasingly, stacks management also refers to the need to develop long-term strategies for the ongoing storage and preservation of the library's physical collections, including the transfer of materials from traditional shelving to high-density storage. Stacks management in this larger sense requires a greater degree of engagement with other units and staff within the library, as well as stakeholders across campus. In order to accomplish these strategic goals, stacks management staff need to actively monitor and analyze circulation patterns, collection growth, and physical space constraints, as well develop a broad understanding of the challenges and opportunities facing collection development and the library as a whole.

STACKS MANAGEMENT WITHIN THE ACADEMIC LIBRARY ORGANIZATION

Depending on various factors, including the size of a library's collections and its larger organizational structure, the various activities associated with stacks management may be distributed across multiple departments within a library, consolidated within an official stacks management department, or incorporated within the duties of an access services department. In general, the smaller the collection, the more likely that a single access services or circulation department will be responsible for stacks management. Conversely, the larger the collection, the more likely many if not all stacks management functions are to fall within a separate stacks management department. Throughout this chapter, we will refer to a stacks management department, irrespective of the size or organization of the unit.

Staffing Models and Training

A stacks management department may rely primarily on full-time employees, part-time (usually student) employees, or a combination of the two. Each staffing model has its strengths and weaknesses. Full-time staff members provide reliable, year-round coverage and less departmental turnover, but may suffer from burnout after years of shelving books for eight hours a day. The absence of a single full-time employee will also have a greater impact on service than that of a single part-time student employee, as students typically work only limited hours per week. Student employees typically don't suffer from burnout, but work fewer hours, work less predictable and reliable schedules, and must be replaced much more often. Many stacks management departments adopt a mixed staffing model in order to take advantage of the strengths of both models.

Whether full-time or part-time employees make up the majority of a stacks management department, training is crucial to the department's success. Standardized, documented training that incorporates ongoing performance assessment and quality control is vital in a work environment in which misplacing a book may result in its loss for days, weeks, or even years. Developing and updating a system of training can also be a valuable opportunity to review and revise procedures and to install a culture of continuous assessment and improvement.

Core Functions of Stacks Management

Regardless of organizational structure or staffing model, there are certain fundamental stacks management functions that all libraries must address. Although the functions vary, all are connected by the mission and values of stacks management to connect users with library materials and services. In order to fulfill that mission, all stacks management functions must balance the tension between the twin goals of accuracy and efficiency. Material must be processed accurately in order to prevent items being temporarily misplaced or even permanently lost, while at the same time workflows must be established to ensure materials are processed as quickly and efficiently as possible so that they can be placed into the hands of users.

Processing, Routing, and Shelving Library Material

All returned library items and in most cases new acquisitions must be scanned into a library's integrated library system (ILS) before being routed or shelved. This work may be done by circulation or stacks management staff. Items must then be sorted based on destination: items to be placed on hold for a patron, items to be routed to another library, items that need preservation treatment or cataloging work, and items that are ready to be shelved. Staff need to create workflows that prevent misrouting items, as this creates delays in making items available to users. This may include the use of colored routing slips, special routing shelves, or some other mechanism.

Once items are ready to be shelved, they are typically sorted onto shelves in a staff-only area and then booktrucks (heavy-duty carts with wheels) in increasing degrees of granularity (e.g., first by floor, then classification, finally into exact call number order).[2] Once that sorting has taken place, books are shelved. Rigorous training and quality control methods should be in place for staff who shelve items, particularly in large libraries, where a misshelved book may be missing for years. Some libraries may use more than one classification system (e.g., Library of Congress and Dewey), making training and quality control even more vital. A variety of training tools may be used, but ongoing quality control is just as vital—this can range from periodically testing or retraining staff to checking a statistically significant sample of books on each cart shelved to ensure ongoing accuracy.

Accuracy is only one side of the equation, however, as stacks management staff must ensure that library materials are returned to the shelves in a timely fashion. The standard measurement of shelving efficiency is referred to as *turnaround*—defined as the time between when an item is returned to stacks management and when it has been reshelved. This can be measured in various ways, depending upon specific workflows, but a good rule of thumb is that turnaround time should not exceed twenty-four to forty-eight hours under normal circumstances. Stacks management staff must keep a close eye on staffing levels, circulation patterns, and the efficiency of the shelving process to successfully manage turnaround.

Shelf Reading and Inventory Control

Once library material has been returned to the shelves or other storage location, it is also the responsibility of the stacks management department to ensure that all items are in their proper location and none are missing. This is particularly true of open stacks, where browsing may be heavy. Shelf reading—checking that each item is in proper call number order—is a time-consuming but vital aspect of stacks management, as a misshelved book is as inaccessible to users as if it were permanently lost or damaged beyond repair. Staff may also look for items with misprinted or missing call number labels, items in need of preservation, and other errors. Books should be straightened on the shelves and provided with bookends to prevent damage. A print or electronic shelf list may be used to determine if items are missing. Whatever the method, some means of capturing statistical data on the number and types of errors found should be integrated into the process.

Technology can be leveraged to make shelf reading and inventory control more powerful and efficient. By scanning books using a built-in ILS inventory control module or electronic shelf list, items can be checked not only for proper call number order, but for whether they have been properly checked in, have been declared missing, etc. Some systems even track the last time an item was scanned using an inventory control system, making it easier to track the library's actual holdings. Electronic solutions also usually capture at least some of the statistical data mentioned above.

Searching and Paging Services

While stacks management functions are all meant to serve our users, many of them do not result in direct interaction with those users. Searching for library materials on behalf of users is an obvious exception. Libraries may employ print or online forms that allow users to submit search requests for items they cannot find themselves, but most libraries also offer immediate assistance in locating items. Searching requires both technical and customer service expertise.

Search services may sometimes be assigned to a dedicated staff member, but all staff in stacks management should expect to search for library materials on behalf of users. Staff must be familiar with interpreting the item records in their library's ILS in order to determine if an item is likely in the process of being reshelved or already checked out to another user, or to generally determine the item's status. Staff should also develop a set of guidelines for searching for missing materials based on common shelving errors, such as reversing two numbers or letters in a call number, routing an item to the incorrect collection, etc. Search services staff will also need to track search requests and to capture statistics on the outcome of those requests.

In addition to these technical skills, staff need to develop good customer service skills in order to best assist users who are often working under deadlines and therefore stressed, upset, or frustrated by the time they encounter stacks management staff. As representatives of the library, search services staff need to develop strong communication skills, both written and oral, as well as customer service skills to de-escalate potential confrontations and provide users with a positive experience, regardless of whether the item requested is located.

Paging services are slightly different from search services. Where searching for an item assumes the user has tried and failed to locate it, paging assumes that staff are retrieving an item on behalf of a user, often in order to route it to another physical library building or to scan a chapter or article for electronic delivery. While the volume of requests is higher for paging services and the task of locating items generally easier, the skills needed are largely the same as those needed for search services.

Shifting and Space Management

Despite budgetary constraints and the increasing popularity of online resources and e-books, physical library collections continue to grow. This may seem like an obvious point, but managing collection growth is in fact one of the primary challenges of stacks management. Space constraints are a constant reality of today's libraries, especially as they are faced with pressure to convert space devoted to storing print collections to other uses, such as collaborative spaces for group study or technology-equipped classrooms. Moreover, collections do not grow at a uniform or constant rate, meaning that one must constantly shift through collections in order to adjust for the ebbs and flows of collection development in new or different areas.

As with all of stacks management, shifting requires accuracy and oversight to avoid mistakes. Shifting materials is time-consuming and, if done improperly, may cause materials to be placed out of order or for collections to run out of space, forcing time-consuming corrections to be made. The calculations involved are not complex: measure the space one has for a given collection, measure the library materials that make up the collection, and divide the latter by the former in order to calculate the fill rate. Measurements must be precise, however, and the shift itself must be carefully overseen in order to prevent errors.[3]

Accurately calculating fill rates become even more pressing when one takes into account the fact that the commonly accepted definition for the maximum working capacity of bookstacks is 85 percent.[4] Fill rates above 85 percent will cause problems for staff shelving materials, users in finding materials, and even staff attempting to preserve collections for future generations.[5] A crowded shelf is much more likely to cause damage to its books than one with a few precious inches of empty space.

When shifting collections, one must also attempt to take into account the aforementioned variability of collection growth. Data about recent collection growth, an understanding of the average size of various library items, and an awareness of the changing trends in scholarship at one's institution are all necessary to make shifting part of an effective stacks management strategy rather than merely a reaction to current space constraints. (See the strategic planning section below.)

Periodicals Management

While in some ways the management of periodicals (journals, magazines, newspapers, and other forms of serial titles) can be considered as a subset of the functions described above, it is worth discussing as a separate category. The latest issues of periodicals are often but not always shelved in a separate location or reading room in academic libraries and frequently do not circulate from that location. In some cases, they are shelved in the same location as the rest of their title. The most recent issues may or may not be assigned a record in the library's ILS.

Typically, periodicals will be assigned a set number of issues (usually based on the number published in a year or other span of time), after which staff will pull them from their current location and send them to be bound together into a single volume by a commercial binder, assigned an item record, and shelved with the rest of the title. In the case of some popular magazines and newspapers, particularly those for which a library subscribes to an electronic version, all but the most recent issues are discarded. The set number of issues varies greatly by title, so staff must develop efficient means of tracking when each title should be retrieved for binding. Once bound, periodicals may be either integrated into the larger collection or shelved separately. In the former case, periodicals will be shelved by call number; in the latter, alphabetically by title. Shelving periodicals by title can be particularly challenging both for staff and users, as periodicals frequently change titles over time, and users may be familiar with a title's colloquial abbreviation or initials rather than its official title, particularly in the sciences, as users familiar with *JAMA* (*Journal of the American Medical Association*) or *PNAS* (*Proceedings of the National Academy of Sciences*) may find themselves looking in quite the wrong place for a familiar title.

Periodical growth represents a special challenge to shifting physical collections, as space for growth should not be distributed evenly throughout a given title, but rather created at the end of the latest volume. Ide-ally, five years of growth should be allowed, which can be calculated by measuring the average width of the latest few volumes. Particularly in areas where space constraints are severe, staff must work to identify active periodicals only. In the past, one might do so by following a simple rubric such as assuming that any title whose latest volume was three or more years old was inactive. As the cancellation of print journals accelerates, however, these rubrics become less meaningful, and data mined directly from the ILS will be more accurate.

In some ways, the challenges associated with managing periodical growth are declining as libraries increasingly depend on electronic-only subscriptions. As this transition gains momentum, however, new chal-lenges emerge. As libraries continue to acquire print collections, space constraints may require librarians to make difficult decisions. Print journals may be transferred to remote or high-density storage or even dis-carded altogether. Stacks management staff may or may not be consulted in the development of criteria for transfer or withdrawal (see below), but will almost always be called upon to assist in the physical removal of print materials and the resulting shifting required to distribute growth space to where it is needed.

Signage and Wayfinding

Although signage and wayfinding should be thought of holistically for an entire library, stacks management staff are often specifically responsible for maintaining the signage at the ends of ranges of shelving indicating the first and last call number or each row. These signs should be updated whenever the collections shift and should be designed to be as legible as possible.

Stacks management staff may also be directly responsible for maps that aid users in finding collections, or at least be expected to com-municate changes or the need for updates. Some libraries have recently implemented interactive online maps that highlight for users the exact location of an item within a building, sometimes highlighting the specific row in which it is shelved. It typically falls to stacks management staff to maintain and update the underlying database of call number locations that power such tools—often a substantial commitment of staff resources. Libraries should carefully assess the need for and (if introduced) effectiveness and popularity of such services, given the budgetary and operational constraints under which most libraries function.

WORKING WITH OTHER LIBRARY UNITS

In addition to the above functions, stacks management staff are increasingly called upon to work with other library units either collaboratively or in a support role. Stacks management staff may work with preservation staff to monitor environmental controls, aid in disaster recovery efforts, and participate in disaster planning. Collection development staff and subject specialists may rely on stacks management staff for data regarding circulation patterns, collection growth, and other factors that impact collection development and management decisions. As many libraries move towards some form of high-density storage, the importance of working with other departments becomes even more critical. High-density storage represents the future of stacks management and as such, deserves a section of its own.

HIGH-DENSITY STORAGE

The history of libraries can in some ways be traced to the ever-present problem of *where to put the books*. Modern bookstacks were introduced in nineteenth-century libraries as a way of storing books more efficiently and in a smaller space than could be accommodated in a reading room. More recently, other solutions have been introduced to increase the number of books that can be stored within a given footprint—all various versions of *high-density storage*.

Compact Shelving

The first of these solutions introduced was *compact shelving*. Compact shelving relies on movable ranges of shelves that allow access to only one aisle at a time within a given unit and can be operated manually or automatically. Compact shelving represents an incremental change from traditional stacks, as it retains most of the characteristics of storing books on open shelving, including shelving by call number and allowing users unmediated access to browse materials, though it can represent challenges in terms of ongoing maintenance and service.

Remote Storage

A more recent form of high-density storage is sometimes referred to as *remote storage*, though the actual distance of these facilities from their home libraries varies greatly. Remote storage may be more properly be thought of as a form of high-density storage that relies on advances in technology to store and retrieve library materials more efficiently than open shelving—though it does so at the expense of users' ability to browse open shelves. Remote storage became increasingly popular starting in the 1980s, as libraries found it difficult to justify the construction of traditional library buildings.[6] Remote storage sorts and stores library materials by size and shape and tracks and retrieves them through a database linking the item's barcode to its physical storage location.

Early forms of remote storage are typically inexpensive warehouses containing several rows of 30-foot-tall shelving on which cardboard boxes or steel bins full of books are stored. Staff, consulting a database and relying on an elevated work platform (or cherry picker) to access the higher shelves, retrieve items requested by users or staff via the online catalog. In addition to greater space efficiency, remote storage generally allows for more precise environmental controls than traditional libraries, thereby creating a better long-term preservation environment for library materials.

Automated Storage and Retrieval Systems

Automated storage and retrieval (ASR) systems represent a further technological advancement in high-density storage. Relying on technology developed for commercial warehouses, ASR systems replace human searching of high-density storage shelves with robotically controlled cranes, which store and retrieve steel bins or modular shelving units within a steel rack framework. Similarly to other forms of high-density storage, ASR systems store library material by size and use a database to track individual items by barcode within the system. However, ASR systems have several key advantages over older forms of high-density storage.

Because the storage and retrieval of bins is performed by the system itself, rather than a human operator, ASR systems can be built at greater heights and densities than high-density storage that requires human access, and typically require one seventh the physical footprint of traditional bookstacks. ASR systems also require fewer staff to operate and can retrieve items much more quickly than traditional high-density storage. ASR systems can also be integrated almost seamlessly with library ILS and online catalogs, allowing user requests to be passed, without human mediation, directly to the system for retrieval, further reducing turnaround time.

Some ASR systems are built in a remote location from campus libraries and require staff to deliver the requested items to campus libraries via an internal or contracted shipping service. However, in order to take advantage of the rapid turnaround time and small footprint of ASR systems, many libraries are building them on campus, either as additions to other campus libraries or, as with the James B. Hunt Library at North Carolina State University, in place of traditional open shelving altogether. The advantages of on-campus locations cannot be overestimated. The Joe and Rika Mansueto Library at the University of Chicago Library, for example, boasts a turnaround time of five to ten minutes between user request and an item being placed on a hold shelf by staff. Because the ASR system is contained within a building adjoining the main campus library, users can literally browse the open shelves one minute and walk over to retrieve items from the ASR system the next.

Unique Challenges of Managing High-Density Storage Facilities

While all forms of high-density storage allow libraries to store more materials in a smaller space than traditional shelving, they also present challenges to stacks management that traditional shelving does not. Those challenges fall into three broad categories—maintenance, user education, and governance and regulation.

The first and most basic challenge of managing high-density storage facilities is one of maintenance. Simply put, all forms of high-density storage rely on either mechanical or electronic systems (or both); unlike traditional shelving, such systems require ongoing maintenance to keep them in operation. Libraries must ensure both that staff are properly trained to provide immediate troubleshooting and routine maintenance and, ideally, that a service contract is in place with the vendor of the high-density storage system in order to ensure smooth and continuous access to collections stored in high-density storage facilities.

Educating users about high-density storage is another key element of managing these facilities. Users must know how to operate compact shelving or how to place requests from remote or ASR systems. Users must also understand the time they should expect to wait for material to be retrieved, especially from remote facilities where that time may be measured in days rather than minutes or hours. Most importantly, users must be educated as to why a library is using high-density storage—its benefits as well as its limitations—and why the library cannot simply build another traditional library on campus (a question often posed by faculty). Since browsing the shelves is not possible with remote storage or ASR systems, libraries should also promote any online virtual browsing tools that may be integrated into the library OPAC or discovery tool.[7]

The final set of challenges that comes with managing a high-density storage facility is one of governance and regulation. High-density storage is almost always a system-wide solution, meaning that libraries that may otherwise function semi-independently must coordinate on questions of operational budgets, reporting structures, and oversight of collection growth within the new facility. Workflows for transferring materials to high-density storage must also be established. These issues are even more pronounced when libraries enter into "shared storage" models, in which a high-density storage facility stores material from multiple unconnected library systems.

Developing transfer criteria is another vital aspect of the governance and regulation of high-density storage. Under the hybrid model that most libraries adopt, some material remains in open shelving while other material is transferred to high-density storage. Various criteria can be used—circulation rates, publication dates, material type, or online availability. The specific criteria used vary greatly, but developing a transparent, documented, and uniform collection management policy—a clear statement of what those criteria are and how they should be implemented—creates a blueprint for moving forward, making the ongoing transfer of library materials a simpler task and reducing potential friction among librarians who feel high-density storage is appropriate for other collections but not for their own. Collection management policies are necessarily the work of many hands, but stacks management staff should advocate strongly for a seat at the table, since stacks management will be responsible for the implementation of those policies.

STRATEGIC PLANNING: FROM STACKS MANAGEMENT TO COLLECTION MANAGEMENT

As the preceding sections hopefully suggest, it is increasingly crucial for stacks management staff to think strategically and to develop both short-term and long-term plans for the management of the library collections of which we are stewards. To do so, we must engage actively and broadly with other units and the library as a whole and must advocate to be included in any long-term planning that impacts the library's collections. It is no longer enough to focus on the daily management of a collection or to respond to unanticipated collection growth by planning an ad hoc shift. Nor is it enough to consider the future only when moving into a new building or storage facility. Stacks management staff must embrace strategic planning and collaboration in an ongoing and active way in order to meet the current and future challenges facing library collections.

For some, this transition may be a painful one, especially in organizations where the purview of stacks management has traditionally been limited to the here and now. Some libraries, in fact, mindful of the new demands being placed on stacks management, have underscored this transition by using the term *collection management* to distinguish between the old and the new. Regardless of the term one uses, however, and regardless of whether one thinks of the transition to greater engagement and strategic planning as a mere shift in focus or a more fundamental transformation, the core mission of stacks management remains the same—placing library materials in the hands of users who need them today and helping preserve access to those same materials for generations of users to come.

NOTES

1. Formal definitions of stacks management are also few and far between. For one useful discussion, see Heather Evans and Gaye Sweeney, "Defining Stack Management," *Library Collections, Acquisitions, and Technical Services* 29, no. 1 (March 2005): 51–60.

2. Various forms of process improvement techniques may be brought to bear on stacks management functions. For a description of one such technique applied to shelving materials, see Nancy Kress, "Lean Thinking in Libraries: A Case Study on Improving Shelving Turnaround," *Journal of Access Services* 5, no. 1/2 (2007): 159–172.

3. If a particular subset of books, for example, measures 2,350 linear inches, and the shelving available measures 2,865 linear inches, the fill rate for that collection is 82 percent. Assuming each shelf is 35 inches long, one needs to leave 6.3 inches of empty space on each shelf. Leaving even 0.7 inch more per shelf would require

2,937.5 linear inches of shelving, meaning that the books need to occupy an additional two shelves. This kind of minor error can compound over the course of a large shift, resulting in a second shift in order to regain the space lost. For more on the dangers of cumulative rounding/shifting errors, see Elizabeth Chamberlain Habich, *Moving Library Collections: A Management Handbook* (Westport, CT: Greenwood, 1998), 9.

4. See Habich, *Moving Library Collections,* 27. Habich follows Keyes Metcalf in suggesting 86 percent as the maximum working capacity of bookstacks.

5. This figure is a moving target, however, as budgetary and physical constraints have forced libraries to store as many books as possible in aging buildings. In fact, the figure itself has been revised upward over the decades, as Kurth and Grim suggest 75 to 80 percent as maximum capacity in 1966, while Fortreide more recently (and grimly) suggests that 90 percent is "a bare minimum," while 80 percent is "adequate." See William H. Kurth and Ray W. Grim, *Moving a Library* (New York: Scarecrow, 1966), 111, and Steven Carl Fortreide, *Moving Your Library: Getting the Collection from Here to There* (Chicago: ALA, 2010), 43.

6. For a solid introduction to the history and issues surrounding high-density storage, see Danuta A. Nitecki and Curtis L. Kendrick, eds., *Library Off-Site Shelving: Guide for High-Density Facilities* (Englewood, NC: Libraries Unlimited, 2001).

7. Many library catalogs and discovery tools incorporate virtual shelf lists, allowing users to see all of their holdings in call number order, sometimes with cover illustrations. Other experiments, such as Harvard's Stack View, go even further by incorporating circulation data and even physical size. See "Stack View," Harvard Library Innovation Lab, http://librarylab.law.harvard.edu/blog/stack-view/.

BIBLIOGRAPHY

Evans, Heather, and Gaye Sweeney. "Defining Stack Management." *Library Collections, Acquisitions, and Technical Services* 29, no. 1 (March 2005): 51–60.

Fortreide, Steven Carl. *Moving Your Library: Getting the Collection from Here to There.* Chicago: American Library Association, 2010.

Habich, Elizabeth Chamberlain. *Moving Library Collections: A Management Handbook.* Westport, CT: Greenwood, 1998.

Kress, Nancy. "Lean Thinking in Libraries: A Case Study on Improving Shelving Turnaround." *Journal of Access Services* 5, no. 1/2 (2007): 159–172.

Kurth, William H., and Ray W. Grim. *Moving a Library.* New York: Scarecrow, 1966.

Nitecki, Danuta A., and Curtis L. Kendrick, eds. *Library Off-Site Shelving: Guide for High-Density Facilities.* Englewood, NC: Libraries Unlimited, 2001.

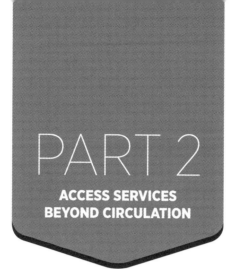

PART 2

ACCESS SERVICES BEYOND CIRCULATION

Interlibrary Loan and Document Delivery

Tom Bruno

Associate Director for Resource Sharing and Reserves,
Sterling and Bass Memorial Libraries, Yale University

INTRODUCTION

This chapter will explore several emerging trends in both interlibrary loan (ILL) and document delivery (DD) services. Some of these trends represent innovations on a local or regional level, while others are attempts by library vendors to incorporate features of the larger online world—such as real-time availability and smart fulfillment options—that we now take for granted as consumers. The silver lining to the fragmentation of ILL is that there is greater tolerance for experimentation, even at institutions that have been traditionally risk-averse. While no one of these potential solutions represents a "magic bullet" that will solve all of the problems facing the postmodern interlibrary loan manager, they should be considered elements in an ever-expanding toolkit for interlibrary loan practitioners.

HISTORY

For as long as there have been libraries, both interlibrary loan and document delivery have existed as well. The earliest recorded instance of interlibrary loan was between the city of Athens and the Great Library of Alexandria. During the reign of Ptolemy III in the third century BCE, the Alexandrians requested the loan of the collected tragedies of Euripides, Sophocles, and Aeschylus so that they might copy the plays and add them to their own burgeoning collection. Fearful that the Great Library, which was already infamous for its questionable collection development methods,[1] would fail to return such precious materials, the Athenians demanded fifteen silver talents—roughly the equivalent of six million US dollars—as security; the Alexandrian librarians kept the scrolls and forfeited the deposit.[2] Despite this ignominious start, the endeavor of interlibrary loan has evolved over the centuries as libraries continue to solve the basic problem of ensuring access to research materials for their own patrons while making their collections available to other libraries in return.

While ancient and medieval European libraries relied upon resource sharing as a means to cope with scarcity, modern interlibrary loan owes its origins, paradoxically enough, to the surpluses brought by industrialization and successive waves of disruptive technologies. From the introduction of paper and the advent of movable type to advances in transportation and communications, ILL has sought to maximize the benefits of innovation both within and without the library world. By the eighteenth and nineteen centuries, the emergence of national libraries in Europe made it possible to conceive of resource sharing on a statewide or even international scope. Although the United States has yet to follow suit in the establishment of its own national library, the American Library Association (founded in 1876) approved its first *Code of Practice for Interlibrary Loan* in 1919.[3]

Interlibrary loan in the twentieth century suffered from an ongoing identity crisis as the service tried to find its home amid the various branches of library services. Was it an outgrowth of reference, for example, or did it belong with access services? As the popularity of just-in-time acquisitions and purchase on demand continue to grow in the twenty-first century, it is entirely possible that interlibrary loan will find itself having more and more in common with collection management. Similarly, as document delivery increasingly finds itself utilized for the purpose of curriculum support, there is a blurring of the distinction between it and course reserves.

The 1980s and 1990s were a period of unprecedented integration for interlibrary loan operations in many research libraries. Robust collections budgets coupled with the enhanced automated discovery and request functionality provided by online catalogs resulted in a bonanza for large academic collections, which were able to capitalize on their statuses as "net lenders" to fund their operations entirely on a cost-recovery basis (and even squirrel money away in some cases). During this period, ILL departments took advantage of relatively straightforward systems of ful-fillment and economies of scale to enable resource sharing at a volume that was an order of magnitude greater than previous decades.

One could argue that the future of interlibrary loan turned on three major events at the turn of the twenty-first century: the growth of elec-tronic resources, which would consume a disproportionate amount of libraries' funds and introduce the problem of licensing into ILL and docu-ment delivery;[4] the Sonny Bono Copyright Term Extension Act of 1998,[5] which represented a shift in Congress's attitude towards the balance of competing rights between content providers and consumers (as well as a nascent hostility towards the proponents of fair use and the exercise of other rights and exemptions under US copyright law);[6] and the dot-com bust of 2000, during which time many colleges and universities found their acquisitions budgets slashed for the first time in years; although many institutions had recovered some of their lost wealth by the middle of the last decade, those gains were wiped out by the sustained economic downturn that followed starting in 2008.[7] Not only was the heyday of the "Big Lender" coming to a close, but the resource-sharing landscape that was emerging in the early years of the twenty-first century was radically different from that of just a few years before.

RESOURCE SHARING TODAY

Although OCLC continues to enhance its holdings, adding national union catalogs from all over the world to its indices, and new databases and discovery platforms are making more and more content known to academic library users, our ability to request such material has fragmented significantly. WorldCat Research Sharing (aka FirstSearch) remains an important tool for the borrowing and lending of library materials, but it is now supplemented by consortial borrowing/lending platforms, third-party article delivery services, pay per view, purchase on demand, and other ad hoc means of resource sharing such as Listservs, message boards, and peer-to-peer file sharing.[8] This multiplicity of modes of fulfillment presents a challenge to interlibrary loan staff as they learn how to transition from doing one thing with expertise to mastering a more nuanced and complicated skill set and obliges managers to work even harder to keep their departments ahead of the curve. Though it is a cliché, change is now the only constant for interlibrary loan and document delivery.

OCLC began as the Ohio College Library Center in 1967 as a cooperative computerized network for Ohio libraries. Since then it has grown into a worldwide tool for cataloging and resource sharing. Millions of interlibrary loan requests have been initiated using OCLC WorldCat Resource Sharing—approximately one every four seconds—from more than forty-six countries, with new libraries being added daily.[9] OCLC has also greatly facilitated the process of library-to-library payments for ILL and other services through its ILL Fee Management (or IFM) service, which eliminates the hassle of cutting and processing checks or dealing with foreign currency exchange rates. OCLC is the primary means for discovery, request, and fulfillment for ILL requests, although medical libraries in the United States continue to utilize the National Library of Medicine's DOCLINE service as an automated solution for sending and receiving article requests.

However, because OCLC depends on a massively decentralized base of participating libraries, each with its own levels of expertise with technology and local support, it is possible for even the best-researched interlibrary loan request to languish. As a result, consortial borrowing/lending arrangements have emerged in order to provide a much-needed fast track for many ILL or document delivery requests. While it would take much more than a chapter to enumerate the many different kinds of library consortia currently in place among academic and research libraries, we can categorize these arrangements into several broad classifications.

Local or regional consortia are the oldest of consortial borrowing/lending agreements. Not necessarily tied to a specific system or platform, they represent an agreement among the constituent libraries to prioritize one another's requests, often subsidizing retrieval, processing, and shipping costs as part of the bargain. An example of a large local or regional US consortium is Kudzu, which includes libraries from the Association of Southeastern Research Libraries (ASERL). Kudzu partners agree to provide expedited processing and delivery to each other without charging lending fees.[10] Although these consortia are optimized to provide faster and more reliable service for members, they still suffer from the same basic problems that libraries using WorldCat Resource Sharing experience, such as lack of real-time availability.

Shared or virtual catalogs solve the problem of real-time availability by collating or aggregating individual library holdings into a shared database, permitting discovery and requesting (often unmediated) across the entire consortium. The original version of OCLC is an example of a shared catalog; integrated discovery platforms, such as WorldCat Local ILL, are examples of virtual catalogs. Many public libraries, for example, now belong to a virtual catalog, as it greatly enhances the borrowing capabilities of its constituent library patrons and therefore the value of their local public library. By extension, college and university libraries can enjoy similar benefits by utilizing a shared catalog, which in effect greatly multiplies any one partner's collections.[11]

Several large academic library consortia have emerged in recent years as a response to shrinking collection development budgets and an explosion in scholarly publishing. Many of these consortial borrowing/lending operations utilize a third-party platform to enable discovery across partner libraries' catalogs and employ circulation interoperability standards such as NCIP[12] in order to effect real-time retrieval requests and holds between one institution's integrated library system and another. Two notable examples of consortial lending in North America are the CIC[13] and Borrow Direct.[14]

Despite the obvious advantage of consortial borrowing/lending arrangements, there are several major drawbacks to such arrangements. As discovery often takes place in a shared catalog or a separate third-party discovery platform, searching for library materials, which may be requested automatically through the consortium, can sometimes take place at the expense of local holdings.[15] Since consortial borrowing/lending operations often exist in isolation from traditional interlibrary loan or document delivery operations, patron expectations may not be adequately managed when transitioning from one service to another; by that same division of library services, library staff's ability to troubleshoot across the various services can also be impacted.

Finally, there is the issue of unintended consequences. A recent study of Borrow Direct data revealed that more than 50 percent of all requests initiated across the platform were for materials that the local library owned but were currently checked out, suggesting that consortial borrowing/lending arrangements are becoming a functional workaround to placing holds or recalls.[16] In fact, many libraries have already de-emphasized or even eliminated patron-initiated recalls in favor of consortial borrowing/lending arrangements. While the complementary advantages afforded by the various resource-sharing services have been rather intensively studied, this new supplementary use of consortial borrowing/lending agreements—as well as a detailed analysis of its hidden costs—is much less well understood. There is also the question of what impact sustained reliance on consortial borrowing/lending arrangements will have on local collection development, especially as acquisitions budgets continue to shrink or are increasingly devoted to purchasing digital content.

The Center for Research Libraries (CRL), based in Chicago, Illinois, puts a new twist on an age-old idea: that of the universal repository of knowledge. Founded in 1949, CRL is a subscription-based consortium of primary source and other library materials that would be otherwise onerous for any one library to collect or maintain—for example, portfolio volumes of newspapers, historical microfilm collections, or international theses and dissertations. CRL re-invests its subscription fees in acquiring and digitizing additional content, particularly from regions of the world that are historically underrepresented in academic research libraries, such as South Asia.[17]

2CUL, on the other hand, represents a more radical collaboration—an agreement between the libraries at Cornell and Columbia Universities encompassing not only reciprocal library privileges and resource sharing but cooperative collection development and shared staff as well. While partnerships such as 2CUL may well presage a future of academic librar-ies where strategic partnerships extend all the way down to the org-chart level, this particular experiment, though eagerly watched by many in the research library community, is still in its infancy.[18]

Document delivery has experienced an even greater degree of frag-mentation and disruption than interlibrary loan. As libraries have tran-sitioned from print subscriptions to digital resources, their ability to share content from these collections has been complicated by licensing terms that supersede the copyright exemptions afforded by Section 108 and CONTU guidelines, which allow for libraries to borrow up to five articles from the past five years of a given periodical without having to pay royalties to the publisher.[19] While some content providers allow for interlibrary loan of electronic resources, others impose cumbersome provisos, such as the need to print out the requested article, then deliver it via rescan, physical mail, or even fax.[20]

The speed of document delivery has improved dramatically over the past several years as digital fulfillment has come into its own. Whereas twenty-four-hour or even same-day electronic delivery was once the purview of expensive document provider services such as CISTI, ISI, or the British Library Document Supply Centre, the ability to purchase or lease content directly from publishers or receive copies through automated consortia has introduced additional options for the resource-sharing librarian. When to use which service instead of another has become a question of critical importance to academic research libraries, as stakeholders must consider the interrelationship of convenience, speed, copyright, and cost when making their decision.

Aside from the multiplicity of request options available in the realm of document delivery, there are also myriad fulfillment mechanisms from which to choose.[21] For more than a decade, Ariel, a product of Infotrieve, was the gold standard for electronic article delivery, but with the widespread adoption of the Odyssey protocol by libraries using ILLiad (as well as non-ILLiad libraries that utilized the Odyssey Standalone application offered for free by Atlas Systems) as their ILL management system, Ariel began to fall into relative disuse. While it has always been possible to e-mail articles directly from one requesting library to another, the problem of file sizes and library or university IT limits on attachments has precluded e-mail as a reliable method of delivery for most ILL operations. However, as campus e-mail services have grown more capable of handling the average file size for an interlibrary loan request and the default file type for electronic document delivery has changed over time from the bulky TIFF file to PDF, e-mail is a more viable option than before. At the same time, Internet "dropbox" services—which deliver content by storing files uploaded to password-protected servers hosted either locally or in the cloud—have emerged as an alternative to others means of electronic delivery.[22]

Many publishers now permit individual or institutional subscribers to purchase content directly from their websites, allowing on-demand access to many digital materials. While this is by any objective measure a boon, because vendor sites are rather cumbersome—often requiring separate login and registration and payment authorization for each item ordered—the process of purchasing said content can be extremely onerous from a workflow optimization perspective. To address this need, several commercial document delivery services have emerged as viable alternatives. Some of these—such as Canada's CISTI or the British Library Document Supply Centre—are adjuncts to existing resource-sharing services, making their collections available via rapid delivery for an additional charge. Others services, like the Copyright Clearance Center's "Get It Now," function as direct intermediaries between requesting libraries and participating publishers, delivering licensed digital content for a fee.[23] In the case of both types of service, a copyright fee is almost always included in the price of delivery. This means that even if the requesting library has not exceeded the "Rule of Five" per CONTU guidelines, it is still paying copyright fees in order to borrow this material. In the interest of exercising their fair use rights, many academic libraries have made a deliberate choice not to use such services except when they are already obligated to pay (i.e., for their sixth and subsequent requests from the same journal for that calendar year).

Another potentially interesting complication to commercial document delivery is the introduction of view-only digital content and expiring or "exploding" digital rights management on PDF articles. While these options for delivery can result in faster access or greater savings over individual purchases, it is unlikely that library patrons would want to request content that they could not save, print, or keep indefinitely. Since these features are already more common in European publishing, however, it is perhaps only a matter of time before they become the norm rather than the exception in North America as well—for better or for worse.[24]

One of the more trying aspects of interlibrary loan is the discovery and request of journal articles. Although electronic databases are making it easier and easier for researchers to find a citation and import it via OpenURL or similar means into an ILL request, the fulfillment process is still fundamentally limited by the level of completeness and accuracy of library serial holdings on OCLC and other shared catalogs, or sometimes in the library's own local catalog. Libraries that invest in exporting and sharing these holdings can benefit by taking advantage of automated request routing, saving time for both staff and patrons; when these holdings are expanded to include licensed electronic resources, the savings are multiplied.

DOCLINE, a service maintained by the National Library of Medicine, was an early pioneer in automated journal article fulfillment. Participating medical libraries upload their holdings into a shared catalog called SERHOLD, from which the DOCLINE system randomly selects a potential library supplier.[25] Despite the obvious advantages of such an arrangement, nonmedical libraries lacked an equivalent service until the development of RapidILL in 1997. Not only does RapidILL utilize a shared database of serial holdings like DOCLINE, but RapidILL members agree to provide article requests within an expedited time frame.[26] OCLC has since developed its own forms of automation for ILL requests and fulfillment. The Direct Request protocol, which allowed libraries to process loan requests without staff mediation, was expanded to include journals and electronic resources. In order to take advantage of this additional functionality, however, libraries must opt in by contributing their own serial and digital holdings.[27]

This has led to a negative feedback loop by which libraries that do not share their holdings are increasingly bypassed in favor of libraries that have opted in: for libraries that have historically depended on their net-lender status in order recover costs or fund other operations, the lack of investment in maintaining current serials holdings on OCLC is now yielding disastrous returns. Not only are these libraries not able to utilize Direct Request functionality for articles and electronic resources to reduce processing time for staff and waiting time for patrons, but they are receiving fewer ILL requests, and therefore less lending revenue if they charge money for providing interlibrary loan services.

THE FUTURE OF RESOURCE SHARING

Where do we go from here? It is clear that the traditional models of interlibrary loan and document delivery as they evolved over the latter half of the twentieth century are under tremendous pressure from a host of internal and external developments. Interlibrary loan librarians are obliged not only to keep abreast of changes in library automation, but also to anticipate changes in scholarly publishing and intellectual property law as well. This strategic view is made all the more complex by the fact that no one library operates in a vacuum—while this is true for any aspect of academic librarianship, it is especially true for resource sharing, where decisions made by a library halfway across the world can have a dramatic effect on one's own local operations.

Several shared or virtual catalogs have already featured real-time availability in their discovery and request fulfillment mechanisms. As interoperability standards for circulation and interlibrary loan permit greater transparency and automation across library catalogs, vendors are now working to incorporate these features into the next genera-tion of resource-sharing fulfillment systems, such as the WorldShare Platform.[28] OCLC has announced that real-time circulation availability will be offered during the request generation phase of its standard ILL borrowing request processing. At the same time, both OCLC and Atlas Systems have been adding remote circulation functionality utilizing the NCIP standard, which would permit borrowing libraries to request items directly through the lending library's ILS—just as many third-party con-sortial borrowing/lending platforms currently allow.

While both of these developments represent important steps for-ward, taken together they will revolutionize the current interlibrary loan landscape. If consortial borrowing/lending platforms have evolved as a response to the extra mediation and waiting times associated with traditional ILL, what will happen when the WorldShare Platform and management tools such as ILLiad permit the creation of similar consor-tial arrangements on the fly, with no extra cost or support required to do so? At the risk of hyperbole, real-time discovery paired with remote circulation interoperability is nothing less than the Holy Grail of interlibrary loan.

Another potential tectonic shift in resource sharing is its realignment with collection development and acquisitions. While in many library academic libraries there is some communication between ILL and book selectors, this usually takes the form of reporting data on borrowing and lending after the fact, or referring hard-to-find interlibrary loan requests to subject specialists for additional assistance.[29] Some resource-sharing operations have always had the ability and funds to purchase materials for library patrons independent of the normal acquisitions process; while originally this was no doubt intended to allow interlibrary loan staff to purchase unusual materials such as dissertations or copies from nonlibrary reprographic divisions (such as museums or historical societies), many ILL operations have extended this buying power to purchase scholarly articles through commercial document delivery providers or to acquire items from Amazon that the library would not normally purchase for the collection.

But why stop there? It has been observed elsewhere that in the process of weeding their collections, libraries have unleashed a virtual torrent of materials on the used book marketplace that are discoverable through Amazon and other secondhand online book vendors such as Better World Books. If an item requested via interlibrary loan can be purchased for the same cost or less than the cost of borrowing it from another library, then why not buy it instead? The idea of patron-driven acquisitions has always enjoyed at best a mixed reaction in academic library circles, especially at institutions where librarians have spent a great amount of time and effort in crafting purchasing plans for their collections.

SUNY Geneseo is pioneering a novel way of bridging patron-driven acquisitions with traditional collection development methodologies through more efficient library automation. The Getting It System Toolkit (GIST) is a series of customizations to Atlas Systems' ILLiad client that enable it to interact directly with collection development and local acquisitions. When a patron submits an interlibrary loan request, its attendant metadata is enriched by querying a series of bibliographic and vendor APIs (such as WorldCat, Amazon, et al.); this metadata is in turn used as the basis for determining whether a requested item meets the established criteria for purchase rather than loan, or vice versa.[30]

GIST makes a radical assumption about patron requests and library services—one that flies in the face of decades of conventional wisdom. As interlibrary loan originally evolved out of the context of reference, even as the function has aligned itself more and more closely with access services, it has always been assumed that the ILL request is fundamentally an extension of the reference interview and therefore a teachable moment for the library patron: for example, "Should I submit a purchase request for this item, or should I ask to borrow it via interlibrary loan?" Services like GIST, however, assume that the patron does not care how he or she gets the item in question.

By putting the responsibility of determining the most appropriate means of obtaining materials on the library and not the patron, libraries are able to take advantage of increasingly sophisticated automation to fulfill any kind of service request. This kind of one-click Get It functionality is consistent with patron expectations when using nonlibrary online services and permits librarians to consolidate myriad request forms and extraneous parallel workflows so as to provide more efficient fulfillment. By utilizing a common request management system, library departments that previously operated in relative isolation from one another may now work collaboratively, with greater transparency both internally among staff and externally for patrons.[31]

Amid these dreams of real-time discovery and universal request buttons lurks a potential nightmare for resource-sharing librarians: e-books. Academic librarians have had the relative luxury of ignoring the broader strategic importance of e-books, as the print monographs that are the stock in trade for college and research libraries have been available only in print; even if e-book versions were available, they were often not acquired due to prohibitive costs, cumbersome delivery platforms, unacceptable licensing terms, or simple lack of demand from library patrons. However, just as journal content has shifted over time from majority print to born-digital publications now being the default, librarians must anticipate a reality where e-books are the norm and not the exception; if the consumer e-book market is any indication, this day will come much sooner than we think.

This of course raises a host of additional factors when dealing with an interlibrary loan request. If a given resource exists in e-book format that can be discovered on OCLC, for example, should the ILL department request this version? Given that every library or library consortium negotiates its own licensing terms for digital content, it can be difficult to determine whether a lending library that lists an e-book as part of their catalog is actually legally permitted to loan a copy of it or not—and if so, they may be able to lend only portions of it, or under highly restrictive terms that may not be optimal for the requesting patron. If the ILL department chooses to purchase the e-book instead, will it be allowed to keep the digital copy for its own collections, or will it only be able to provide the content to that individual patron?

What if the patron would prefer a print copy to the e-book version? Or what if a patron would accept an e-book copy, but only in a format that is readable on their platform of choice (such as MOBI or EPUB)? These considerations do not apply solely to new electronic acquisitions, but increasingly come up in the context of retrospective digitization as well. For example, libraries that have scanned their older materials through Google Books or HathiTrust may be less willing to lend the physical copies of these items via ILL.

But what if a patron requests the print copy anyway? Some libraries are exploring the possibility of providing "use copies" using online print services such as Lulu[32] or offering on-site print-on-demand services using Espresso Book Machines or similar equipment, but even with these novel solutions available, the needs of primary-source scholarship will never vanish entirely. The Association of College and Research Libraries (ACRL) has long recognized this basic tension between academic research and library preservation and in recent years has worked to develop a protocol for the borrowing and lending of rare and fragile library materials.[33] Although these guidelines were originally envisioned as providing a framework for archives and special collections, as our aging general print collections are digitized and moved to high-density storage, they may find themselves increasingly referred to in the future.

The changing nature of interlibrary loan and document delivery is not happening in a void, however, but within a context of a rapidly evolving conceptual framework for access services, where traditional boundaries are eroding in favor a more fluid and dynamic operational whole. Take, for example, the recent trend of academic libraries launching "scan on demand" services, whereby they make their print collections accessible online to library patrons. While many of these services take advantage of existing ILL systems and workflows, many of them cross several unit or departmental lines in the course of providing such popular (and hence high-demand) new functionality.

That this kind of internal document delivery service is often used to request materials for curriculum support leads us back to the fundamental questions of streamlined services and the goal of one-click fulfillment. Although many college and university library systems are currently trying to distance themselves from the messy and potentially legally actionable business of electronic reserves[35]—with some even exiting e-reserves entirely—other libraries are approaching the problem from the opposite tack by making discovery easier, making the request process more intuitive and less cumbersome, leveraging existing internal document workflows to meet increased demand, and developing new methods of reporting and data analysis to make better decisions in real time.

On many occasions, this author has jokingly claimed that resource sharing is always trying to take over the library world; although this has been said with tongue firmly in cheek, like all jokes it has an element of truth to it. After operating in their own silos for the latter half of the twentieth century, interlibrary loan and document delivery have become critical components of the dynamic and interconnected academic research library of the twenty-first century. As college and university libraries turn to more cooperative strategies for meeting the research needs of their faculty, students, and staff, the resource-sharing endeavor that began with the ancient Alexandrians finds itself at the vanguard of librarianship. Though only time will tell how libraries will weather the perfect storm of digitization, declining budgets, and decreased relevance among the "Google generation," it is clear that interlibrary loan and document delivery will continue in the spirit of innovation, collaboration, and experimentation for many years to come.

NOTES

1. One of the Alexandrians' more innovative schemes was to seize any books that arrived in port and have them copied. These copies would be returned to the owners, while the originals themselves would be added to the Great Library's collection.
2. Collected Works of Galen, ed. C. G. Kühn, vol. 17a (Leipzig, 1828, reprinted in facsimile by Georg Olms, Hildesheim, 1965), 607; English translation of pages 605–608 available at "Extracts from Greek and Latin Writers in Translation," Attalus website, accessed April 26, 2013, http://www.attalus.org/translate/extracts.
3. For more information about the development of interlibrary loan in the nineteenth and twentieth centuries, see Margaret W. Ellingson and Susan D. Morris, "Interlibrary Loan: Evolution to Revolution," in *Interlibrary Loan Practices Handbook*, ed. Cherié L. Weible and Karen L. Janke, 3rd ed. (Chicago: ALA Editions, 2011), 1–16.
4. For an excellent overview of the pressures that were facing academic librarianship at the turn of the twenty-first century, see Glenda A. Thornton, "Impact of Electronic Resources on Collection Development, the Roles of Librarians, and Library Consortia," *Library Trends* 48, no. 4 (Spring 2000): 842–856.
5. Sonny Bono Copyright Term Extension Act, Pub. L. No. 105-298, 112 Stat. 2827 (1998).
6. For discussion on the implications of copyright on course reserve, see chapter 4 of this book and Howard Besser, "The Erosion of Public Protection: Attacks on the Concept of Fair Use" (paper, Town Meeting on Copyright and Fair Use, College Art Association, Toronto, February 1998) accessed 14 May 2013 http://besser.tsoa.nyu.edu/howard/Papers/caa-fairuse/sld013.htm.

7. State and public libraries were the first to endure the hardships of the new fiscal reality; ironically, these early budgetary pressures spurred a great deal of innovation, especially in the field of resource sharing. An inspiring example of this triumph under adversity is the IDS Project, a partnership of over seventy private, public, and special libraries in New York state providing free reciprocal interlibrary loan and document delivery services.

8. Much of this alternative resource-sharing traffic is now happening without the assistance (or even knowledge) of many ILL librarians; an example of this is the subreddit Scholar, http://www.reddit.com/r/scholar, where users place requests for articles and library patrons with the appropriate licensed resource at their college or university fulfill these requests anonymously.

9. "WorldCat Resource Sharing Facts and Statistics," OCLC, accessed April 4, 2013, https://www.oclc.org/en-US/resource-sharing/statistics.html.

10. "Kudzu ILL Policies and Procedures," Association of Southeastern Research Libraries, accessed March 18, 2013, http://www.aserl.org/programs/wrlc-ill/kudzu-ill-policy.

11. An excellent example of a shared catalog is InRhode, a catalog composed of eleven academic libraries and fourteen health sciences libraries in Rhode Island, including Brown University, Bryant University, the Community College of Rhode Island, the Dominican House of Studies, Johnson and Wales University, Providence College, Rhode Island College, Roger Williams University, Salve Regina University, University of Rhode Island, and Wheaton College; see "InRhode Library Catalog," HELIN Library Consortium, accessed March 18, 2013, http://inrhode.uri.edu/.

12. "NCIP: NISO Circulation Interchange Protocol," National Information Standards Organization, accessed March 18, 2013, http://www.niso.org/workrooms/ncip.

13. Committee on Institutional Cooperation homepage, accessed April 18, 2013, http://www.cic.net/home.

14. "Borrow Direct," Yale University Library, accessed March 18, 2013, http://guides.library.yale.edu/bd.

15. Although some systems are able to prevent patrons from ordering items that are currently available at their home institution, this is by no means an exact science; conversely, libraries with complicated local holdings often struggle to make all of their materials available for requesting.

16. Bart Hollingsworth and Carol Jones, "Borrow Direct" A Vision for Excellent Service" (presentation, NELINET Resource Sharing Conference, Danielson, CT, June 19, 2009).

17. For a list of CRL's active collection areas, see "Collecting Areas," Center for Research Libraries, accessed March 18, 2013, http://www.crl.edu/collections/collection-building/collecting-areas.

18. Damon Jaggers and Scott Wicks, "2CUL Resource Sharing in 2015," 2CUL website, February 2011, http://2cul.org/sites/default/files/resourcesharing.pdf.

19. "The CONTU Guidelines," *The Campus Guide to Copyright Compliance*, Copyright Clearance Center, 2005, http://www.copyright.com/Services/copyrightoncampus/content/ill_contu.html.

20. The author of this chapter has recently encountered licensing terms that specify electronic transmission only by certain proprietary formats, such as Ariel. It is unclear what happens when these methods become obsolete or are discontinued.

21. For an excellent overview of the ILL management systems landscape see Tina Baich and Erin Silva Fisher, "Technology and Web 2.0," in *Interlibrary Loan Practices Handbook*, ed. Cherié L. Weible and Karen L. Janke, 3rd ed. (Chicago: ALA Editions, 2011), 93–108.

22. Not only has Ariel recently rebranded itself as a secure dropbox file server, OCLC now has its own proprietary dropbox delivery service as well called Article Exchange; see "Article Exchange: Secure, Copyright-Compliant Delivery of Documents," OCLC, accessed April 8, 2013, http://www.oclc.org/resourcesharing/features/articleexchange/default.htm.

23. "Get It Now," Copyright Clearance Center, accessed March 18, 2013, http://www.copyright.com/content/cc3/en/toolbar/productsAndSolutions/getitnow.html.

24. Rafal Kasprowski, "Perspectives on DRM: Between Digital Rights Management and Digital Restrictions Management," *Bulletin of the American Society for Information Science and Technology* 36, no. 3 (February/March 2010): 49–54.

25. "DOCLINE," National Library of Medicine, accessed March 18, 2013, https://docline.gov/docline/index.cfm.

26. "Announcements," RapidILL, Colorado State University Libraries, accessed March 18, 2013, http://rapid2.library.colostate.edu/Default.aspx.

27. "Direct Request: Automated Fulfillment You Control," OCLC, accessed March 18, 2013, http://www.oclc.org/resourcesharing/features/directrequest/default.htm.

28. "WorldShare Interlibrary Loan," OCLC, accessed March 18, 2013, http://www.oclc.org/migrate-worldshare-ill/.

29. On the topic of referring patron inquiries to subject specialists, see Louise Mort Feldman, "Information Desk Referrals: Implementing an Office Statistics Database," *College and Research Libraries* 70, no. 2 (March 2009): 133–141.

30. "Using GIST GDM to Find Textbooks to Place on Reserve," Getting It System Toolkit, February 6, 2013, SUNY Geneseo, http://www.gistlibrary.org.

31. Cyril Oberlander, director of the Milne Library at SUNY Geneseo and one of the creators of GIST, sums it up: "We must retain our strengths as successful advanced problem solvers and searchers, willing to innovate, adapt, and redesign our services around user requests. We can do by asking, 'What are users trying to achieve?' and 'How can we best serve them?'" (Cyril Oberlander, "The Future of Interlibrary Loan," *Interlibrary Loan Practices Handbook,* ed. Cherié L. Weible and Karen L. Janke, 3rd ed. [Chicago: ALA Editions, 2011], 118).

32. Lulu homepage, accessed April 8, 2013, http://www.lulu.com/.

33. *ACRL/RBMS Guidelines for Interlibrary Loan and Exhibition Loan of Special Collections Materials* (Chicago: ACRL, January 2012), http://www.ala.org/acrl/standards/specialcollections.

34. The topic of reserves is beyond the scope of this chapter, but for an excellent analysis of the recent Georgia State copyright lawsuit and its relevance to the future of libraries, see Kevin Smith, "Another Fair Use Victory for Libraries," *Scholarly Communications @ Duke* (blog), Duke University Libraries, November 26, 2012, http://blogs.library.duke.edu/scholcomm/2012/11/26/another-fair-use-victory-for-libraries/.

BIBLIOGRAPHY

Association of College and Research Libraries. *ACRL/RBMS Guidelines for Interlibrary Loan and Exhibition Loan of Special Collections Materials.* Chicago: Association of College and Research Libraries, January 2012, http://www.ala.org/acrl/standards/specialcollections.

Association of Southeastern Research Libraries. "Kudzu ILL Policies and Procedures." Association of Southeastern Research Libraries, accessed March 18, 2013, http://www.aserl.org/programs/wrlc-ill/kudzu-ill-policy.

Baich, Tina, and Erin Silva Fisher. "Technology and Web 2.0." In *Interlibrary Loan Practices Handbook*, 3rd ed., edited by Cherié L. Weible and Karen L. Janke, 93–108. Chicago: ALA Editions, 2011.

Besser, Howard. "The Erosion of Public Protection: Attacks on the Concept of Fair Use." Paper, Town Meeting on Copyright and Fair Use, College Art Association, Toronto, February 1998 accessed 14 May 2013 http://besser.tsoa.nyu.edu/howard/Papers/caa-fairuse/sld013.htm.

Center for Research Libraries. "Collecting Areas." Center for Research Libraries, accessed March 18, 2013, http://www.crl.edu/collections/collection-building/collecting-areas.

Colorado State University Libraries. "Announcements." RapidILL, Colorado State University Libraries, accessed March 18, 2013, http://rapid2.library.colostate.edu/Default.aspx.

Committee on Institutional Cooperation. Homepage. Accessed April 8, 2013, http://www.cic.net/home.

Copyright Clearance Center. "The CONTU Guidelines." *The Campus Guide to Copyright Compliance*. Copyright Clearance Center, 2005, http://www.copyright.com/Services/copyrightoncampus/content/ill_contu.html.

————. "Get It Now." Copyright Clearance Center, accessed March 18, 2013, http://www.copyright.com/content/cc3/en/toolbar/productsAndSolutions/getitnow.html.

Ellingson, Margaret W., and Susan D. Morris. "Interlibrary Loan: Evolution to Revolution." In *Interlibrary Loan Practices Handbook*, 3rd ed., edited by Cherié L. Weible and Karen L. Janke, 1–16. Chicago: ALA Editions, 2011.

Feldman, Louise Mort. "Information Desk Referrals: Implementing an Office Statistics Database." *College and Research Libraries* 70, no. 2 (March 2009): 133–141.

HELIN Library Consortium. "InRhode Library Catalog." HELIN Library Consortium, accessed March 18, 2013, http://inrhode.uri.edu/.

Hollingsworth, Bart, and Carol Jones. "Borrow Direct: A Vision for Excellent Service." Presentation, NELINET Resource Sharing Conference, Danielson, CT, June 19, 2009.

Jaggers, Damon, and Scott Wicks. "2CUL Resource Sharing in 2015." 2CUL website, February 2011, http://2cul.org/sites/default/files/resourcesharing.pdf.

Kasprowski, Rafal. "Perspectives on DRM: Between Digital Rights Management and Digital Restrictions Management." *Bulletin of the American Society for Information Science and Technology* 36, no. 3 (February/March 2010): 49–54.

Lulu. Homepage. Accessed April 8, 2013, http://www.lulu.com.

National Information Standards Organization. "NCIP: NISO Circulation Interchange Protocol." National Information Standards Organization, accessed March 18, 2013, http://www.niso.org/workrooms/ncip.

National Library of Medicine. "DOCLINE." National Library of Medicine, accessed March 18, 2013, https://docline.gov/docline/index.cfm.

Oberlander, Cyril. "The Future of Interlibrary Loan." In *Interlibrary Loan Practices Handbook*, 3rd ed., edited by Cherié L. Weible and Karen L. Janke, 109–120. Chicago: ALA Editions, 2011.

Online Computer Library Center. "Article Exchange: Secure, Copyright-Compliant Delivery of Documents." Online Computer Library Center, accessed April 8, 2013, http://www.oclc.org/resourcesharing/features/articleexchange/default.htm.

———. "Direct Request: Automated Fulfillment You Control." Online Computer Library Center, accessed March 18, 2013, http://www.oclc.org/resourcesharing/features/directrequest/default.htm.

———. "WorldCat Resource Sharing Facts and Statistics." Online Computer Library Center, accessed April 4, 2013, https://www.oclc.org/en-US/resource-sharing/statistics.html.

———. "WorldShare Interlibrary Loan." Online Computer Library Center, accessed March 18, 2013, http://www.oclc.org/migrate-worldshare-ill/.

Smith, Kevin. "Another Fair Use Victory for Libraries." *Scholarly Communications @ Duke* (blog), Duke University Libraries, November 26, 2012, http://blogs.library.duke.edu/scholcomm/2012/11/26/another-fair-use-victory-for-libraries/.

SUNY Geneseo. "Using GIST GDM to Find Textbooks to Place on Reserve." Getting It System Toolkit, SUNY Geneseo, February 6, 2013, http://www.gistlibrary.org.

Thornton, Glenda A. "Impact of Electronic Resources on Collection Development, the Roles of Librarians, and Library Consortia." *Library Trends* 48, no. 4 (Spring 2000): 842–856.

Yale University Library. "Borrow Direct." Yale University Library, accessed March 18, 2013, http://guides.library.yale.edu/bd.

Course Reserves Management

Brice Austin

Head of Access Services, University of Colorado Libraries, Boulder, CO

SINCE ITS inception, course reserves have been seen as a logical component of access services. An early 1990s Association of Research Libraries (ARL) study of the then-recent organizational trend found that 70 percent (53) of the libraries surveyed had placed reserves within an access/circulation–type department.[1] This comes as no surprise given the traditionally close relationship between reserves and circulation; indeed, reserves came into being (as early as the 1870s) precisely to satisfy a need to better manage the checkout of materials that had been assigned for courses and were therefore in high demand.[2]

In spite of the dramatic changes course reserves have undergone during the past two decades, the service is just as likely to reside under the circulation/access umbrella today. In fact, a subsequent ARL study, conducted almost fifteen years after the one referenced above, found that the percentage of access/circulation departments that included course reserves had actually increased.[3]

Whether or not this trend continues remains to be seen as the rate of change, not only for course reserves but for access services, academic libraries, and higher education, seems to continually accelerate. However, for the moment at least, reserves continue to be found, more often than not, within an access/circulation–type department, though it is a service that bears little resemblance now to its original nineteenth-century form. The checkout of physical objects from a restricted collection, once the very definition of course reserves, is now only one offering among a modern suite of services.

AN OVERVIEW OF RESERVES SERVICES

Traditional Reserves

Origin and Description

As noted above, "traditional" reserves came into being at least as early as the 1870s, when librarians at Harvard and Yale Universities first began to pull materials from the stacks at the request of faculty members and to place them in a restricted area, often behind the circulation desk. The materials were then added to the professor's course listing, and he instructed students to request them at the library. The checkout period is generally short—hours rather than days—and late fees are often high in order insure the materials' prompt return. This portion of what began in the 1870s still remains today.

While the ways in which libraries provide traditional reserves have evolved over the past century (materials are now listed and checked out electronically) and while reserves have expanded to include other formats of physical materials (e.g., videos, CDs, DVDs, even e-readers), the general concept and purpose remain the same: to provide access to high-demand information resources for as many users as possible within a narrow window of time.

Traditional (Print) Reserves

When taken within the context of the academic library as it was defined until roughly the mid-twentieth century, traditional reserves provided a very straightforward, even elegant solution to the problem of managing access to information resources in high demand. It allowed more students to use the same materials. It provided one-stop shopping in the sense that students had to visit only one place—the reserve desk—in order to find all library materials on a professor's reading list or, for that matter, all library materials on multiple professors' reading lists.

Challenges

While traditional reserves do provide a very simple solution to the problem of giving access to multiple users, in practice there are issues that make (and always have made) that solution less than ideal. Some of the most vexing issues are as follows:

- **Access, while improved, is still limited**. While there is no doubt that placing an item on traditional reserve makes it available to more students, the laws of physics still limit the number of possible users. A book with a two-hour checkout period, for instance, can in theory be circulated twelve times in one day; however, in practice the number of circulations is generally far smaller. The library may not be open all twenty-four hours. Some students may require more than two hours in order to complete the assignment. It is unlikely that students will queue up at two-hour intervals in order to check out the book one after another, so there are periods when the book is not in use.
- **High-demand materials may be damaged.** Reserve materials by definition tend to be used very frequently and by a large number of patrons, which naturally raises the risk that those materials will be damaged. Yet removing them from reserve for repairs is generally not an option until the end of the term, by which point the damage has likely grown worse.
- **Reserved materials require space**. Traditional reserves deal with physical objects and physical objects that require space—usually space within what might be termed prime real estate, as these materials are generally housed behind or adjacent to a circulation desk.

Early attempts to address some of the above challenges focused upon purchasing or (for a brief time) renting additional copies of materials; however, by the 1930s it had become apparent that these strategies were not viable given limited library budgets and the unwillingness of faculty or departments to fund such initiatives.[4] Thus, when new technologies began to emerge mid-century, librarians looked to them to provide better information delivery methods, methods that have now largely supplanted the need for traditional reserves.

Still, while changes over the last half century have altered the ways both in which courses are taught and in which information is delivered, even today, at least in certain situations, traditional reserves sometimes remain the best method for managing information resource access.

Photocopied Reserves

Origin and Description

During the latter part of the 1930s through the 1950s, libraries experimented with making mimeographed, photostatted, or even hand-typed copies of materials for reserves, though adoption of these methods appears to have been scattered at best. However, with the introduction by Xerox of the modern copy machine in the late 1950s, use of photocopies for reserves became a viable alternative, one that academic libraries quickly embraced. By the end of the 1960s, photocopied reserves were firmly established and remained the dominant paradigm well into the 1990s.[5]

In terms of process, photocopied reserves follow the service model established for traditional reserves: professors simply supply photocopies instead of books to library staff (some libraries do the copying for faculty) to place on reserve for short-term checkout. However, using copies instead of originals has many advantages.

What Photocopied Reserves Do Well

Photocopied reserves improve access to materials because more copies mean more students can use the materials at the same time, without libraries having to invest their limited resources in purchasing additional originals, which may be used only during times when a particular course is being taught. Additionally, using photocopies mitigates completely any concerns regarding wear and tear upon the original items purchased by either the library or the faculty member, as damaged photocopies may be replaced while the original work remains protected from heavy use. Finally, photocopies take up less physical space than books; thus, the same amount of material can be housed in a much smaller area.

Challenges

While photocopied reserves did address many of the most vexing problems posed by traditional reserves, they presented problems of their own. For one, simple and cheap photocopying often led to an explosion in the use of course reserves, such that staffing and space efficiencies gained by using photocopies were sometimes negated by increased volume. At the author's institution, for example, at the peak of the paper reserves era in the mid-1990s, more than 22,000 items were stored in folders behind the service desk, items that were checked out more than 140,000 times in one year, representing nearly 20 percent of all circulation!

A larger concern, however, was one which had not existed for course reserves before: the question of whether or not the practice of making photocopies for such a purpose was legal under United States Copyright Law. This is a particularly complicated issue, one which will be given more attention below, but it is one that has become rather a moot point in recent years for photocopied reserves, because in large measure the service model has been replaced by electronic reserves.

Electronic Reserves

Origin and Description

While photocopied reserves were generally seen as a rather large service step forward, by the early 1990s new technologies were emerging that suggested to librarians that an even better model might be possible. At its heart, the idea of providing reserves in electronic rather than paper format is a simple one: rather than checking out copies that students will immediately copy again anyway, why not scan the item once and post it where students in the course may access it remotely? In the beginning, this was easier said than done, of course, but by the mid- to late 1990s technology had caught up with librarians' imaginations and the dream became feasible.

In terms of process, electronic reserves differ considerably from photocopied reserves. Professors still identify library materials (or provide their own) to be placed on reserve, but instead of photocopying those materials and housing them behind a circulation desk, library staff (or sometimes the professors themselves) make digital copies and place them on a server or other such storage device. The materials are still attached to each professor's course listing, but no longer do library staff need to check them in or out; students access the materials over the campus network or Internet.

What Electronic Reserves Do Well

There are considerable advantages to using such an information delivery method for reserves:

- **Loss or damage of materials is prevented**. As is the case with photocopies, using electronic copies of reserve materials prevents damage to the original, but the process represents a further improvement as even the copies themselves are unlikely to be damaged. While photocopies are relatively easy and cheap to replace, keeping copies intact for continued use in a high-circulation environment can tax staff's time and patience.
- **Access to materials is vastly improved.** Even assuming photocopies are not lost or damaged, they may be unavailable simply because all copies are checked out or the library is closed. With electronic reserves, this is not an issue as items may be accessed simultaneously by the entire class, if need be, at any hour of the day or night.

- **Very little physical space is needed.** Traditional reserve rooms occupy considerable space within libraries for the storage of books and photocopies. E-reserves take up only disk space.
- **Staff workload is improved**. While little if any labor savings may be realized in the initial processing of materials for electronic reserves—scanning may in fact require more time than photocopying—considerable staff time is saved after the materials have been placed in an electronic reserves system, as there is no longer any need to check items in or out or reshelve them.

Challenges

Early on, electronic reserves challenges centered upon technical issues such as inadequate bandwidth, user authentication, and so on, but as noted above those had largely been resolved by the late 1990s. As with photocopied reserves, the primary concern regarding electronic reserves has been, from the outset, copyright law. If anything, the digital nature of electronic reserves, providing users with the ability to easily copy and share reserved readings, has ratcheted up these concerns. Again, this will be discussed in detail below.

Streaming Audiovisual Reserves

Origin and Description

In recent years, as computer memory and bandwidth have improved dramatically, many libraries have begun providing a new reserves service to their patrons, streaming audio and audiovisual content across the campus network. In a sense, this is an analogue to the evolution of print reserves from paper copies to digital files, though audiovisual content brings with it certain additional complexities.

In terms of process, streamed reserves are very much like electronic reserves, in that content is digitized and placed on a server or other storage device and then links to the files are attached to a professor's course listing for remote access by students.

What Streamed Reserves Do Well

Streamed reserves provide the same advantages for audiovisual material that electronic reserves do for print, only more so given that with audio and video material a student does not even have the option of copying the material to take home for later study. Generally, students are expected to check out physical materials and listen to or watch them inside the library, sometimes within restricted listening or viewing rooms. Particularly for music and film studies scholars, who may need to replay portions of a song or movie over and over again, the ability to do so at any hour of the day or night, from virtually any location, is a liberating experience.

Challenges

Even more so than with electronic reserves, adoption of streamed reserves has been hampered by technical problems. Greater bandwidth requirements (particularly for video), issues of quality for both music and film, and the lack of interoperability among players have all contributed to less widespread use of streamed reserves. In addition, digitizing audio or audiovisual content can be much more complex than digitizing print and often requires more expertise than most reserves staff and teaching faculty possess. Thus, conversion of these files cannot always be done in house at the library, but must be outsourced to others with greater technical skill, often staff within campus information technology departments.

As with both photocopied and electronic reserves, streamed reserves are subject to the barriers of copyright law, of course, but frequently have even steeper hurdles to overcome. Often audio and audiovisual content is subject to license agreements that may forbid streaming or copying altogether, and content may be "wrapped" in digital rights management (DRM) access controls that prevent copying even for uses that may qualify as fair use.

A further barrier, particularly to the use of streaming video for reserves, has come from requirements embedded in the 2008 reauthorization of the Higher Education Opportunity Act (HEOA).[6] The HEOA, which applies to United States academic institutions that receive federal monies for student aid programs, includes provisions requiring those institutions to combat the unauthorized distribution of copyright material by affiliated users. One way in which institutions are encouraged to do this is through "bandwidth shaping"; that is, reducing throughput on campus networks. In theory, this discourages illegal downloading of large quantities of audio and audiovisual content, but it sometimes has the unintended effect of stifling transmission of high-bandwidth library services such as streamed reserves.

RESERVES, COPYRIGHT, AND FAIR USE

When the 1909 revision of the nation's copyright law went into effect, course reserves had already been in existence for more than three decades, yet were essentially unaffected as only "originals"—that is, only imprints of materials sold and distributed by publishers—were placed on reserve at that time. By the 1970s, however, when copyright law again came under review, use of photocopy machines had become widespread and copies of book chapters and journal articles had become an essential component of reserves collections. While many had hoped for clarity within the new law regarding the legality or limits of this practice, no such clarity was forthcoming. The 1976 revision as finally enacted by Congress made no mention of course reserves specifically, thus setting the stage for considerable uncertainty.[7]

In the more than thirty years since, that uncertainty has raged unabated, with librarians and content providers staking out very different positions. While various attempts have been made to draw up guidelines or model policies, nothing has ever been set forth that both sides have been willing to endorse. During this period publishers have engaged in considerable saber-rattling, and occasionally have initiated legal action against commercial entities engaged in reserves-like practices, but until very recently there had not been any actual lawsuits implicating a library reserve operation.[8]

The Case for Fair Use

Many librarians have felt for a long time that copying for reserves—whether in paper or digital format—very likely falls under fair use, arguing that, viewing the library as an extension of the classroom, this practice is precisely one of those which Section 107 of the law was designed to exempt from strict copyright limitations. The preamble to Section 107 specifically lists "multiple copies for classroom use" as an example of fair use, and many have felt that three of the four factors the law says should be considered in any fair use determination (purpose and character of the use; nature of the copyrighted work; and amount used in relation to the entire work) would generally favor reserves copying.[9] However, in the absence of any pertinent court rulings coupled with a steady stream of rhetoric to the contrary from the content industry, many academic institutions, especially those with risk-averse legal counsel, chose to take very conservative positions. Recently, however, a case specific to reserves was finally brought before a court and resulted in a largely favorable ruling for libraries.

In 2008, several publishers funded by the Copyright Clearance Center (CCC) and the Association of American Publishers (AAP) brought suit against Georgia State University, challenging GSU's use of copyrighted material for electronic reserves. In *Cambridge University Press et al. v. Mark Becker et al.,* publishers argued that fees should have been paid for copies of scholarly book chapters that were used for reserves without obtaining permission from rights holders. However, Judge Orinda Evans, in a ruling finally made in 2012, did not accept that argument.[10] Since that time, publishers have appealed, but if the ruling stands it will represent a significant victory for reserves.

Even assuming that Judge Evans's ruling is upheld on appeal, however, questions surrounding reserves and copyright are likely to remain far from settled. As Kevin Smith, Scholarly Communications Officer at Duke, and others suggest, the GSU ruling has some troubling aspects to it.[11] Only scholarly book chapters, which is but one class of materials frequently placed on reserve, were included in the decision. Judge Evans somewhat arbitrarily set 10 percent or one chapter as the threshold for the permissible fair use amount for any one work. And her approach to the fourth factor, effect on the market, left open some serious questions as to how fair use may be applied in an increasingly digital world. Overall, however, as noted by Brandon Butler, Director of Public Policy Initiatives at the Association of Research Libraries (ARL), this ruling represents "an overwhelming victory for Georgia State" and an "overall a positive development for libraries."[12]

Many questions remain, of course, regarding the extent to which fair use may be claimed for reserves material, and therefore uncertainty will almost certainly continue, yet the GSU decision should at least encourage libraries to be less self-restrictive in terms of their policies and practices. As one writer recently suggested in his conclusion to a survey of copyright policies and practices among ARL libraries, perhaps the best advice for librarians engaged in making fair use determinations for e-reserves is "simply to relax."[13]

THE FUTURES OF COURSE RESERVES

In 2004, the author wrote somewhat at length regarding three possible futures that might be in store for course reserves: that the service may cease to exist; that it may continue to exist but in a limited form; or that it may continue to exist but in an expanded or diversified form.[14] While much of what was written still holds true, academic libraries and their parent institutions have continued to undergo dramatic change over the past decade, and that change could hardly help but have some effect upon the outlook for reserves. While it still seems reasonable to suggest the same three broad categories of reserve futures set forth almost ten years ago, with the benefit of both hindsight and new foresight some amendments need to be made.

Future One: Libraries Will No Longer Provide Course Reserves Services

The possibility that reserves will cease to exist altogether must still be considered, though perhaps for slightly different reasons than previously suggested. In 2004 it seemed plausible to speculate that reserves might fade into history due to what was termed either Death by Irrelevance or Death by Copyright. While Death by Copyright could certainly still come to pass, that outcome seems much less likely in the wake of the Georgia State ruling (assuming that ruling is upheld on appeal). The possibility of Death by Irrelevance, however, appears stronger than ever, especially in regard to electronic reserves. Moreover, another related candidate has emerged given recent difficult economic times: Death by Selective Budget Cuts.

Death by Irrelevance

Currently, there are a number of information trends in progress that could potentially lead to the obsolescence of course reserves, especially as they tend to reinforce one another:

- **Increased faculty use of personal web pages and courseware.** As web tools and courseware have become more powerful and user-friendly, more faculty members have adopted them in order to facilitate "one-stop shopping," places where class readings, discussion, testing, and grades all may be accessed by their students. This trend has been further reinforced as some institutions have actively encouraged courseware use as a means of providing a common student experience.
- **The continued growth of electronic resources.** As more and more material becomes available online, the value of reserves is bound to diminish, for there is little advantage to grouping lists of links together through the library catalog over grouping them through a professor's website or courseware. In fact, there is a *disadvantage* to doing so as it involves another step for the student.

- **The rise of electronic books.** In 2004, the availability and usability of e-books lagged far behind that of electronic journals, making it unlikely that traditional reserves, at least, would become obsolete in the immediate future. Almost a decade later, however, given that vastly more titles have been published in digital format and given that e-readers such as Amazon's Kindle, Apple's iPad, and others have become fairly ubiquitous, it no longer seems a stretch to suggest that e-books may soon obviate the need to have physical materials placed on reserve. That many libraries already offer to-the-desktop delivery of content scanned from their print collections further contributes to this trend.

- **The emergence of electronic textbooks.** A related trend is the emergence of a specific sort of e-book: e-textbooks. While thus far, campus bookstores and students have been slow to adopt them, it seems inevitable that e-textbooks will eventually become the dominant paradigm in higher education. As functionality such as highlighting and note taking continue to improve, combined with the considerable advantages of portability and text searching, which are already offered, e-textbooks seem poised to replace one of the major categories of physical materials currently placed on reserves.

- **The emergence of massive open online courses.** The very nature of what a "course" is may be changing. In the last few years, massive open online courses (MOOCs) have begun to be offered through some of the nation's major universities. MOOCs, as the name implies, are courses that are taught online and are available to practically anyone, worldwide. While it is still unclear how or if MOOCs will be integrated into a university's curriculum, if they are the effect may be profound, not only upon reserves and libraries, but upon institutions of higher education as a whole. In terms of reserves it seems unlikely that professors would be able to use physical content in the teaching of MOOCs, and even proprietary local e-content might be only minimally useful.

Rather, it seems likely that professors teaching such courses would seek out freely available online content, accessible by students practically anywhere. Such a world might not have a need for what we now think of as course reserves.

Death by Selective Budget Cuts

The flip side of this Irrelevance coin is that libraries may, of their own volition, eliminate course reserves as part of budget-cutting strategies that target services that can be provided elsewhere. Given that faculty *can* use courseware or webpages and many already do, and given that doing so actually provides some advantages to students, the option of eliminating reserves services is one that many libraries are seriously considering. Even if libraries decide not to do away with reserves completely, continuing economic pressures may, in many cases, lead them to scale back the scope of their services.

Future Two: Libraries Will Offer Only Very Limited Course Reserve Services

In 2004, the author wrote that while the extinction of reserves was by no means impossible, it was rather more likely that reserves might shrink to the point of filling only a minor niche within the suite of services libraries offer. For some institutions, this has indeed become a reality, driven largely by the Death by Selective Budget Cuts scenario described above, which itself is a product of the diminished relevance of reserves in what is increasingly an electronic information world. Recently an "environmental scan" of more than one hundred academic reserves operations found that while only one library surveyed (the University of Arizona) had eliminated reserves entirely, a significant number had either stopped providing electronic reserves or were considering doing so in the near future.[15] In fact the author's institution, while not included in this environmental scan, is among those that have decided to eliminate e-reserves in the year ahead.

It remains to be seen, of course, whether this path will be the one taken by the majority of academic libraries; some institutions have decided to go in a quite different direction.

Future Three: Libraries Will Offer Expanded or Diversified Course Reserve Services

Ten years ago, it seemed reasonable to speculate that there might be a third possible future for course reserves, one in which the service would expand rather than contracting or simply disappearing. In spite of many changes to the information landscape of higher education since that time, this still seems possible, though it is probably true that if libraries wish to see this future materialize they will have to make a concerted effort to create it. The three essential components to bringing about such a future are likely the same ones set forth in 2004—strong leadership, collaboration, and flexibility—though perhaps it no longer makes sense to discuss those three components separately as was done then, given that any expanded role for reserves staff in the future will necessarily require a combination of all three. What follows is a list of services that libraries might offer in the future under the umbrella of reserves, either in addition to the full suite of services they offer now, or in combination with some subset of that full suite. Some of these services are already being offered by some library reserves operations now; others are more speculative in nature.

- **"Embedded" reserves staff in faculty courseware.** Staff might continue to be responsible for posting and linking PDFs or audiovisual streaming files, but instead of linking those files to a reserves system, they might link them directly to faculty courses within a course management system. While this could well prove more time-consuming and perhaps arduous than working with a single reserves platform, it might present an opportunity to forge closer personal relationships with individual faculty members.

- **Copyright support.** Many libraries already manage copyright for faculty using course reserves, determining fair use and seeking permissions for material when necessary, and this service could certainly be offered by libraries even should they decide to no longer provide electronic or streaming reserves.
- **Copyright education.** Again, many libraries already provide copyright education to their campuses, or share a role in it with others, and could do so regardless of what other reserves services they might offer.
- **Technical support.** Reserves staff might work with campus information technology (IT) departments to provide technical support for streaming or scanning—digitizing or posting files— even should the library no longer be responsible for hosting those files. In a sense, many libraries do this already through their electronic document delivery services, providing digital files for professors' use; it seems likely that in some cases those professors are already posting those files to courseware or class websites.
- **Class capture.** Reserves staff might, either independently or in collaboration with campus IT, take on responsibility for filming and hosting video of class sessions.
- **Support for MOOCs.** MOOCs, which offer a potential threat to reserves, could also present opportunities as libraries might offer their expertise to assist in locating course readings that are both relevant and open access.
- **Electronic bookstore.** As textbooks evolve from print to electronic format, it may be that library staff will find a place at this table as well, in partnership with campus bookstores.

Any such list must necessarily be incomplete as it is difficult to predict all the ways in which information delivery, teaching methods, and technology will evolve in the next ten or perhaps even five years. Yet it seems likely that as the need to provide traditional reserves naturally diminishes and library catalogs give way to course management systems as the gateway to class information resources, there will be many opportunities to gather new and reimagined old services under the course reserves umbrella. Again, though, it is probably true that expanded or diversified reserves services will not come to pass if librarians simply sit back and wait to be asked to participate in the changes that are sweeping through higher education; we will need to envision the future we want for reserves and then plan an active role in creating it.

Course reserves, indeed libraries and higher education in general, are in a state of transition. Undeniably, there are sweeping trends at play (trends in technology, pedagogy, and service philosophy) that may render reserves obsolete. However, there are also opportunities available for libraries to preserve still-relevant portions of reserves, to reimagine others, and to add new services. The direction each library chooses will, in large part, determine whether this suite of services best fits within its particular organizational structure, but given past history and possible future directions it seems likely that in a majority of instances, course reserves will continue to be seen as a logical component of circulation and access services departments.

NOTES

1. Virginia Steel, *Access Services: Organization and Management: SPEC Kit 179* (Washington, DC: ARL, 1991), 5.

2. Brice Austin, *Reserves, Electronic Reserves, and Copyright: The Past and the Future* (Binghamton, NY: Haworth Information Press, 2004), 3–4.

3. Trevor A. Dawes, Kimberly Burke Sweetman, and Catherine Von Elm, *Access Services: SPEC Kit 290* (Washington, DC: ARL, 2005), 20.

4. Austin, *Reserves, Electronic Reserves, and Copyright,* 5–7.

5. Ibid., 1–12.

6. Higher Education Opportunity Act, Pub. L. No. 110-315, 122 Stat. 3078 (2008).

7. Copyright Act of 1976, Pub. L. 94-553, 90 Stat. 2541 (1976).

8. For an historical overview of copyright law and reserves from the mid-1970s through the 1990s, see Austin, *Reserves, Electronic Reserves, and Copyright,* 13–31, 37–42.

9. Copyright Act of 1976.

10. Cambridge University Press v. Becker, 863 F. Supp. 2d 1190 (N.D. Ga. 2012).

11. Kevin Smith, "The GSU Decision—Not an Easy Road for Anyone, *Scholarly Communications @ Duke* (blog), Duke University Libraries, May 12, 2012, http://blogs.library.duke.edu/scholcomm/2012/05/12/the-gsu-decision-not-an-easy-road-for-anyone/.

12. Brandon C. Butler, *GSU Fair Use Decision Recap and Implications,* ARL Issue Brief (Washington, DC: ARL, May 15, 2012), 1

13. David R. Hansen, William M. Cross, and Phillip M. Edwards, "Copyright Policy and Practice in Electronic Reserves among ARL Libraries, *College and Research Libraries* 74, no. 1 (January 2013), 78.

14. Austin, *Reserves, Electronic Reserves, and Copyright.*

15. Kymberly Anne Goodson and Linda Frederiksen, "E-Reserves in Transition: Exploring New Possibilities in E-Reserves Service Delivery," *Journal of Interlibrary Loan, Document Delivery, and Electronic Reserve* 21, no. 1–2 (2011): 33–56; "Electronic Course Reserves Move to D2L," University Libraries, University of Arizona, February 11, 2009, http://www.library.arizona.edu/news/entries/view/2353.

BIBLIOGRAPHY

Austin, Brice. *Reserves, Electronic Reserves, and Copyright: The Past and the Future.* Binghamton, NY: Haworth Information Press, 2004.

Butler, Brandon C. *GSU Fair Use Decision Recap and Implications,* ARL Issue Brief. Washington, DC: Association of Research Libraries, May 15, 2012, http://www.arl.org/storage/documents/publications/issue-brief-gsu-decision-15may12.pdf.

Dawes, Trevor A., Kimberly Burke Sweetman, and Catherine Von Elm. *Access Services: SPEC Kit 290.* Washington, DC: Association of Research Libraries, 2005.

Goodson, Kymberly Anne, and Linda Frederiksen. "E-Reserves in Transition: Exploring New Possibilities in E-Reserves Service Delivery." *Journal of Interlibrary Loan, Document Delivery, and Electronic Reserve* 21, no. 1–2 (2011): 33–56.

Hansen, David R., William M. Cross, and Phillip M. Edwards. "Copyright Policy and Practice in Electronic Reserves among ARL Libraries." *College and Research Libraries* 74, no. 1 (January 2013): 69–84.

Smith, Kevin. "The GSU Decision—Not an Easy Road for Anyone." *Scholarly Communications @ Duke* (blog), Duke University Libraries, May 12 2012, http://blogs.library.duke.edu/scholcomm/2012/05/12/the-gsu-decision-not-an-easy-road-for-anyone/.

Steel, Virginia. *Access Services: Organization and Management: SPEC Kit 179.* Washington, DC: Association of Research Libraries, 1991.

University of Arizona. "Electronic Course Reserves Move to D2L." University Libraries, University of Arizona, February 11, 2009, http://www.library.arizona.edu/news/entries/view/2353.

Building Management Responsibilities for Access Services

David W. Bottorff
Head of Collection Management, Regenstein
Library, University of Chicago

Katherine Furlong
Director, Access and Technical Services, Lafayette College

David McCaslin
Head of Access and Fulfillment Services,
California Institute of Technology

ACCESS SERVICES staff, especially those in circulation, often act as the conduit for space management and library building maintenance. Overseeing the physical aspects of a library can encompass a variety of challenges. The access services department possesses a unique perspective from its frontline service point and is able to oversee certain facility-related issues within a library operation.

The following chapter provides a brief overview of many of those issues, from managing the use of study rooms to planning a new library facility. As will become clear, the range of these issues is far-reaching and, regardless of where direct responsibility for them may fall within a given library, access services staff will often find themselves involved, formally or informally, in many if not most of the areas discussed in the following pages. Successful access services librarians will find that knowing at least a little about each of these areas will serve them well. To be forewarned is to be forearmed.

GROUP STUDY ROOMS

Study spaces on campuses are not easy to come by, and group study rooms have become a haven where students can collaborate on class projects, practice presentations, or simply study quietly in an enclosed space.[1] Libraries are increasingly asked to build and manage rooms for groups of students to work. Scheduling and technology are two major factors with library group study rooms.

Group study rooms can vary in size, but each room should be able to accommodate approximately four to six students. More than six people, and the room might become too noisy for those studying outside it. Libraries should have clear policies in place regarding the number of students permitted to reserve a room.[2] For example, a student reserving a group study room for individual use could be considered to be wasting available space for others, especially during a high-volume time like finals or midterms. Libraries should also restrict the monopolizing of study rooms through consecutive reservations by the same group of students. Scheduling software can provide libraries with a system to accept study room reservations and keep statistics on use of the rooms, thus lessening the staff time devoted to scheduling issues.[3]

When creating group study rooms, strong consideration should be given to technology for the space. To provide spaces for students to practice presentations or collaborate on projects, libraries should offer large screens with laptop/network connectivity for easier viewing, whiteboards or smartboards, and multiple docking stations to connect several laptops. If groups of students interested in collaboration are steered into group study rooms, quiet study spaces in other parts of the libraries could become available for individual students. Flexible furnishings, adequate lighting, power, and network access (through either wireless or wired connectivity) are essential aspects for successful group study spaces.

LIBRARY CLASSROOMS

Like group study rooms, library classrooms can be in high demand for students or groups because of the space and technology they can provide.[4] These spaces present the library with opportunities to become active partners in the learning or teaching process. Instructors can offer the classroom as a way to introduce the library and its resources to students. Librarians can give instructional presentations on library resources or research methods. Library staff can use the space for training purposes. Groups can offer speakers to give presentations around related topics to their groups.

To offer a palatable learning environment, a library classroom will require adequate space for a standard number of students, presentation space for an instructor, and technology support, which could include individual workstations or projection capabilities. Whether planning a classroom for a new library or retrofitting classroom space into an existing library, library planners should ensure that the classroom be adaptable so that users can move around and work collaboratively, as well as being flexible enough so that the space can accommodate new technology when it becomes available. Aspects of adaptability can include moveable furnishings, laptops for instruction, wireless and wired network access, and variable lighting controls.

Scheduling a library classroom could be similar to scheduling group study rooms, with some form of appointment software providing support for booking the classroom. In addition, to ensure that the classroom is booked for its intended purpose, staff could require that the use planned be disclosed upon scheduling. Libraries may want to think carefully about what purposes are appropriate for library classrooms (e.g., library instruction sessions, faculty-led courses that rely on library resources) and what purposes might be less appropriate. In a landscape in which teaching spaces are at a premium, libraries may find themselves struggling to retain control over classroom spaces rather than cede ownership of the spaces to the course registrar or the university as a whole.

24/7 (OR 24/5 OR 24/6) OPERATIONS

Just as a library's electronic resources are available twenty-four hours a day, the demand for access to a library's physical confines has resulted in many libraries remaining open for twenty-four hours for five to seven days a week. While use between midnight and 6:00 a.m. may not be as high as other times of the day, the accessibility can provide users with a safe and quiet alternative that may not be available to them elsewhere. Providing twenty-four-hour access to a library is no small undertaking, and several things must be considered before leaving the doors open. Physical access to the library, staffing, and security must be addressed.

Several libraries offer twenty-four-hour access, but to only a part of the library.[5] A university library can be a very large building, and providing staff and security for the whole facility may not be feasible or cost-effective. Given that use during the late hours will likely be lower, a smaller space within the library may be acceptable. Ideally, the space should have its own entrance, and any internal doors that lead to the rest of the library should be lockable. Closing procedures for the majority of the library should include filtering students towards the twenty-four-hour or extended hours area. Once the twenty-four-hour area is secure, the area should have only one or two entry points. Access to the areas of the library that are open during the overnight hours could be limited through use of ID cards. This could involve either key card technology, such as RFID that unlocks a door, or a security checkpoint where identification is presented to a security guard or staff member for entry. If using key cards, library staff should work with student life or public safety personnel to ensure that part-time students and students living off campus have access to the building.

Staffing a library space for twenty-four hours can be difficult. The level of staffing might be dictated by what services will be offered in the space. For instance, can patrons check out or return materials? Some libraries rely heavily on student staff. For the overnight hours, student staff may be an option if students need the work to earn their living expenses and are able to keep odd hours. However, relying on students to staff this area may not be the best option, given that students' lives can often be dictated by their academic responsibilities. Employing full-time staff for a twenty-four-hour space might be ideal, but hiring and keeping staff for these nontraditional hours could be an ongoing problem. This is particularly true if the library does not have overnight operations for some periods during the year, such as the summer, and the overnight staff will not be employed during that time. If the twenty-four-hour space provided by the library is purely study space with no circulation services available, staffing the area with a security guard could be adequate.

Whether security is the primary source of staffing or the library relies on student or library staff for the after-midnight hours, the presence of a uniformed security guard in the space during the overnight hours can provide a sense of safety for the patrons. If an academic library is unable to provide a security guard within the twenty-four-hour space, it is recommended that the library consult with on-campus security to ensure staff receive the proper training and support in case a security situation arises.

DISABILITY SERVICE CONSIDERATIONS

Not all libraries have the ability to offer dedicated personnel to offer services to those with disabilities. Access services staff are often, and should be, trained to assist patrons with disabilities. The Americans with Disabilities Act (ADA) legally obligates libraries to provide public accommodations to those who need assistance. Examples of assistance might include ensuring appropriate physical access to the library building, retrieving items for users with physical or mobility disabilities, or providing assistive technologies, such as screen-reading equipment for users with visual disabilities or assistive listening devices for users with hearing disabilities. The American Libraries Association (ALA) provides a framework of guidelines for libraries to follow in order to be in compliance with the ADA.[6]

In a college or university environment, users may need official documentation of a disability to qualify for some accommodations, and this may often be coordinated through a campus office for disability services or office of student life. Policies and interpretations of ADA and related matters are always changing, so liaise with your appropriate campus office to ensure seamless service, and advocate for universal design principles in any library renovation.

SIGNAGE AND WAYFINDING

The area of signage and visual communication for wayfinding, perhaps one of the more neglected aspects of library buildings, often falls into the realm of access services. A coherent wayfinding scheme, combined with well-placed and clearly worded signs, can greatly reduce the number of directional questions received at service points and serve to communicate a welcoming and inclusive atmosphere.

Wayfinding is an umbrella term used for indicators (light, color, design elements) that guide patrons to a destination. Signs, directories, and digital displays are some of the tools in a wayfinding scheme. For large and complicated library buildings, use of a design consultant may be considered. It may also be helpful to perform a wayfinding study of one's users to identify failure points in one's current signage system.[7]

Above all else, a wayfinding system should be as simple and intuitive as possible, and librarians should restrain the impulse to label everything. Too many signs create information overload and can actually cause users to ignore potentially helpful signs. There may always be a need for temporary signs, but use of them should be limited. Well-designed and simple signs can be created using office productivity software, but a template should be used to maintain some uniformity. Signs will need to comply with all state and local building codes, and permanent signage must meet ADA requirements for braille and tactile graphics.

A recent trend in libraries is to integrate physical signage and virtual wayfinding tools more directly. Particularly in large buildings, some libraries have leveraged technology to provide interactive maps that link from the library catalog and show the user the precise location of a book on an online map.[8] Given the ongoing investment in keeping systems like these accurate and up-to-date (see chapter 2 on stacks management), libraries should consider carefully how many users will take advantage of these systems, both before implementing or updating them.

PEST MANAGEMENT AND ABATEMENT

Access services personnel are often the first to notice and respond to pest threats in a library. Your institution may have a contract with a pest management service, or it may need to coordinate services with custodial and plant operations. While common pests (mice and roaches, for example) may be covered by standard pest management, more exotic library menaces, such as silverfish, firebrats, bedbugs, and cigarette beetles, may need special consideration. Working with your plant operations personnel and developing an integrated pest management solution to prevent and control infestations are key to success. Any change in food policies or the introduction of a library cafe will merit a review of pest management and custodial procedures. Your pest management program should not be limited to public areas of the building; ensure that any staff lounge and office areas are also covered.

Controlling climate and climate fluctuations in a library building is also vitally important to preserving collections. Mold outbreaks can happen with little notice following a seemingly innocuous event that alters the environment in your library building. Even the most modern HVAC systems can create microclimates, or pockets of humid air, that allow molds to flourish. High relative humidity encourages both mold growth and insect activity. Extremely low relative humidity brings its own risks of desiccation for materials. Installing and maintaining a climate control system providing a stable environment with a temperature no higher than 70°F/21°C and a stable relative humidity between a minimum of 30 percent and a maximum of 50 percent is a common standard for preserving collections and maintaining a healthy building for patrons and staff. Due to the potential health hazards in any large mold outbreak, professional advice and mold remediation are recommended. Take protective measures, such as using respirators, gloves, and protective eyewear, when handling moldy materials. In general library collections, the cost of cleaning materials might outweigh the value of the volumes; prudently evaluate collections before proceeding.

DISASTER PLANNING

Preparing for a disaster can be a daunting task because it requires foresight to imagine what damaging event might occur and what effect it might have on the library. Access services, especially circulation, is often involved in this type of planning given that it has a very public location within a library building and that access services staff are generally available whenever the library building is open. While entire books are written about library disaster planning and all aspects of the topic cannot be covered here, it is worth noting that access services personnel are key players in any disaster response team.[9]

Disasters can come in many forms. Earthquakes and weather-related events can cause flooding, power outages, structural problems, and fires. Regardless of the circumstances the focus during and immediately after should be on safety. The safety of personnel and patrons is the key driver of any disaster response. Above all, stay safe, and keep people in your department safe.

Once patron and staff safety is assured, a disaster plan must involve the cleanup and preservation of potentially damaged materials. Libraries that have preservation experts should include them in the planning as their insight will be helpful in creating preventive measures and documenting postdisaster protocols. Just as the immediate response to a disaster is likely to involve security and emergency personnel from the campus or community, the overall disaster plan should integrate and liaise with safety personnel on the campus (for an academic library) or in the community (for a public library) to ensure the library's disaster planning corresponds with the campus or community disaster plan.

PLANNING FOR A NEW LIBRARY OR RENOVATING AN EXISTING LIBRARY

Planning for a new library or renovation of existing library space can be an exciting and challenging endeavor. Access services librarians and staff must advocate for a seat at the table early in the process to ensure that our ideas and concerns are incorporated into any final design. Access services staff are often best situated to keep two factors in the forefront of planning discussions: the pragmatics of workflows and staff processes and, more importantly, the user experience itself.

On a practical level, access services staff are well positioned to address questions of how proposed building plans would impact daily workflows and staff processes. Where are books returned? Is it close to where they are processed and shelved? Do pathways allow book carts and other equipment to be moved where needed efficiently and with minimal disruption to users? Are staff workstations designed in ways that encourage interaction with users? In other words, designers of these spaces should engage staff on the daily tasks of staff and practices of library patrons. Access services librarians should prepare themselves for these planning meetings by meeting with staff and students to understand different points of view on what is desired in a library.

More important than staff processes, however, is the user experience. What is the first impression the building will make on users? How easy is it for users to find someone to help them? How do the library's physical spaces create expectations for behavior, whether of quiet studiousness or active group inquiry? What paths will users take through the building in a given visit? In short, how can users' needs and desires be anticipated by the building itself, and how can universal design principles be incorporated to ensure access for all? Access services staff should be willing and able to engage in discussion with other public services staff, with outside architects and consultants, and most importantly with the users themselves to understand users' needs and to help translate those into a compelling vision for new or renovated library spaces.

The user experience and workability for staff are two important issues, but there are a few other preliminary actions that should take place. Communication is vitally important during a construction project. Updates should be shared early and often with staff and patrons. Disruptions will likely occur with renovations or through moving collections to a new library, and announcing these disruptions early and often will avoid patrons and staff being caught by surprise. As a major public service point, access services staff should have a communication plan in place to answer questions from patrons on the construction project. Staff should also be prepared to manage service interruptions or to provide additional services to minimize patron inconvenience.

Along with communication, protection of collections should be a focal point during the construction project. Collections may not move during a renovation project. In these cases, preservation should be a paramount concern due to the risks, such as dust or sprinkler leaks. If collections need to be moved to a new library, careful planning must be done to ensure the materials are moved in a safe manner and are shelved in the proper order.[10]

CONCLUSION

As this chapter outlines, access services may take many and varied roles in building management. From mediating group study spaces to battling mice to planning major renovations, anything and everything may fall into our purview. It's what makes working in access services so interesting and, at times, exhausting. Participating in a new library space planning process or creating and managing collaborative spaces like group study rooms can be intellectually stimulating, while planning for an impending disaster or dealing with pest issues will not make the front page of a library newsletter. Building management for access services staff can span the spectrum from exciting to monotonous, but all are vital services that take organization, foresight, and commitment.

Keeping signage current or dealing with construction dust is probably not the reason many have chosen librarianship. However, access services casts a wide net of responsibilities, and building management is included. More importantly, the space and facilities issues that the access services department manages are essential to creating and maintaining a clean, safe, and appealing library. If we think of building management in terms of serving our users, even the seemingly mundane can be imbued with significance. By focusing on our users, we are also more likely to make better choices—both small and large—about the spaces we manage: choices that will have a lasting impact on how our users experience and perceive libraries. Ultimately, building management can be a rewarding and deeply satisfying task.

NOTES

1. See Harold B. Shill and Shawn Tonner, "Does the Building Still Matter? Usage Patterns in New, Expanded, and Renovated Libraries, 1995–2002," *College and Research Libraries* 65, no. 2 (March 2004): 123–150, and Heather V. Cunningham and Susanne Tabur, "Learning Space Attributes: Reflections on Academic Library Design and Its Use," *Journal of Learning Spaces* 1, no. 2 (2012), http://libjournal .uncg.edu/ojs/index.php/jls/article/view/392/283.

2. For policy examples, see "Policies on Room Use at the University of Chicago Library," University of Chicago Library, accessed March 28, 2013, http://www.lib .uchicago.edu/e/using/rooms/policies.html, and "Group Study Rooms," New York University Libraries, January 2013, http://library.nyu.edu/services/group_study .html.

3. Scheduling software options run the gamut from open-source programs such as PhpScheduleit and OpenRoom, to modestly priced SAS options like LibCal (by Springshare, the same company behind the popular LibGuides platform), to expensive, enterprise-level solutions such as MeetingRoomManager.

4. For research on classrooms in libraries, see Shill and Tonner, "Does the Building Still Matter?" and Cunningham and Tabur, "Learning Space Attributes."

5. For examples of twenty-four-hour access to library spaces, see "24-Hour Study Room," UC Davis University Library, accessed March 28, 2013, http://www .lib.ucdavis.edu/ul/services/computers/wireless/ehrr.php; "24/7 Study Space in Hayden Library," MIT Libraries, accessed March 28, 2013, http://libraries.mit. edu/hayden/24study.html; and "Goldstein Undergraduate Study Center," Penn Libraries, December 9, 2009, http://www.library.upenn.edu/access/gusc.html.

6. See *Library Services for People with Disabilities Policy* (Chicago: ALA, January 16, 2001), online at ASCLA website, accessed March 22, 2013, http://www.ala.org/ ascla/asclaissues/libraryservices.

7. See Nancy Kress, David Larsen, Tod Olson, and Agnes Tatarka, "Wayfinding in the Library: Usability Testing of Physical Spaces," in *Proceedings of the Library Assessment Conference: Building Effective, Sustainable, Practical Assessment (September 25–27, 2006; Charlottesville, Virginia)*, ed. Francine DeFranco, Steve Hiller, Lisa Janicke Hinchliffe, Kristina Justh, Martha Kyrillidou, Jim Self, and Joan Stein (Washington, DC: ARL, 2007), 33–41, and David Larsen, and Agnes Tatarka, "Wayfinding Revisited: Improved Techniques for Assessing and

Solving Usability Problems in Physical Spaces," in *Proceedings of the 2008 Library Assessment Conference: Building Effective, Sustainable, Practical Assessment (August 4–7, 2008; Seattle, Washington)*, ed. Steve Hiller, Kristina Justh, Martha Kyrillidou, and Jim Self (Washington, DC: ARL, 2009), 65–73.

8. An example of this kind of tool is StackMap, accessed May 6, 2013, http://www.stackmap.com/.

9. See Emma Dadson, *Emergency Planning and Responses for Libraries, Museums, and Archives* (Lanham, MD: Scarecrow, 2012); "Preservation," Library of Congress, accessed March 22, 2013, http://www.loc.gov/preservation/; and Miriam B. Kahn, *Disaster Response and Planning for Libraries* (Chicago: ALA Editions, 2012).

10. See Philip C. Leighton and David C. Weber, *Planning Academic and Research Libraries* (Chicago: ALA Editions, 1999), and Jeannette Woodward, *Creating the Customer-Driven Academic Library* (Chicago: ALA Editions, 2009), which address the challenges and issues around a new library or renovated facility.

BIBLIOGRAPHY

American Library Association. *Library Services for People with Disabilities Policy.* Chicago: American Library Association, January 16, 2001. Available online at ASCLA website, accessed March 22, 2013, http://www.ala.org/ascla/asclaissues/libraryservices.

Cunningham, Heather V., and Susanne Tabur. "Learning Space Attributes: Reflections on Academic Library Design and Its Use." *Journal of Learning Spaces* 1, no. 2 (2012), http://libjournal.uncg.edu/ojs/index.php/jls/article/view/392/283.

Dadson, Emma. *Emergency Planning and Responses for Libraries, Museums, and Archives.* Lanham MD: Scarecrow, 2012.

Kahn, Miriam B. *Disaster Response and Planning for Libraries.* Chicago: ALA Editions, 2012.

Kress, Nancy, David Larsen, Tod Olson, and Agnes Tatarka. "Wayfinding in the Library: Usability Testing of Physical Spaces." In *Proceedings of the Library Assessment Conference: Building Effective, Sustainable, Practical Assessment (September 25–27, 2006; Charlottesville, Virginia)*, edited by Francine DeFranco, Steve Hiller, Lisa Janicke Hinchliffe, Kristina Justh, Martha Kyrillidou, Jim Self, and Joan Stein, 33–41. Washington, DC: Association of Research Libraries, 2007.

Larsen, David, and Agnes Tatarka. "Wayfinding Revisited: Improved Techniques for Assessing and Solving Usability Problems in Physical Spaces." In *Proceedings of the 2008 Library Assessment Conference: Building Effective, Sustainable,*

Practical Assessment (August 4–7, 2008; Seattle, Washington), edited by Steve Hiller, Kristina Justh, Martha Kyrillidou, and Jim Self, 65–73. Washington, DC: Association of Research Libraries, 2009.

Leighton, Philip C., and David C. Weber. *Planning Academic and Research Libraries.* Chicago: ALA Editions, 1999.

Library of Congress. "Preservation." Library of Congress, accessed March 22, 2013, http://www.loc.gov/preservation/.

Massachusetts Institute of Technology. "24/7 Study Space in Hayden Library." MIT Libraries, accessed March 28, 2013, http://libraries.mit.edu/hayden/24study.html.

New York University Libraries. "Group Study Rooms." NYU Libraries, January 2013, http://library.nyu.edu/services/group_study.html.

Shill, Harold B., and Shawn Tonner. "Does the Building Still Matter? Usage Patterns in New, Expanded, and Renovated Libraries, 1995–2002." *College and Research Libraries* 65, no. 2 (March 2004): 123–150.

University of California-Davis University Library, "24-Hour Study Room." UC Davis University Library, accessed March 28, 2013, http://www.lib.ucdavis.edu/ul/services/computers/wireless/ehrr.php.

University of Chicago Library. "Policies on Room Use at the University of Chicago Library." University of Chicago Library, accessed March 23, 2013, http://www.lib .uchicago.edu/e/using/rooms/policies.html.

University of Pennsylvania. "Goldstein Undergraduate Study Center." Penn Libraries, December 9, 2009, http://www.library.upenn.edu/access/gusc.html.

Woodward, Jeannette. *Creating the Customer-Driven Academic Library.* Chicago: ALA Editions, 2009.

Emerging Technologies and Spaces in Access Services

Katherine Furlong
Director, Access and Technical Services, Lafayette College

David McCaslin
Head of Access and Fulfillment Services,
California Institute of Technology

THE EMERGENCE of new technologies and alternative uses of space increase opportunities for access services departments to offer better resources and services to their users. As technology becomes more entwined in people's lives, libraries will be expected to address their patrons' digital needs. Access services departments that embrace new technology can circulate new hardware to their users or provide unique services and become collaborative partners in research or education. The shift towards technology and digital resources over traditional print creates opportunities for library space to become adaptable and collaborative.

CIRCULATING TECHNOLOGY

Over a decade ago, libraries began to introduce laptop computer lending to their patrons.[1] Offering laptops for checkout provides users the opportunity to work in comfort or mobile freedom from a computer lab. However, the circulation of laptops presents access services staff with a number of issues to address. The circulation staff must define a policy for laptop lending to protect the library and inform the user of his or her responsibilities when borrowing a laptop. This includes the length of loan period, whether the laptop can leave the building, and what is permissible use of a library laptop. Staff should explain the responsibility for the equipment a user assumes while using a laptop at the time of checkout. While laptops have consistently declined in price since their introduction, the cost is still higher than that of the typical lost or damaged book.

A longer loan period and freedom to leave the library could increase the chances of damage or theft. Yet these risks must be weighed against a desire to give users opportunities with the laptops. Server restrictions may protect a library resource from possible theft or damage, but they will also discourage users from benefiting from the service or device. A balance must be struck to ensure security for the laptop and maximize use by the patron.

The library's user population and the number of available laptops will play a role in determining an ideal loan period. The integrated library system (ILS) may also have prescribed loan period parameters that must be used in determining a loan period. It is good practice to offer a shorter loan period if a library has a high user population and few laptops to lend. This will assure reasonable availability for users. A longer loan period is generally an indication that the laptop may be used outside the library; shorter loan periods may not offer the borrower sufficient time to leave the library facility. Some libraries with less than a twenty-four-hour loan period do not allow circulating laptops to leave the building. Libraries that offer a loan period of twenty-four hours or more usually allow users to leave the building with library these materials.

While the checkout process for a laptop will resemble that for a book, it could include a written authorization form that allows users to read the rules related to use of the laptop and sign, accepting those responsibilities. A written acknowledgement would provide possible recourse for the library if a laptop is damaged or altered while checked out to a patron. It may be prudent to consult with the library's general counsel when drafting such authorization forms. Before checkout and upon return, staff should inspect the laptop to confirm it is in good condition and proper working order. This information can also be noted on the authorization form, which again verifies any damage or alterations that occurred while the laptop was checked out.

The circulation of laptops must include collaboration with the library technology staff. Procedures should be developed to address the cleaning, housing, and charging and replacement cycle for the laptops. In addition, their assistance would be needed to provide troubleshooting support for issues that might occur with a laptop.

Circulating just laptops may not satisfy users' needs. Libraries should be prepared to offer laptop accessories to patrons. For many years, libraries have circulated non-book items such as headphones, dry-erase markers, and Ethernet cables. Libraries should be willing to circulate computer mice and battery chargers for use with laptops, in addition to headphones and Ethernet cables. The circulation of these accessories can mirror the process for laptop checkout, with a similar loan period and a written authorization form.

Laptop lending is a large component of non-book lending for libraries, but other electronic hardware can be circulated to library patrons. Patrons now expect more from libraries than just providing content through print and digital resources; they expect that libraries will also offer tools for creating content and mobile devices that store content. The circulation of these types of hardware can mirror the process developed for laptop circulation, but each offers unique challenges and requires special attention.

Digital cameras for still photography or high-quality video recording have become popular for patrons to check out to produce visual projects or document research. This type of hardware can be very sensitive with regard to lenses and settings. Staff should be trained on the basic handling and operation of circulating camera models and share this knowledge with users. Documentation should be available for staff and users to refer to. In addition, libraries should clarify if they offer memory cards or expect patrons to provide their own memory cards. Digital cameras usually have a small internal memory capacity. Staff must review this space and erase files to ensure privacy from one user to the next.

Gaming systems, such as Sony's PlayStation and Nintendo's Wii, have grown popular with libraries that seek to engage their young users with technology that promotes problem solving, creative thinking, and teamwork.[2] The use and circulation of gaming systems can vary between libraries depending on space limitations and available funds. Libraries with adequate space could furnish designated space, gaming systems, monitors, and furniture for use within libraries. Circulation staff could be called upon to administer and schedule the gaming space as well as circulating gaming units and individual games. For libraries unable to offer this type of space, staff may decide to circulate gaming systems for use outside of the library. Like laptops and cameras, this type of hardware must be treated with care by users and staff to ensure longevity of use.

Digital projectors are a great resource to offer patrons, who may use them for class presentations or to display a popular film. In a sense, a digital projector can be viewed as a computer accessory and treated as such. However, the sheer size and cost of this type of equipment warrant special care. Training on how to properly operate the projector may be a precondition to checking out the device.

Tablet computers, or simply tablets, combine high mobility and easy-to-use functionality with the strong productivity capabilities of a laptop computer to form a very popular electronic device. Apple's iPad, Google's

Nexus, and Samsung's Galaxy are examples of a highly mobile computer with a touchscreen in place of a static keyboard. The use of these devices can alternate between entertainment options like reading books, watching movies, or playing games and production tasks like statistical manipulation, presentation creation, or academic research. Due to their user-friendly interfaces, they have grown in popularity and may become highly requested by library patron populations. Libraries that invest in tablet hardware must recognize the risk of tablets becoming outdated by newer models. Competition among tablet manufacturers and advancement of technology have ensured that new tablets could be substantively superior to models produced a year or two previously. If libraries choose to circulate tablets, policies should be in place to address the prospect of replacing tablets with newer models. Library budgets could limit the possibility of refreshing the collection with newer tablets or the frequency with which this could be done. However, these limitations could affect the circulation rate or popularity of the devices for patrons.

The circulation of tablets could emulate the laptop process, with some exceptions. Library staff must decide how the tablet will be used and can shape how it is used by adding software applications, or apps, to it. Using Apple's iPad as an example, apps are added through Apple's iTunes website. The apps range from games to office production to reference to entertainment. While some apps are free, others are not, and the cost of the apps should be considered when budgeting for tablet circulation. Upon checkout, users should be informed of the restrictions on use on the tablet. When the device is returned, staff should inspect the tablet to confirm it is in good working order, but also to check for any software or app updates. Many software developers are constantly improving their apps to add new features or better operability. Staff must be attentive when inspecting tablets and update apps when needed.

For those who enjoy having several books at their fingertips in a small, easy-to-handle device, e-readers have become extremely popular. Amazon's Kindle and Barnes and Noble's Nook are two of the most recognized e-reader models. While Amazon and Barnes and Noble have expanded the functionality of the Kindle and Nook to include models that are essentially tablets, their basic e-reader models are purely devices to provide electronic access to books and magazines. The circulation of e-readers can also resemble the laptop and tablet process.

The major difference between the e-reader and other circulating e-devices is content. With laptops, projectors, and even tablets, the devices themselves will likely be used to produce content for the user. The e-reader, much like a book, already contains content.. Many libraries include the e-books found on the reading device in their online catalog for users to discover. Content may be added to e-readers in various ways. Collection development librarians could select a pool of titles to be available on the e-readers, or the reader could select the content.

Patron-driven acquisitions (PDA) is a concept in which the user selects titles and initiates a library purchase request independent of any collection development decision by a librarian. Some models of PDA involve vendors making the available title lists display in the library's online catalog; titles are added the collection only when certain predefined conditions are met. The conditions generally include the number of times a particular title is accessed, after which a copy will be added to the library's permanent collection. Allowing users to select and add titles to the e-readers would be another form of PDA. Just like circulation of the device, patrons would need to be educated on the rules for adding materials to the e-readers. Libraries would also have to clearly define the parameters for allowing patrons to acquire titles with library funds and add the titles to the e-readers. A number of issues must be addressed before engaging in such a service. Publishers' licensing for e-readers, simultaneous access on multiple e-readers, and sustainability must be investigated to ensure success.[3]

To offer a successful circulation program for any nontraditional item, such as electronic devices, circulation staff should be thoroughly trained on how to operate the hardware and provide troubleshooting assistance when needed. Developing a wiki or creating easily accessible documentation will provide staff with a go-to reference in times of need. In addition, library policies must clearly define the loan period and inform patrons of rules on what use of the device is acceptable and unacceptable. In addition, procedures must be formed to address issues that might arise. Circulation staff are in a unique position to provide education to patrons on proper operation and responsibilities for use the hardware as well as report anecdotal feedback to the library administration on lessons learned from providing the service.

PATRON-DRIVEN ACCESS SERVICES

Technology has improved circulation processes since the days of staff waiting for books to be brought to the desk and stamped with the due date. Integrated library systems (ILSs) have provided for a smooth process with barcodes and automated due dates generated, but staff may still be required to complete the process. With self-check machines and radio-frequency identification (RFID) tags, the time required for staff to check out books to patrons has decreased; in fact, staff time may no longer be needed. For libraries with few staff members performing many tasks, the labor costs and staff time saved from performing routine circulation tasks could be valuable.

Self-check machines are not a recent development, but technology has improved their performance and reliability.[4] In the past, dependability was a concern for libraries where self-check machines received high use. If a library changed its ILS, there might be compatibility issues between a self-check system and the new ILS. Some self-check machines with card swipe technology required ID cards in good condition. Students, who use their ID cards for dormitory access and meal purchases as well as for the library, could have damaged ID cards. Some self-check machines require a book to be placed in a specific spot or angled so a barcode reader can scan the item's barcode. These conditions require patience from the patron.

Due to advances in technology[5] and competition among vendors, self-check machines have become more dependable and easier to use.

Investigating and testing self-check machines is an important key to possible implementation of the service to a library. A library should choose self-check machines that meet the needs of its patron population and also provide security for the library's collection. An unreliable self-check machine could result in missing or stolen materials, leading to staff needing to spend time conducting shelf searches or purchasing replacement copies, as well as patron frustration and dissatisfaction.

The improved performance of self-check machines could partially be due to increased use of RFID chips in library books and ID cards. Like self-check machines, RFID is not new to libraries. The appeal of RFID is rooted in the benefits it can deliver to circulation and inventory maintenance. For manual circulation, using books with RFID tags could reduce repetitive motions and prevent occupational injuries such as carpal tunnel syndrome for library staff. Self-check machines with RFID-reading technology are easier to use and less intimidating for patrons, who need only place the books and ID card within range of the RFID reader. For collection maintenance, RFID offers library staff the ability to examine and correct collection location without having to touch multiple items. However, cost has been a major obstacle to integrating RFID into more libraries. RFID technology has declined in cost in the past decade but still remains an issue for libraries that might consider retroactively tagging their collections and installing RFID hardware. Staff working with RFID must also be successfully trained with the technology.[6]

STUDENT WORKSTATIONS

A mainstay in academic libraries in the twenty-first century is student access to computing. Many libraries designate space for public computer workstations to be grouped together in a computer lab, while others disperse public workstations throughout the library building. Some libraries provide both arrangements. Given the public space these workstations often occupy, access services staff are often called upon to monitor and possibly troubleshoot problems that might occur with public computers. Access services staff should be trained to triage technical problems and have procedures in place to refer difficult issues to the appropriate staff.

Not every student user owns a computer or has access to a high-speed Internet connection, so these workstations fill a need for these patrons. In addition, these workstations may offer software applications otherwise unavailable to users. Student computing spaces could also allow small groups of users to work collaboratively on assignments or projects. All of these factors could lead to crowded computer labs or long waits for individual workstations. Access services staff should rely on their public service training to manage problems that might arise with open computing spaces. Staff should also be trained to address computer use that may be offensive to other patrons. For example, a patron who uses a public computer to view pornographic or potentially insensitive images can upset others in view of the computer. Access services staff must meet with the individual and explain the acceptable use of public computers within that library—assuming the library has such a policy.

MERGED SERVICE POINTS/NEW AND ALTERNATIVE SERVICE POINTS

Learning Commons

A learning commons (also called information commons, knowledge commons, or reference studio, among other names) is a space that combines traditional reference and research services with new elements supporting emerging technologies or student services in a larger and more integrated environment. Some learning commons include writing centers, information technology help desks, math or quantitative learning support centers, and a variety of other student support services. In the best models, students can experience the support and expertise of library, computing, media, and other professionals all in one combined learning space. The concept emerged in the early 1990s and has quickly become a key design element of new and renovated academic library buildings.[7]

Creating a learning commons can represent a major capital expense and require many dedicated staff. The Tombros and McWhirter Knowledge Commons at the Pennsylvania State University, for example, was a multiyear building project and includes video production areas, living room areas, podcasting facilities, green "living" walls, service kiosks, and integrated help desk areas, all carved out of prime first floor space in the historic library. The knowledge commons, a collaboration between Penn State's University Libraries and Information Technology Services, is envisioned as a student-centered space featuring areas for relaxation and collaboration and full of the just-in-time help needed for academic research and multimedia creation.[8]

Sometimes, a smaller-scale learning commons can be created through more informal partnerships and by repurposing existing staff and space. Often legacy library services or areas where collections are shrinking (such as print periodicals or reference collections) can be repurposed into a learning commons. No matter how the commons is created, the goal of student-centered, integrated services remains. Whether the commons is large or small, the same issues are at stake for providing fluid services in a library that respects and makes the most of both print and digital environments.

While the learning commons model often centers around services that have traditionally been part of reference's milieu, access services often gets pulled into the mix. From integrated circulation and reference service desks to building maintenance issues, serving patrons in a learning commons brings its own challenges. Whatever the interaction within the learning commons model is called—a consultation, a drop in, or a reference interview—providing the right support for students and faculty is key. Properly staffing the support desks and clearly communicating available levels of support can help to manage student and staff expectations and experiences. Providing this staffing requires clear reporting lines, defined service goals, and flexible referral and tracking systems.

Circulation of a variety of equipment to support multimedia creation is often one of the services offered in a learning commons environment. From digital video production cameras to music keyboards and FireWire drives, the array of devices in circulation can quickly become overwhelming. Some low-tech items, like headphone splitters, seemingly require little or no staff intervention, while other items require specialized training and software to operate. While access services staff may not need to be experts in using the equipment, their expertise in policy making and in labeling and circulating items will enhance any program. Most ILS systems can be used in robust ways to display messages, track inventory, book items, and collect statistics. Consider customizing the records for each piece of equipment so a pop-up message appears at checkout and checkin reminding staff to look for all the various pieces and parts. Custom hang tags and labels can also assist in tracking each item. Include a photograph on each hang tag showing what should be contained in each case and information for patrons on where to find assistance or the online manuals for each piece of equipment. Adequate space for secure equipment storage and battery charging can be a challenge but needs to be incorporated into your service area.

If your information commons includes large-format-poster printing or the more cutting-edge 3D printers, access services may also be called upon to coordinate cost-recovery measures.[9] Tracking payment for print jobs is a thankless task, but one made easier by a variety of print management solutions on the market, such as Pharos. One should be aware of what systems may already be in place on your campus and consider a system that directly interfaces with your campus enterprise system for ease of tracking and billing and to help provide a unified user experience across the institution.

In some learning commons, circulation and access functionalities are being provided by self-serve kiosks and high- and low-tech vending machines. Automated laptop-vending kiosks have the ability to let users obtain laptops or tablet computers as intuitively as using an ATM at a bank. When the patron swipes an ID card or credit card, the kiosk authenticates the patron, tracks circulation, and imposes any necessary fees. Once an item is returned, the kiosk has the ability to erase data on the device and ensure that the machine is charged and ready for the next patron. Other vending machines serve up everything from office supplies to books and DVDs.[10]

Collaborative Spaces

Related to both learning commons and group study spaces, collaborative community spaces in libraries are flexible and modular environments where the social learning needs of patrons can be met. In some ways, collaborative spaces are a natural outgrowth of the learning commons trend and research into constructivist learning theory. Constructivist theory holds that learning occurs when students have to create—or construct—meaning for themselves.[11] Collaborative spaces allow students free rein to work with others to learn as part of an active, social process. From rather extreme experiments in library innovation such as Harvard's 2012 LABrary to more permanent spaces such as the University of West Florida's Great Good Place, collaborative spaces can take many forms to meet local needs.[12] While many well-publicized collaborative spaces are large undertakings, some needs can be met on a smaller scale by outfitting nooks within the library for collaborative teamwork.

The design of the collaborative space is crucial, and the design process should involve campus stakeholders including faculty, students, librarians, technicians, and custodial personnel (after all, if the collaborative space is not well maintained, no one will want to stay). Consider a variety of low- and high-tech solutions for sparking discussion and creativity. A whiteboard and AC outlets for charging personal devices may be more crucial to success than the latest projection equipment. Some students want a degree of privacy during their collaboration—moveable partitions and flexible seating options can help to meet this need. Try to avoid using single-purpose furnishings that cannot be reused in the future.

The common thread linking collaborative spaces, large and small, is a sense of community involvement in what sociologist Ray Oldenburg termed a "third place" (with the first and second places being home and work).[13] Collaborative "third" spaces celebrate informal public gathering places that support the communal production and sharing of knowledge and resources in a creative, flexible environment. Ubiquitous wireless connectivity, a wide array of digital multimedia creation tools, and human-centered furnishings coalesce into a "collaboratory" for constructivist learning.

Communal spaces in libraries offer many outreach and programming possibilities, and the open nature of the space echoes the inter- and cross-disciplinary aspects of the work that can happen there.

Partnership Service Strategies

Managing learning commons, collaborative spaces, and shared service points is not easy, and often not exclusively under the library's purview. Models for service in partnered spaces vary based on the structure and philosophy of organization. Collaborative management, flexibility, and clear communication are keys to success.[14]

Most learning commons and communal spaces are in some way shared spaces within the library. Space is often the most valuable asset on a college or university campus, and if the library is providing space for non-library departments, then the guest relationship should be clearly delineated. Agreements with outside departments may be formal or informal, but a memorandum of understanding (MOU) outlining expectations and providing a framework for partnership is a vital tool for avoiding conflict. Clearly outline items for which the library is responsible (power, coordinating access, etc.) and items the guest department must provide (e.g., staffing and training, office supplies, specialized equipment). You don't want service in the shared area to break down because of disputes over trivial matters like changing (or paying for) batteries or toner cartridges. The best MOUs are designed to allow for flexibility and evolution, and any agreement will need to be reviewed on a regular basis to ensure it remains in line with current needs and supports best practices in service delivery. The process of crafting and revising an MOU can also help to defuse misunderstandings that may arise when differing organizational cultures are brought together in a shared service environment. Addressing these organizational differences directly can empower staff to move beyond seeing differences as problems and into a space where differences can be used to provide the best possible service to the community.

Consider creating an advisory stakeholders group to ensure clear communication and foster a true sense of collaborative decision making for the shared space. Partner departments in the learning commons should also be taken into consideration during any library-specific training. If a service is offered in the library, then not only should service providers be aware of library policies in general, especially policies surrounding patron confidentiality and copyright, but the staff providing the service should be included in crucial activities such as the library disaster response plan. Formalizing shared training expectations in the MOU can help to ease the process.

If your shared service point combines only library departments (such as a consolidated reference and circulation desk), something like an internal memorandum of understanding should still be crafted between departments. Culture and work expectations can vary between reference and circulation staff even in a small library, and while consolidating service points might make perfect sense from the patron's point of view, the day-to-day operating details will still need to be carefully considered and mutually agreed upon.

One of the most compelling arguments for a single library service point is that it alleviates any uncertainty on the part of the patron. Patrons no longer need to figure out which desk to approach or whether their question is important enough to "bother" a reference librarian. All issues can be brought to one place for service. Public services staff who are appropriately cross-trained can gain confidence and, hopefully, increased job satisfaction through a more varied skill set.

Ultimately, the success of any shared service point depends upon the training, talents, attitude, and knowledge of the workers. Provide (and budget for) continuous training, and foster an environment that encourages staff at all levels to try new technologies and experiment with new services and ideas. It's not easy sometimes to determine the difference between a tech problem, an information problem, and a circulation problem, and often desk personnel must multitask or find the right person for a job. Establish and follow a robust workflow/referral/problem-tracking and resolution system. There are a variety of high- and low-tech tools available to help with tracking. Use the data from your tracking system to analyze staffing and use patterns. But don't rely on quantitative data alone in making decisions; talk to the various desk workers, as well as students and researchers using the space, to ensure that needs are being met and resources are adequately distributed. The best decisions are made with both quantitative and qualitative data, providing a robust picture of what's really happening within your organization. Once you achieve that clear picture, you can make adjustments to services as necessary. More information on data-driven decision making and survey methodologies can be found in chapter 10.

Finally, remember that a staff member with a strong service orientation who is dedicated to finding answers will often outperform those personnel with extremely strong technical skills. As always seems to be the case, the quality of the personal interaction is key to any successful library transaction.

NOTES

1. See Doris Munson and Elizabeth Malia, "Laptop Circulation at Eastern Washington University," *Journal of Access Services* 5, no. 1–2 (2008): 211–219, and Jason Vaughan and Brett Burnes, "Bringing Them In and Checking Them Out: Laptop Use in the Modern Academic Library," *Information Technology and Libraries* 21, no. 2 (June 2002): 52–62.
2. See Suellen S. Adams, "The Case for Video Games in Libraries," *Library Review* 58, no. 3 (2009): 196–202, and James Paul Gee, *What Video Games Have to Teach Us about Learning and Literacy* (New York: Palgrave MacMillan, 2007).

3. See David A. Swords, ed., *Patron-Driven Acquisitions: History and Best Practices* (Berlin: De Gruyter, 2011).

4. For a historical perspective, see Jackie Mardikian, "Self-Service Charge Systems: Current Technological Applications and Their Implications for the Future Library," *Reference Services Review* 23, no. 4 (1995): 19–38.

5. For more information, see "NISO Publishes New Version of NCIP-NISO Circulation Interchange Protocol" (news release), National Information Standards Organization, August 22, 2012, http://www.niso.org/news/pr/ view?item_key=c914d849ab4a5f9912495395049737482fd3b9f0.

6. See Linda Howard and Max Anderson, "RFID Technology in the Library Environment," *Journal of Access Services* 3, no. 2 (2005): 29–39, and Laura Smart, "Making Sense of RFID," *netConnect,* supplement to *Library Journal,* October 14, 2004: 4–14.

7. See Elizabeth K. Heitsh and Robert P. Holley, "The Information and Learning Commons: Some Reflections," *New Review of Academic Librarianship* 17, no. 1 (2011): 64–77; see also Russell D. Bailey and Barbara Tierney, *Transforming Library Service through Information Commons: Case Studies for the Digital Age* (Chicago: ALA, 2008).

8. "Tombros and McWhirter Knowledge Commons," Penn State University Libraries, 2013, http://www.libraries.psu.edu/psul/kc.html.

9. For a discussion of 3D printing, see Yvette M. Chin, "University of Nevada Offers 3-D Printing across the Board," *Library Journal Academic Newswire,* August 7, 2012, http://lj.libraryjournal.com/2012/08/academic-libraries/u-nevada-library -offers-3d-printing-across-the-board/. For an example of cost-recovery measures, see "Makerspace," NCSU Libraries, accessed April 4, 2013, http://www.lib.ncsu .edu/spaces/makerspace.

10. For an example, see "Drexel Introduces Kiosk That Dispenses MacBooks for Student Use" (news release), Drexel University, January 9, 2013, http://www .drexel.edu/now/news-media/releases/archive/2013/January/Drexel-Libraries- Introduces-MacBook-Kiosk/.

11. Constructivist theory is based on the work of Jean Piaget; for a brief overview, see Mary Lamon, "Constructivist Approach," *Encyclopedia of Education,* ed. James W. Guthrie (New York: Macmillan Reference, 2002), 1463–67. For an overview of the constructivist approach in libraries, see Bryan Sinclair, "Commons 2.0: Library Spaces Designed for Collaborative Learning," *EDUCAUSE Quarterly* 30, no. 4 (2007): 4–6.

12. Jennifer Korber,"The Harvard Labrary: A Design Experiment in Library Futures." *Library Journal Academic Newswire,* December 13, 2012, http://lj.libraryjournal .com/2012/12/future-of-libraries/the-harvard-labrary-a-design-experiment -in-library-futures/; "The Great Good Place—Now Open!" University of West Florida Libraries, accessed April 4, 2013, http://library.uwf.edu/about/spaces/ great_good_place/.

13. Ray Oldenburg, *The Great Good Place: Cafés, Coffee Shops, Bookstores, Bars, Hair Salons, and Other Hangouts at the Heart of a Community* (New York: Marlowe, 1999).

14. For more on service strategies, see Kay Vyhnanek and Christy Zlatos, *Reconfiguring Service Delivery: SPEC Kit 327* (Washington, DC: ARL, 2011).

BIBLIOGRAPHY

Adams, Suellen S. "The Case for Video Games in Libraries." *Library Review* 58, no. 3 (2009): 196–202.

Bailey, Russell D., and Barbara Tierney. *Transforming Library Service through Information Commons: Case Studies for the Digital Age.* Chicago: American Library Association, 2008.

Chin, Yvette M. "University of Nevada Offers 3-D Printing across the Board." *Library Journal Academic Newswire,* August 7, 2012, http://lj.libraryjournal.com/2012/08/ academic-libraries/u-nevada-library-offers-3d-printing-across-the-board/.

Drexel University. "Drexel Introduces Kiosk That Dispenses MacBooks for Student Use," news release. Drexel University, January 9, 2013, http://www.drexel.edu/ now/news-media/releases/archive/2013/January/Drexel-Libraries-Introduces -MacBook-Kiosk/.

Gee, James Paul. *What Video Games Have to Teach Us about Learning and Literacy.* New York: Palgrave MacMillan, 2007.

Heitsh, Elizabeth K., and Robert P. Holley. "The Information and Learning Commons: Some Reflections." *New Review of Academic Librarianship* 17, no. 1 (2011): 64–77.

Howard, Linda, and Max Anderson. "RFID Technology in the Library Environment." *Journal of Access Services* 3, no. 2 (2005): 29–39.

Korber, Jennifer. "The Harvard Labrary: A Design Experiment in Library Futures." *Library Journal Academic Newswire,* December 13, 2012, http://lj.libraryjournal .com/2012/12/future-of-libraries/the-harvard-labrary-a-design-experiment-in -library-futures/.

Lamon, Mary. "Constructivist Approach." *Encyclopedia of Education*, edited by James W. Guthrie, 1463–67. New York: Macmillan Reference, 2002.

Mardikian, Jackie. "Self-Service Charge Systems: Current Technological Applications and Their Implications for the Future Library." *Reference Services Review* 23, no. 4 (1995): 19–38.

Munson, Doris, and Elizabeth Malia. "Laptop Circulation at Eastern Washington University." *Journal of Access Services* 5, no. 1–2 (2008): 211–219.

National Information Standards Organization. "NISO Publishes New Version of NCIP-NISO Circulation Interchange Protocol," news release. NISO, August 22, 2012, http://www.niso.org/news/pr/view?item_key=c914d849ab4a5f9912495395049737482fd3b9f0.

North Carolina State University Libraries. "Makerspace." NCSU Libraries, accessed April 4, 2013, http://www.lib.ncsu.edu/spaces/makerspace.

Oldenburg, Ray. *The Great Good Place: Cafés, Coffee Shops, Bookstores, Bars, Hair Salons, and Other Hangouts at the Heart of a Community.* New York: Marlowe, 1999.

Penn State University Libraries. "Tombros and McWhiter Knowledge Commons." Penn State University Libraries, 2013, http://www.libraries.psu.edu/psul/kc.html.

Sinclair, Bryan. "Commons 2.0: Library Spaces Designed for Collaborative Learning." *EDUCAUSE Quarterly* 30, no. 4 (2007), 4–6.

Smart, Laura. "Making Sense of RFID." *netConnect,* supplement to *Library Journal,* October 14, 2004: 4–14.

Swords, David A. ed., *Patron-Driven Acquisitions: History and Best Practices.* Berlin: De Gruyter, 2011.

University of West Florida Libraries, "The Great Good Place—Now Open!" University of West Florida Libraries, accessed April 4, 2013, http://library.uwf.edu/about/spaces/great_good_place/.

Vaughan, Jason, and Brett Burnes. "Bringing Them In and Checking Them Out: Laptop Use in the Modern Academic Library." *Information Technology and Libraries* 21, no. 2 (June 2002): 52–62.

Vyhnanek, Kay, and Christy Zlatos. *Reconfiguring Service Delivery: SPEC Kit 327.* Washington, DC: Association of Research Libraries, 2011.

PART 3

**SPECIAL TOPICS IN
ACCESS SERVICES**

Access Services within Campus and Library Organizations

Stephanie Atkins Sharpe

Head of Access Services, Washington University in St. Louis

DESCRIBING THE organizational structure of access services is not as easy as it would seem. No two access services departments are exactly the same. Each department reflects the unique organizational culture and history of its library. In some libraries, the strong service orientation of access services makes it a natural fit for the public services side of the organization. However, the department's operations and processes behind the scenes have similarities with technical services. The heavy reliance on various systems for circulation, interlibrary loan, and reserves requires strong working relationships with the library and campus technology units. Because the department keeps the building open, access services personnel are the first responders to building issues and emergencies. Access services touches on all aspects of the library organization. This chapter will explore the organizational history and reporting structures, as well as go into detail about the various relationships that access services has with other departments in the library and units on campus.

BEFORE ACCESS SERVICES ───────────────────────────

Appreciating access services as it exists today requires a brief introduction to its origins. In their classic work, *Circulation Work in College and University Libraries*, Brown and Bousfield describe a loan or circulation department where the librarian not only circulates books, maintains loan records, and shelves books, but also plays an important role in the intellectual lives of undergraduate students. The circulation/loan librarian recommends and purchases titles in support of undergraduate education, instructing undergraduates in the use of the library catalog and reference resources.[1] Brown and Bousfield go so far as to discourage instructors from themselves providing library instruction in first-year English courses. They argue that circulation/loan librarians have a better understanding of "the difficulties encountered by students in their use of the library" and "are more familiar with the books most used."[2] Brown and Bousfield also stress the importance of the loan department in students' views and future usage of the library resources. They note that the loan department's "practices will in many cases determine whether students continue the use of books throughout their college course, or whether they become discouraged at failures to obtain desired materials promptly."[3]

After World War II, the growth in collections,[4] coupled with a shortage in trained librarians,[5] forced libraries to reconsider the division of responsibilities. Circulation became less involved in reader services, collection building, and instruction as libraries departmentalized these functions.[6] More emphasis was placed in the efficient circulation and maintenance of the rapidly growing collections. Keeping track of the collection required more time devoted to filling out cards, typing notices, and shelving books. Circulation staff focused on checking out materials to users and referred questions to the reference librarians. Library administrators chose to rely on nonprofessional and student staff for these tasks, moving the professional librarians to other areas of the organization where their expertise would be better utilized. If a library retained a librarian in the circulation department, it was for supervision of the clerical and student staff and oversight of policies and procedures.

Stanley Gwynn lamented this evolution as the "stripped-down, mechanized, clerically-staffed general circulation" with staff members who are unable "to give complete and accurate information about resources and services in other subject or general departments of the library" to library users.[7] The growth of collections and the departmentalization of libraries created a complex environment, making users' dependence on human guidance even greater. Gwynn contends that as the most frequent point of contact with the users, circulation staff are "perhaps in a better position than any other class of staff members to hear of the inadequacies of the library's resources and services."[8] Either the circulation staff can ask the user to take his or her question to another service point, which users are reluctant to do, or the library needs to provide channels so that the information will reach the right individuals in the library. One of Gwynn's contemporaries, Philip McNiff, went even further by recommending that well-trained circulation staff can handle quick reference and directional questions so that reference librarians can devote their time to more in-depth questions. McNiff surmised that this level of cooperation could go a long way toward eliminating user complaints about "being shunted back and forth between service units to get answers to simple requests."[9]

Deborah Carver noted that by the mid-1970s, declining budgets, rising labor and acquisition costs, and growing user expectations forced libraries to reexamine their emphasis on efficiency alone.[10] Library administrators began to review operations for overall effectiveness and service quality. Betty Young's 1976 article suggests that some libraries did not heed Gwynn's and McNiff's suggestions. User surveys at Syracuse University, Northwestern University, and Ohio State University pinpointed lack of satisfaction with the level of service at the circulation desk.[11] As Gwynn feared, the most frequent point of contact for users was with the least trained staff members in the library. Users were not aware that the staff members assisting them at the circulation desk were not librarians, taking the circulation staff's lack of helpfulness, inability to locate books, and

other failings as reasons not to use the library. Young concluded by arguing that "students and faculty are more critical about the help they receive
[the level of service] than about specific services offered by the library."[12]
Improving the image of the library and librarians could be as simple as
providing "well-trained, serviced-oriented librarians at circulation."[13]

Around the same time that libraries were focusing on service quality,
the nature of circulation work was changing as well. Automation did
away with many of the labor-intensive tasks. The introduction of the
integrated library system meant that less time needed to be devoted to
manual tasks (e.g., filling out cards) and more to taking on more complex tasks.[14] For example, circulation staff needed more training to assist
cataloging and technical services staff in maintaining the bibliographic
database. The need for better customer service plus a higher level of skill
among the frontline staff brought changes to circulation that led to this
new organizational model: access services.

THE DAWN OF ACCESS SERVICES

In the inaugural issue of *Journal of Access Services* in 2002, leaders in the
field shared their insights on the emergence and evolution of access services. New technologies, new mechanisms for the delivery of information,
increased availability of digital content, the move away from "ownership"
and toward "access" to content, collection maintenance, and management
of storage facilities were some of the trends mentioned at that time. One
constant in many of the comments, however, was a renewed emphasis
on customer service. Mary Anne Hansen gave the following reason for
the genesis of this new organizational unit:

> Access services as an umbrella term came about as library
> administrators recognized that a circulation department does
> far more than just circulate materials and provide stacks main-
> tenance to facilitate the circulation of materials. Further, the

concept of access services places more emphasis on the user as
a consumer of information who needs access to information
in a variety of formats.[15]

Brown and Bousfield might find the concept of "consumer of information" foreign and the numerous formats of today's information quite
dizzying, but they would likely have agreed wholeheartedly with the
essence of Hansen's observation. The circulation department is doing
more than simply circulating and managing collections. Libraries in the
1940s through the 1970s may have lost sight of the importance of the
circulation department, but Hansen's echo of their basic argument nearly
seventy years later is perhaps a validation of their original convictions.

Pat Weaver-Myers also suggested that the Association of Research
Libraries (ARL) Management Review and Analysis Program in the late
1970s played a role by bringing together a number of services that did
not fit under other service units into a single unit called access services.[16]
Dawes, Sweetman, and Von Elm's survey of ARL libraries support this
observation, as few libraries had a unit named Access Services prior to
1981.[17] The number of libraries using the name grew steadily between
1991 and 2005, with fifteen libraries adopting the term in the years from
1996 to 2000 alone.[18] By 2005, forty-six libraries had a department called
Access Services.[19] Some libraries simply renamed the circulation unit,
while others created access services by merging circulation with other
departments, such as current periodicals, microforms, information desk,
and interlibrary loan departments.[20] The decade between 1995 and 2005
also witnessed the consolidation of service points as well as increased
service hours.

Not all changes were a result of organizational reshuffling. Dawes,
Sweetman, and Von Elm found relative consistency in the core services,
circulation, stacks maintenance and shelving, billing, entry/exit control,
and course reserves among ARL libraries, but also observed a broadening
of service offerings to on-campus document delivery, laptop circulation,
and electronic reserves.[21] In some instances, access services expanded

services into nontraditional areas. Services for users with disabilities, computer lab maintenance, copyright clearance, and mail services are a few examples. Further automation enabled access services to provide "do-it-yourself" options for renewals, interlibrary loan requesting, and document delivery.

REPORTING STRUCTURE

Since the functions in access services may be considered part of technical or public services, the reporting structures will vary accordingly. Mary Anne Hansen, Virginia Steel, and Joan Ellen Stein argue that since access services has direct dealings with the public, the department is more closely aligned to the public services side of the organization.[22] Based on the data, the most consistent reporting structure is to have access services report to the assistant or associate dean or director of public services. Steel's 1991 *SPEC Kit 179* found that 33 out of 55 (60 percent) departments reported through public services,[23] which is fairly consistent with the numbers reported in Dawes, Sweetman, and Von Elm's 2005 *SPEC Kit* 290: 36 out of 73 (49 percent).[24] Fewer departments report directly to the dean or director, and even fewer report to the assistant or associate dean or director of technical services.

While the evidence supports access services as a part of the public services realm, a few wonder if these distinctions matter. Mary Anne Hansen was an advocate for the inclusion of access services in public services, but she also viewed the staff serving as "intermediaries between the materials as they are acquired and processed and the patrons waiting for access to these materials."[25] In this capacity, access services can bridge the gap between the two sides of the organization. Pat Weaver-Myers, whose library has access services in technical services, believed that libraries should focus their energies more on providing services that support the institution's goals and less on whether access services fits on one side of the organization or the other.[26] Weaver-Myers's observations are prescient of today's libraries. Libraries are marshaling all of the organization's resources towards meeting the mission of the university and college.

UNIVERSITIES AND COLLEGES

Access services as a distinct unit of the library is more prevalent in academic libraries. This is not to say that some large public and special libraries will never have a similar department responsible for services and operations that assist users in accessing the library's collections. The trend started in university and college libraries, and that possibly explains why it remains most common in these libraries.

In many ways, the service orientation of access services dovetails nicely with the university's mission to serve the research and scholarly needs of faculty and students. Access services may no longer provide reader services and instruction to students, but the department strives to provide the highest level of service to users in accessing the collections that will support teaching and learning on campus. Access services is the one department within the library that is in the best position to serve as library ambassadors. Any student or faculty member who comes to the library will invariably come into contact with access services staff. Brown and Bousfield made a similar observation that students' first contact with the library is through the loan department.[27] What was true eight years ago is still true now; the frontline staff members represent the library to the community.

INTERNAL RELATIONSHIPS

Technical Services

To serve users' needs and manage the collection effectively, access services staff need to build close working relationships with the technical service departments. Once materials leave the cataloging department, access services staff may be the only ones in a position to alert it to any problems with items' records and markings. The need for this oversight is becoming even greater as more libraries are moving to shelf-ready materials. The shelf-ready items may go directly to the shelf with only minimal processing on the library's end. Even though errors may be negligible, even a simple error in the record or call number may render an item lost in the collection. Access staff responsible for shelving and checking in materials will notice anomalies in call numbers, errors in item and holdings records, and other problems that will make it difficult for users to find items in the stacks.

Access services staff members are another set of eyes for the library's preservation unit as well. They will notice items with pages falling out, torn covers, or excessive highlighting. In extreme cases, staff may identify evidence of mold and pest infestation. Quick action can save the library money in the treatment and replacement of items. Occasionally, a staff member may see a rare item come to the desk for checkout. Instead of checking the item out to a patron, access services may recommend a title be transferred to special collections or scanned for the library's digital collections.

For years, access services departments dutifully collected circulation and interlibrary loan statistics for library administration, external organizations, and federal agencies. Now these data are examined with a renewed vigor, as libraries are looking for ways to reclaim parts of the stacks for user spaces. Libraries can easily identify low-circulating items for removal through the integrated library system. On the flip side, high circulation can help the library in identifying subject areas that need more collection funding. Where circulation data can provide evidence of high or low use, interlibrary loan's borrowing data can identify areas of weakness in the collection. Academic libraries have struggled to keep pace with changes in the curriculum and the research needs of new faculty members and academic units. Collecting information on requests of titles not held locally may assist bibliographers in modifying approval plan profiles and pinpointing titles for firm ordering.

Most academic libraries have a mechanism for faculty and students to request titles for purchase by the library. However, more libraries are enabling users to purchase print titles directly through the catalog. Many libraries simply call this service "Patron Driven Acquisitions" or "User Driven Acquisitions". While the title bypasses acquisitions for ordering, it may lack cataloging records and call number markings once it arrives at the library. Instead of sending the title for cataloging and thus creating delays in availability, access staff can create a brief record in the integrated library system, barcode the item, and put it on the hold shelf for pick-up. When the patron returns the item to the library, it can go to cataloging for further processing.

Information Services

Reference, or information services, has been a part of the library as long as circulation has. Both departments have similar goals in providing the best level of service to users. There are natural tie-ins between the departments. However, differences in culture and the professional and paraprofessional divide have created barriers in understanding and cooperation in the past.[28] The consolidation of service departments to create a single service point has brought the staff of access services and information services closer together. Although merging the two cultures may take time, the new service model has created new opportunities for circulation and information services staff to acquire new knowledge and skills and to rethink their job responsibilities. The single service desk allows for cross-training of circulation staff in basic reference and database searching. The professional librarians benefit by reducing their desk hours so that they can provide assistance to their faculty and students outside of the library. The tiered service model not only gives users a single point at which to seek assistance, but it allows the library to deploy the staff and librarians where they are most effective in serving users' needs With that said, Naismith's survey of libraries with merged service points stresses the importance of communication, referrals, and definition of roles in making a successful partnership.[29]

EXTERNAL RELATIONSHIPS

Information Technology

Access services is heavily dependent on various systems to keep its operations going. Whenever a system crashes or is unavailable, the collective groans of the access staff can be heard throughout the library. Access services depends on the information technology staff within and outside of the library to manage and maintain the servers loaded with its software. Some software companies are very responsive to the user community, and as a result, they are constantly releasing upgrades. To ensure that the department is using software that is still supported by the vendor requires vigilance on the part of the manager to keep up with these updates. No matter if it is a minor or major upgrade, occasionally a function of the system will cease to work properly. Access services managers must possess enough of an understanding of the software in order to articulate the problem to IT staff. The problem can be a local one, or it may require the software company to develop a fix. Nevertheless, access services cannot rely on IT to understand how its systems are supposed to function. Access services managers may need to advocate for their staff and their users when software is not performing optimally. Occasionally this requires applying some pressure on IT to resolve the software issues.

Access services may also need to work with IT over user authentication issues. Before the advent of e-journals and electronic databases, access services staff simply required a person's university identification card to check out a print book or journal. With increased availability of electronic content, libraries need the ability to verify users' status electronically. University IT can help by creating a single sign-on system for the campus community. This allows faculty and students to access a variety of university applications, including the library's resources, with a single logon name and password. This satisfies the vast majority of library users, as most of the library's electronic resource licenses restrict access to current faculty, students, and staff.

It becomes more challenging when a visiting scholar or student or guest to the university needs access to electronic resources. In some instances, the visiting faculty member is teaching a class for a semester or is assisting another faculty member in her research. These situations suggest that definitions of faculty and student can be fluid when the university develops partnerships with other universities, think tanks, and other organizations around the world. However, the library is in the unenviable position of acting as the gatekeepers to resources with strict user restrictions. And the problem is only growing. Authentication is required not only to access e-journals and databases but increasingly for e-books as well. Access services staff may need to negotiate on behalf of these users to get the necessary credentials for remote access and at the same time make sure that providing this access will not be in violation of electronic resource and e-book licensing agreements.

Facilities

Access services will occasionally receive complaints about broken chairs, lost faculty carrel keys, burned-out incandescent lights, malfunctioning compact shelving, and a myriad of other equipment and facility problems. In some libraries, it will be responsibility of access services staff to contact campus facilities or an outside vendor for repairs and replacements. At larger institutions, library policies may dictate sending all reports to a central unit (e.g., library administration) for handling. In either event, it is always most satisfactory if access services has the ability to resolve the user's problem. This may not always be possible. For instance, the temperature control in buildings is usually handled centrally by the university. Conditions may be freezing in the summer time and hot in the winter, but little can be done to modify the temperature on demand. The only recourse is simply to advise users to wear layers at all times of the year.

With academic libraries running out of room for new acquisitions in their crammed stacks, library administration will find places to house older collections acquired during the book-buying craze in 1950s and

1960s. In some instances, libraries will build high-density shelving facilities or participate in a shared storage facility with other libraries. These facilities can hold millions of items on thirty-foot shelves accessible only via a cherry picker. At many of these facilities, access services will assume responsibility for managing these facilities as well as providing retrieval and scanning services to users.

As the only department that is open for all the hours that the library is open, access services usually handles building situations and emergencies at the main library as well. Incidents can range from overflowing toilets to fire and tornado alarms. For instances when collections are endangered due to water or fire, access services staff need training in how to handle these situations so as to stem further damage.

Campus Security/Police

Occasionally, access services will need to deal with the theft of a patron's belongings, inappropriate patron behavior, or similar incidents that require immediate attention. Oftentimes, these situations require the assistance of campus security or police. Building a good rapport with campus security or police will assist the library in getting these situations handled quickly. For academic libraries open to the public, access services may also receive no-trespass lists from the campus police. Access services staff need training in order to know what to do if an individual violates a no-trespass order. Staff members also must be familiar with relevant campus rules and policies as well as local and state laws to report these incidents properly.

Academic Departments and Faculty

Access services will occasionally receive requests from academic departments to provide library access to participants in a summer institute or conference at the university. Access services will negotiate the terms based on the length of time of the participants' visit on campus as well as level of access (only print collections? borrowing privileges? or electronic access too?).

Access services also provides faculty support with print and electronic course reserves. Staff may assist the faculty members in loading the content themselves through the reserves system. Some academic libraries use a campus-wide course management system for course reserves. Access services staff members simply need the correct permissions to post content to the course page.

Some libraries enable faculty members to designate their campus office for delivery. Access services can make the deliveries itself, or in some instances utilize campus or library mail services. Regardless of the delivery method, the service is another way that access services can provide fast and convenient service to users.

Consortial Relations

No library can serve all of the needs of its clientele. Shrinking or flat collection budgets compounded by increases in inflation and exchange rates make it impossible for a library to acquire every possible item that its users may need. Although some libraries have valiantly tried, most academic libraries have ceased debating access versus ownership. Access is the only viable option. Oftentimes, libraries depend on consortial partnerships to serve as the only or second copy of materials. Although these partnerships extend the library's collections, these arrangements may introduce a whole new set of policies and rules for users. Libraries with liberal loan and renewal policies may need to explain to a frustrated user, for example, why the book borrowed from another institution can be renewed only two times for a total of six weeks, when a local copy can circulate for a month with unlimited renewals. Access services staff may also serve as the intermediary in disputes between the local patron and the consortial library over lost and damaged materials. While the benefits of consortial partnerships outweigh the challenges, streamlining of policies and rules would improve service to all users in the consortium.

CONCLUSION

Over the last twenty-five years, these changes to the service model have brought about a resurgence of circulation/access services in libraries. Margery Closely Quigley described the role of the circulation librarian in 1957 as "the most uninspired, unprogressive, and unrewarding" job in libraries.[30] The opposite can be said about today's access services. The enhanced duties and expansion of services suggest that access services is a very dynamic and progressive department. Although they might not have anticipated some of the changes in the last eighty years, Brown and Bousfield might take comfort in the fact that the department continues to play a significant role in the lives of students and faculty on today's campuses.

NOTES

1. Charles Harvey Brown and H. G. Bousfield, *Circulation Work in College and University Libraries* (Chicago: ALA, 1933), 106–120.
2. Ibid., 110–112.
3. Ibid., 11–12.
4. Stanley E. Gwynn, "Departmentalization and Circulation Work: Problems and Relationships," in "Current Trends in Circulation Services," ed. Wayne S. Yenawine, special issue, *Library Trends* 6, no. 1 (Summer 1957): 87–100.
5. Ralph E. McCoy, "Personnel in Circulation Service," in "Current Trends in Circulation Services," ed. Wayne S. Yenawine, special issue, *Library Trends* 6, no. 1 (Summer 1957): 42–51.
6. Deborah Carver, "From Circulation to Access Services: The Shift in Academic Library Organization," *Collection Management* 17, no. 1/2 (1992): 26–29.
7. Gwynn, "Departmentalization and Circulation Work," 92.
8. Ibid., 96.
9. Philip J. McNiff, "Administration of Circulation Services," in "Current Trends in Circulation Services," ed. Wayne S. Yenawine, special issue, *Library Trends* 6, no. 1 (Summer 1957): 16.
10. Carver, "From Circulation to Access Services," 30–31.
11. Betty Young, "Circulation Service—Is It Meeting the User's Needs?" *Journal of Academic Librarianship* 2, no. 3 (July 1976): 122–123.

12. Ibid., 124.

13. Ibid.

14. Carver, "From Circulation to Access Services," 33.

15. Mary Anne Hansen, Jakob Harnest, Virginia Steel, Joan Ellen Stein, and Pat Weaver-Myers, "A Question and Answer Forum on the Origin, Evolution and Future of Access Services in Libraries," *Journal of Access Services* 1, no. 1 (2002): 10.

16. Ibid., 12.

17. Trevor Dawes, Kimberly Burke Sweetman, and Catherine Von Elm, *Access Services: SPEC Kit 290* (Washington DC.: ARL, 2005).

18. Ibid., 18.

19. Ibid.

20. Ibid., 11–12.

21. Ibid., 12.

22. Hansen et al., "A Question and Answer Forum," 12–13.

23. Virginia Steel, *Access Services: Organization and Management: SPEC Kit 179* (Washington DC: AR:, 1991): 3.

24. Dawes, Sweetman, and Von Elm, *Access Services,* 29.

25. Hansen et al., "A Question and Answer Forum," 12.

26. Ibid., 13-14.

27. Brown and Bousfield, *Circulation Work in College and University Libraries,* 11.

28. Ken Johnson, Susan Jennings, and Sue Hisle, "Ending the Turf War: Circulation, Reference, and Instruction on One Team," *Journal of Access Services* 8, no. 3 (2011): 107–124.

29. Rachael Naismith, "Combining Circulation and Reference Functions at One Desk," *Journal of Access Services* 2, no. 3 (2004): 15–20.

30. Margery Closely Quigley, "A Reporter at Large," in "Current Trends in Circulation Services," ed. Wayne S. Yenawine, special issue, *Library Trends* 6, no. 1 (Summer 1957): 7.

BIBLIOGRAPHY

Brown, Charles Harvey, and H. G. Bousfield. *Circulation Work in College and University Libraries.* Chicago: American Library Association, 1933

Carver, Deborah. "From Circulation to Access Services: The Shift in Academic Library Organization." *Collection Management* 17, no. 1/2 (1992): 23–36.

Dawes, Trevor, Kimberly Burke Sweetman, and Catherine Von Elm. *Access Services: SPEC Kit 290.* Washington DC: Association of Research Libraries, 2005.

Gwynn, Stanley E. "Departmentalization and Circulation Work: Problems and Relationships." In "Current Trends in Circulation Services," edited by Wayne S. Yenawine, special issue, *Library Trends* 6, no. 1 (Summer 1957): 87–100.

Hansen, Mary Anne, Jakob Harnest, Virginia Steel, Joan Ellen Stein, and Pat Weaver-Myers. "A Question and Answer Forum on the Origin, Evolution and Future of Access Services in Libraries." *Journal of Access Services* 1, no. 1 (2002): 5–24.

Johnson, Ken, Susan Jennings, and Sue Hisle. "Ending the Turf War: Circulation, Reference and Instruction on One Team." *Journal of Access Services* 8, no. 3 (2011): 107–124.

McCoy, Ralph E. "Personnel in Circulation Service." In "Current Trends in Circulation Services," edited by Wayne S. Yenawine, special issue, *Library Trends* 6, no. 1 (Summer 1957): 42–51.

McNiff, Philip J. "Administration of Circulation Services." In "Current Trends in Circulation Services," edited by Wayne S. Yenawine, special issue, *Library Trends* 6, no. 1 (Summer 1957): 13–19.

Naismith, Rachael. "Combining Circulation and Reference Functions at One Desk." *Journal of Access Services* 2, no. 3 (2004): 15–20.

Quigley, Margery Closely. "A Reporter at Large." In "Current Trends in Circulation Services," edited by Wayne S. Yenawine, special issue, *Library Trends* 6, no. 1 (Summer 1957): 6–12.

Steel, Virginia. *Access Services: Organization and Management: SPEC Kit 179.* Washington DC: Association of Research Libraries, 1991.

Young, Betty. "Circulation Service—Is It Meeting the User's Needs?" *Journal of Academic Librarianship* 2, no. 3 (July 1976): 120–125.

Access Services Department Organization

Brad Warren
**Director of Access Services, Sterling Memorial
and Bass Libraries, Yale University**

WHEN LOOKING at the organization of an access services department, it is important to note that just as each library is a unique reflection of the community and organization in which it serves, access services departments can vary quite widely in how they are organized and staffed. As library organizations continue to shrink while finding ways to offer new services and maintaining core traditional services, the structure of a particular access services department must be adaptable and flexible to ensure that services and the processes that support them can remain responsive to the changing needs of library users. Because access services departments need to provide both public frontline services and technical processing skills, they are often the right environment to attract librarians and staff who are deeply committed to assisting the public while also solving complex problems and developing innovations to benefit users or create workflow efficiencies. Regardless of the library in which the access services department is located, there are the following commonalities:

- staff comprised of librarians, managers, clerical staff, and a large number of student workers
- emphasis on customer service skills
- high attention to detail and problem solving
- flexibility and ability to work in a stressful environment

This chapter will address the overall structure of an access services department with a particular focus on the types of staff and the associated responsibilities, education, training, skills, recruitment, and developmental needs of each category. Illustrations will be drawn from a case study of the recent reorganization of the Yale University Library Access Services Department. The explanation of requirements for each of the roles in an access services department will illuminate how the department is organized and will suggest language that can be used in specific job descriptions. Emphasis will also be placed on discussing the affinities that may exist between departmental functions so that a flexible structure for an access services department can be realized with both small and large staffing models.

ACCESS SERVICES ORGANIZATIONAL STRUCTURE

While any library will obviously have a structure in place for providing access services, it is important to understand the philosophy and decisions that led to any department's current organization before determining what changes, if any, need to be made. Access services departments are usually hierarchical with an emphasis on supervision and accountability while also having teams that work in common areas of specialization. In a survey for a 2005 ARL *SPEC Kit*, research libraries were asked to answer questions on the existing and changing needs of their departments and to submit their organizational charts, mission statements, and job descriptions.[1]

The areas of specialization in access services generally were

- circulation
- interlibrary loan and resource sharing
- shelving maintenance
- reserves

Some access services departments were also responsible for IT functions relating to the circulation module of the integrated library system (ILS), preservation triage, security, periodicals and microforms, and technical services related to updating and maintaining item records and holdings in the catalog, although these responsibilities were not as common. The needs of the parent organization will always determine to what department specific areas of responsibility are assigned; however, these tasks, which are frequently assigned outside of access services, might be performed more efficiently within an access services department. The *SPEC Kit* revealed that in every example submitted, access services departments are led by a librarian, at either the department head or the assistant university librarian level. If a department had more than one librarian in access services, the most common area of specialization was interlibrary loan, followed by circulation and reserves. While most access services departments are overwhelmingly comprised of clerical staff and student workers, the need for librarians in this area is becoming greater as users' needs are changing rapidly as technology grows explosively and as academic libraries take a more service-oriented, patron-centric focus. Access services librarians are able to work collaboratively across department lines, understand the needs and desires of their user base, and analyze and implement improvements to functions and workflows in order to reallocate staff resources to new services. These librarians perform outreach functions with the understanding that staff members in access services departments are highly visible assets in shaping a library's public image with its users by virtue of the thousands of daily interactions between those staff members and patrons.

As of the publication of the *SPEC Kit* in 2005, access services had developed into a recognizable department handling the core work necessary to maintain, track, and use the print collection. While access services departments at several institutions had also begun to handle electronic reserves, equipment checkout, information services, and on-campus document delivery, departments were about to experience other changes as budgets tightened, information and learning commons were developed, and changes were made to traditional reference desk work.

In the last eight years, access services departments have experienced several changes resulting from external monetary pressures, significant paradigm shifts in user desires and behavior, and a rethinking of the role of traditional library service provision in an increasingly electronic world. As every university budget suffered in some sense from the US recession that began in 2007, libraries have seen drastic cuts to their operating budgets, resulting in fewer staff members and smaller collections. Since these cuts often happened intermittently and unevenly across department lines, most access services departments have undergone some sort of restructuring as a result of decreased staffing. In addition, these changes have been coupled with an increasing emphasis on the importance of service provision and convenience as university communities have also had to do more with less. *Ithaka's 2006 Studies of Key Stakeholders in the Digital Transformation of Higher Education* states:

> If attention and support fades from the library, its ability to contribute to the intellectual work of the campus diminishes, and its continuing institutional well-being may be threatened. Libraries should be aware of this decreasing visibility and take steps to improve the value of their brand by offering more value-added services to raise their profile on campus. It is essential to their long-term viability that libraries maintain the active support of faculty on their campuses, a factor which will be most effectively obtained by playing a prominent, valued, and essential role in the research process. By under-

standing the needs and research habits of scholars in different disciplines, libraries can identify products and services which would be appreciated by and of use to these scholars. Such efforts to be involved in the research process offer benefits to scholars, by providing them with services to improve their efficiency and effectiveness, as well as to libraries, recapturing the attention of scholars and contributing to a general awareness of and respect for the library's contributions.[2]

This report made it clear to academic libraries that they needed to rethink their traditional roles by making sure that they provided the services most useful to faculty—their very existence depended on it. In 2006, OCLC published its *Perceptions* report with a special emphasis on college students. In gathering responses, students offered advice on improving customer service and access to collections, expanded hours, rethinking loan periods and assisting users with the actual retrieval of materials.[3] Academic libraries' key stakeholders were clearly asking for changes, many of which needed to happen in access services.

It is no surprise that many access services departments have changed significantly since that 2005 *SPEC Kit*. Presentations at the first Access Services Conference, held in November 2009, discussed issues such as RAPID interlibrary loan services, library commons and access services, merging service points, managing change, and a wide range of tools and technologies to improve customer service. The importance of these issues has continued and expanded over all four years in which the conference has been held. While the 2005 *SPEC Kit* provides a good basis for understanding core access services roles, it is clear that understanding the current makeup of a department and its roles requires an understanding of how these roles and new work are put together to best serve the public. This chapter will discuss these various roles, responsibilities, training, recruitment, development, and retention based on a case study of Yale University Library's Access Services Department and its reorganization, which occurred in 2012.

YALE UNIVERSITY LIBRARY: A CASE STUDY ————

Background

When the US economy suffered with the stock market crash in September 2008, many libraries that were considered immune to the challenges of tightened state budgets and reduction in staff were no longer safe. Some of the largest academic library systems in the United States had to rethink how their budgets and staff were allocated, as had already been experienced by many state-funded institutions since 2001. In the case of Yale University Library's Sterling Memorial Library, the staff of the Access Services Department had been reduced by 14 percent through attrition, but the department had not undergone any serious changes to staffing or service provision in recent memory. As a result, some units experienced no changes, and others were down several staff members while also experiencing significant increases in usage of some services, such as electronic reserves. New leadership in 2009 and new units joining the department in 2011 led to a serious reorganization effort, which was completed in 2012 and implemented in January 2013. This section will discuss the business reasons behind the reorganization, give an overview of the process, and describe the final structure, which will provide the framework for the positions covered in this chapter.

Operational Reasons behind Reorganization

Before the reorganization process began, the department had a total of five service points in three different locations. Four of the service points were administered by different managers or staff, and there was little flexibility in providing staff who could work at more than one desk. Circulation managers held additional responsibility for significant processing operations, while the stacks operation handled retrievals for one location and shelving for two locations. There was rapid expansion in electronic reserves and equipment checkout with a recognized difficulty in meeting the needs of greatly expanding resource-sharing operations and user expectations for scanning and office delivery services. As a result, the following business reasons were drafted, which became the framework for making decisions in the changes to the overall department structure and jobs:

- Creating a single point-of-service desk at each of the three locations.
- Identifying common work across existing units to seek affinities and reduce unnecessary duplication of effort.
- Empowering staff to make decisions and exceptions and assist patrons without referral.
- Ensuring staff play a more active role with student employees.
- Ensuring staff are covering service points during all hours of operation.

Process of Reorganization

Reorganization activities took place in two phases over the course of fourteen months. The first phase began in August 2011 and was completed in November 2011. It involved restructuring the management of the department to better reflect how services and the processes that support them should be overseen and developed. Two new librarian positions were created to oversee information services and play an expanded role in overseeing resource sharing and reserves across the entire Yale University library system. In addition, IT positions were created to ensure responsive oversight of the circulation module of Yale's ILS, and a business systems analyst position was added to assist managers in actively seeking and implementing improvements to complicated workflows. These were not new positions in the sense of requiring new ongoing money to fund them, but they were a natural result of finding the mix between the department's operational needs and the skills and interests of existing managers.

The second phase commenced with a complete restructuring of the clerical and technical positions in March 2012. Since Yale is a unionized environment, the project was approached as a joint union/management project that involved several meetings with union leadership and employees during every milestone of the process. The department used a process similar to one that was developed in 2011 when the Kline Science Library and the Social Science Library were combined into the new Center for Science and Social Science Information. The phase two process fell into the following activities:

- introduction of business reasons for reorganizing
- manager discussions to create new framework: four months
- creation of task lists for each new area
- creation of new job descriptions
- classification of positions and mapping of staff to new positions
- creation of training plans for each new job
- notification of final job placement and commencement of training

Introduction of Business Reasons for Reorganizing

As mentioned above, the management team had outlined the reasons behind the reorganization, which were introduced to the staff in a meeting. These reasons were echoed several times during the process in order to remind staff about why the changes were happening.

Manager Discussions to Create New Framework: Four Months

The managers met as a team to tackle all of the services and processes that occurred in the department. Everything was broken down into its component parts and put back together again with the idea that the following principles would guide decisions:

- Any process that supported more than one service should be considered for centralization.

- There would be exceptions to centralization if the department needed specialization within the services and the processes that support them.
- The more staff understood the supporting processes, the better service they would provide.
- Relationships between services and processes needed to be understood through training and structure regardless of role. Many staff had hazy or incomplete knowledge of anything outside of their current unit.
- Staff should be exposed to all services and processes to increase understanding.
- Staff jobs should be reasonably attainable.
- Staff should have a sense of ownership of their work.
- Learning was continuous and staff could develop training for other staff.
- Reporting lines needed to be clear.

All past arrangements and ties were disregarded as management discussed and made decisions on how to structure the department. This work took at least twenty-four hours of meetings distributed over four months. The result was the broad framework of the new structure with a basic understanding of the types of jobs needed to support it. This structure was presented to the staff.

Creation of Task Lists for Each New Area

Once the structure had been presented and modified based on staff input, managers created task lists for each job necessary to perform the work of the new department structure. These task lists also reflected the type of staff member needed for the work (e.g., staff vs. student) and the level of expertise or specialization to do the task. Hence, each task list suggested the hierarchical level of that job and where it would fall on a job ladder by which staff could advance to higher positions. This strategy would lead to a methodology allowing staff to advance within the department or to other library jobs within the university.

Creation of New Job Descriptions

Once the task lists had been settled, they had to be translated into recognizable job descriptions that could be presented to union leaders and staff for input and discussion. The descriptions were fairly lengthy because they needed to clearly communicate how significantly the jobs and the department were changing. The descriptions were presented to staff before the jobs were graded so that discussions and input would not be colored by a perception of how much any particular position would be paid.

Classification of Positions and Mapping of Staff to New Positions

After several revisions, the job descriptions were finalized and classified by human resources. Managers also created a two-phase mapping plan to ensure that staff who clearly mapped to new jobs would not have to bid on them. Because of the degree of change in the department, only 10 percent of staff clearly mapped to the new jobs. The remaining 90 percent had to go through a formal mapping process in which they had to apply and interview for jobs in which they were interested.

Creation of Training Plans for Each New Job

While mapping discussions were occurring, managers also developed training plans for each job in the new structure. Since it was desirable to have the new structure begin during the break between the fall and spring semesters, training fell into an intensive period of basic training during December and ongoing training that would continue over the course of the next year. Although much of the training focused on learning new tasks and software, emphasis was placed on training that would help foster a new culture of collaboration and teamwork.

*Notification of Final Job Placement
and Commencement of Training*

Once the mapping decisions had been finalized and discussed with union leaders, staff were notified of their new positions and given training plans for those positions. Training commenced immediately afterward with the new structure going into place six weeks later at the beginning of 2013.

Final Structure

Once the process was completed, Yale's Access Services Department was completely unrecognizable. Every staff member had to go through some sort of training, some of it quite extensive. New positions had work that at the most contained only half of what any staff member had experience with. While it was a fairly dramatic change, the process had been conducted in such a way that all staff, although understandably skeptical of the success of the new structure, clearly understood the reasons and were ready to take on the new changes. The new Access Services Department structure fell into four broad categories (see figure 8.1). They were

- administration and IT
- frontline services
- resource sharing and reserves
- operations

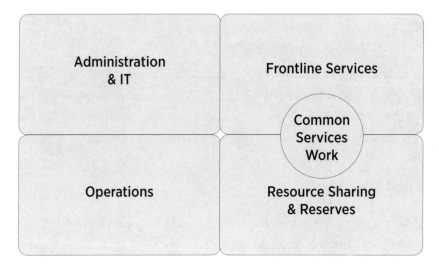

Figure 8.1
Broad organization of the new Access Services Department

Administration and IT

The area of administration and IT encompassed the activities that provided either oversight or direct support to the success of the department. Staff included the department head, an administrative assistant, and three IT positions, which covered the circulation module of the ILS, technical help for workstations, circulating equipment, reporting, business systems analysis, and project management support with library IT.

Frontline Services

The frontline services unit encompassed all of the service desk support for three different locations, including circulation, information, microforms, privileges, bills and fines, virtual reference, and equipment checkout. The expectation was that staff in this unit would work 80 percent of their time providing services in these areas regardless of location and 20 percent of their time doing work in the other major service unit—resource sharing and reserves (see figure 8.2). Jobs in this area and in resource sharing and reserves were structured to share common services work:

- knowing library policies for services
- searching in the library catalog, other catalogs, and electronic databases with incomplete information
- corresponding with patrons
- resolving problems
- resolving patron accounts for all services
- working at frontline service points

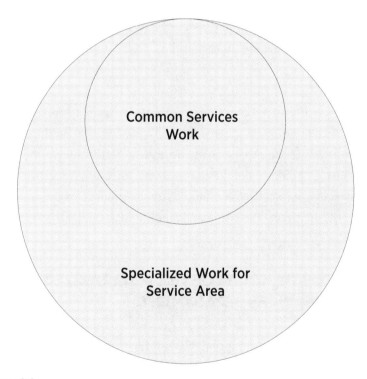

Figure 8.2
Division of work in the frontline services and resource sharing and reserves units

Resource Sharing and Reserves

The resource sharing and reserves unit was intended to provide services for interlibrary loan, document delivery, scan-on-demand services, and print and electronic reserves. Its organization was similar to that of the frontline services unit; the staff were expected to work about 80 percent of their time in their primary unit and 20 percent of their time at one of the service points. Some other significant changes involved getting rid of the divide between borrowing and lending and consolidating all scanning activities into one unit. The goal was having staff in this unit and in frontline services spending regular time doing each other's work in order to reduce the need for internal referrals while also accommodating the need for specialization in each unit.

Operations

All of the behind-the-scenes operational work was consolidated into a single unit. The unit was expected to provide retrieval and processing support for all of the service areas, while also performing shelving and delivery work. As a result of the changed structure, this unit retrieves and processes approximately 1,000 items daily to support internal requests and interlibrary loan borrowing and lending.

DETAILED STRUCTURE OF THE REORGANIZED ACCESS SERVICES DEPARTMENT

This section will go into more detail on the professional, clerical, and student positions necessary to support this particular structure. It is important to note that although this reflects one particular model, the requirements can be mixed according to the needs of any particular department structure.

Administrative and IT Positions

Department Head

The department head is responsible for providing leadership and direction for an access services department. The head is creating, leading, and developing a reader-centric environment of discovery, research, and engagement. The head is leading staff and librarians from multiple library units and university departments to develop creative and innovative strategic service initiatives while instilling high service standards in a fast-paced and stressful work environment. Innovation through effective leadership, application of new technologies, and assessment of user experiences and expectations is critical to the success of this position. This position, having significant managerial responsibilities, must work collaboratively with direct and indirect reports, supervising and coaching a team of librarians, managers, support staff, and a large pool of student assistants. Placing emphasis on data-based decisions and heading a department rich in objective statistics, the head should establish, monitor, and incorporate performance indicators and benchmarks to assess and improve the quality of services provided by the access services department. While a department's size may dictate how hands-on a department head can be, it is important for the department head to develop and lead staff and make strategic and deliberative efforts to delegate, coach, and provide new developmental opportunities for staff.

Since this is often a senior level position in a library, the position requires a master's degree from an ALA-accredited library school program and at least five years of progressively responsible administrative and managerial experience. Previous experience should include demonstrated success in initiating service improvements, customer service orientation, leading a diverse group of staff, excellent communication skills, and successful project management experience.

RECRUITMENT

As in many specialized areas of librarianship, certain affinity groups focus particularly on access services. Recruitment efforts take a traditional posting route on common library and higher education job websites. However, other avenues for recruiting for this position can include the various conferences, e-mail discussion lists, and organizations discussed in chapter 11.

DEVELOPMENT

If access services department head is expected to lead and develop innovative user services, development activities may draw from both traditional and unexpected sources. It is common to stay connected and active professionally through some of the outlets suggested for recruitment above, but with emphasis on areas such as leadership, management, and innovation, it is important to provide the department head with development opportunities in the following areas:

- management and leadership
  - classes and programs offered by the parent institution in management, conflict management, communication skills, facilitation skills, coaching, and customer service
  - leadership and management institutes

    - Leading Change Institute (previously the Frye Leadership Institute): http://www.leadingchangeinstitute.org/
    - Harvard Leadership Institute for Academic Librarians: http://www.gse.harvard.edu/ppe/programs/higher-education/portfolio/leadership-academic-librarians.html
    - leadership and management institutes periodically conducted by many state libraries or state library membership organizations

  - active participation and leadership in conferences, library professional organizations, and program planning

- innovation
  - developing an understanding of user experience design (UXD)

- offering new services and initiatives at beta level with a commitment to conducting simple usability surveys to make key decisions in the life of the service
- understanding the environment of the parent institution; its faculty, staff, and students; and the library's role within that organization (This is often the key area in which department heads can drive innovation to meet unmet needs that may be quite different from other institutions' needs.)

Access Services IT Manager

Access services has a high need to manage and maintain circulation systems, a wide variety of circulating equipment, workstations, and infrastructure. While these responsibilities may traditionally lie with a library IT department, having a position with this focus in access services results in having embedded in the department an individual with technical abilities and a high degree of understanding of the priorities and unique nature of access services. Responsibilities can include troubleshooting of circulation database administration activities, performing weekly monitoring and troubleshooting of patron update and bursar transfer output, complying with university regulations regarding storage of personal information, maintaining library calendars in systems administration, running reports, updating circulation matrices as needed, and assisting staff with workstation and equipment needs. It is also important for someone in this position to have an active relationship with the overall library IT department.

RECRUITMENT

While this could be a librarian position, it can also be filled with a systems or database administrator. It is important for the person to have a thorough understanding of access services functions, including circulation, reserves, patron accounts, and inventory functions of ILSs; experience with SQL and reporting; and excellent analytical and organizational skills. Just as important, having a person well versed in both IT and access services ensures a deep commitment to making sure that work can be prioritized and responsiveness to a department that traditionally makes significant demands for IT assistance. Recruitment efforts would most likely revolve around normal outlets for IT database administrator positions. It is also possible to build these skill sets with existing staff members who have a particular affinity for IT systems.

DEVELOPMENT

As with many IT positions, it is important for this individual to continually develop and expand his or her knowledge of IT systems and library ILS applications. This need is usually served with training provided by the university or the library IT department. It is equally important for this individual to attend user group conferences for the various systems for which he or she is responsible.

Business Systems Analyst

Access services departments are challenged by being frontline service providers while also seeking to implement new services or improve the operational efficiency of existing services and workflows. It can be particularly challenging to move forward when most day-to-day activities involve keeping the operation running, addressing customer service needs, and managing staff and student workers. A business systems analyst can provide assistance by analyzing the department's services and workflows, prioritizing based on the impact made by changes, and making recommendations or even implementing those improvements. Responsibilities include analyzing complex procedures to make improvements and efficiencies; testing, analyzing and making recommendations for improvements in business systems; identifying, suggesting and implementing new technological tools to improve internal processes; and running reports to track process efficiency.

RECRUITMENT

This position is usually considered an IT position. Recruitment efforts would most likely revolve around normal outlets for business systems analyst positions. It is important to identify a person with excellent analytical and customer service skills who would excel in a library environment. Experience in using SQL for complex data analysis is also essential. It is also possible to build these skill sets with existing staff who have a particular affinity for IT systems or are particularly skilled at workflow analysis and improvement.

Administrative Assistant

A department administrative assistant assists with coordinating office functions for the department, ensuring that orders are made and tracked and deposits are generated and providing direct administrative support to staff in the department.

Technical Assistant

A technical assistant can provide support for equipment checkout programs, run routine reports, or perform basic analysis of problems with technical systems supported by the department. Depending on the need, this person can also train others in how to use the circulation system.

Frontline Services Positions

Providing comprehensive frontline services is the hallmark of access services work. This role has evolved from the circulation desk and now includes direct support for collections access, privileges, information, and even basic reference work. The mix of staff and student desk workers should reflect the complexity of the services being offered and at what times. In Yale's experience, this work is becoming increasingly complex, providing assistance with everything from directional questions to basic ready reference work. This mix of services requires higher-level staff for more open hours with a higher mix of student workers in the evening hours when some of the services drop off or are not offered. This section outlines the types of positions necessary to run an effective frontline services operation (see figure 8.3).

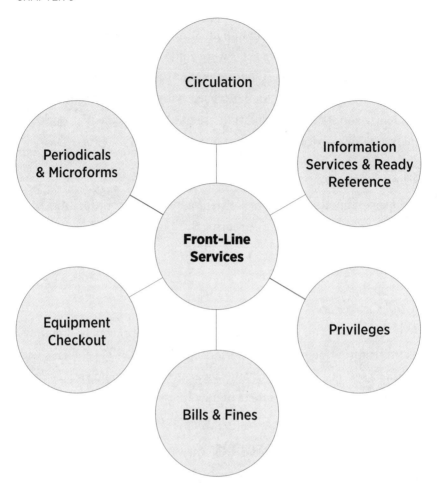

Figure 8.3
Functions of a frontline services unit

Frontline Services Librarian

With a mix of circulation, equipment checkout, privileges, information services, and virtual reference, it is essential to have a librarian head up the programmatic activities of the department's frontline services. Because of the mix of traditional circulation activities and information services work, an individual in this position needs to develop strengths in both access services and reference. Responsibilities include programmatic development of all frontline service points, development and execution of training programs to ensure an environment of constant learning, and an awareness of customer needs and alteration of service offerings accordingly. This librarian also works closely with librarians performing outreach activities, collection development, usability, and systems support. Because of the linking of frontline services staffing with reserves and resource sharing work, the person needs to be skilled in collaboration and work closely with other managers and librarians in the department to ensure seamless service.

This can be an entry-level position, but it may also benefit from an individual with two years of experience. It requires a master's degree from an ALA-accredited library school, and the individual should have direct management experience, an excellent record of customer service, organizational skills, and the ability to communicate effectively with a diverse group of people.

RECRUITMENT

Since this role bridges between access services and reference, it can benefit from a two-pronged approach in recruiting a librarian for the position. Access services outlets are highlighted in the department head recruitment section. Other avenues for this position include the following:

- E-mail discussion lists such as LIBREF-L@listserv.kent.edu (general reference Listserv) and INFOCOMMONS-L@listserv.binghampton.edu (information commons Listserv)
- ALA: RUSA-RSS (Reference and User Services Association—Reference Services Section)
- Reference Renaissance conference in Denver, Colorado (held biennially)

DEVELOPMENT

Aside from involvement in professional organizations and committees outlined in the recruitment section above, it is important to allow a librarian in this position the ability to experiment and expand services to meet and exceed users' unmet needs. This calls for allowing experimentation and expansion with the understanding that most services are in a perpetual state of evolution. Collaboration with other public services librarians, as well as developing expertise in usability and user experience design, can also be beneficial.

Evening and Weekend Manager

Since frontline services are usually offered for all the hours in which the library is open, this unit requires an evening and weekend manager to ensure smooth functioning of services and processes that can be performed in nontraditional hours such as shelving, scanning, and retrievals. This position would usually report to the librarian for frontline services. Since a library's population and service needs in the evening and on weekends can vary significantly from daytime operations, it is important to allow some latitude for this manager to develop services and operations that mesh well with the needs of the unit during these times. Finally, this position can oversee both services and operations work. Responsibilities include directly managing staff and students working in the evenings and weekends, ensuring that service points are staffed and running smoothly, actively communicating with daytime librarians and managers to ensure smooth handoffs between shifts, handling security responsibilities, and working well with a diverse staff and student population. The position requires direct managerial experience, excellent communication skills, the ability to prioritize and be responsive to user needs, the ability to solve problems with little or no direction, and direct customer service experience.

Frontline Services Team Leader

Frontline services team leaders are responsible for running day-to-day operation activities, ensuring that a service point is adequately staffed, training staff and ensuring that service standards are met, hiring and training student workers, making exceptions to policy as necessary, and referring problems as needed to the frontline services librarian. Multiple team leaders are needed if there is more than one service point, and it is equally important that team leaders communicate daily with each other to ensure smooth operations throughout the day and evening.

Student Assistants

Because of the hours of operation and the varying peak busy times, students are necessary to running a successful frontline services operation. Since student workers often work six to eight hours a week, tasks assigned to them need to focus more on transactional activities such as circulation and directional questions, with clear training on how to handle referrals. It is also beneficial to place student workers at service points after they have spent at least a semester doing operational work such as shelving, retrieving, or scanning. This background not only allows for a broader understanding and ability to answer questions, but also funnels the most reliable and high-performing students to frontline services operations where performance issues can be more detrimental.

Resource Sharing and Reserves Positions

Because of the affinities between reserves and interlibrary loan operations, it is becoming increasingly common to combine the leadership of those functions into a single librarian position. The tasks, clientele, operational workflows, and copyright needs can be combined in such a way as to provide new and innovative ways to provide and develop these service areas (see figure 8.4).

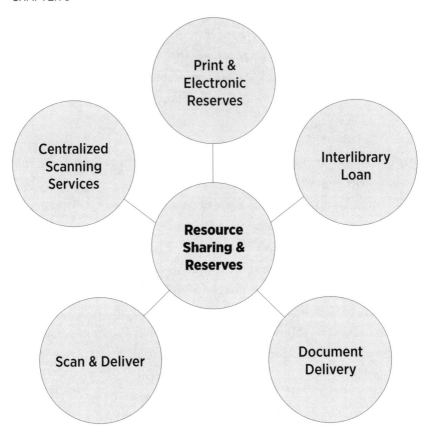

Figure 8.4
Functions of a resource sharing and reserves unit

Resource Sharing and Reserves Librarian

As resource sharing activities increase with more and more consortial partnerships across multiple library types, increasingly complex copyright issues, the need to find synergies with electronic reserves, and expansion of services such as RAPID and scan and deliver, a librarian is needed to head up resource sharing and reserves operations in access services. Responsibilities include providing direction and leadership in all areas of resource sharing and reserves, assessing resource sharing and reserves programs, and implementing improvements in workflows and productivity, technology, and service to users. It is essential for this librarian to keep abreast of new technologies, enhancements, and trends in the field, working collaboratively with librarians and managers in the department as well as librarians at other institutions. This librarian serves as a resource for questions about copyright and fair use as they apply to resource sharing and reserves services and often works with library IT to coordinate and schedule upgrades to resource sharing and reserves hardware and software. This position is a senior level librarian position with a minimum of three years of experience and a master's degree from an ALA-accredited library school. This librarian must have significant managerial experience, project management skills, excellent communication skills, and a history of successful collaborative projects. This individual should also have expertise in either interlibrary loan or reserves work and management software, with experience in implementing such software, training, and developing statistical information and reports. Since this area both generates and spends income, strong budgetary experience is also important.

RECRUITMENT

Recruitment for this position can use similar outlets as those for the department head.

DEVELOPMENT

Development activities are essential to the success of a resource sharing and reserves librarian. It is essential for the librarian to stay active with user groups and vendor meetings at the ALA annual or midwinter conferences to ensure constant development of the software necessary for performing interlibrary loan and reserves functions. In addition, because of the collaborative nature of the work, opportunities to network and stay active professionally should be sought. This can include a combination of conferences, user groups, and affinity organizations. For more information about affinity and user groups as well as conferences, see chapter 11.

Borrowing and Lending Team Leader

The borrowing and lending team leader is a high-level staff position responsible for the day-to-day operations of the borrowing and lending functions of the department's resource sharing and reserves unit. This staff member ensures that borrowing and lending requests are being processed and benchmarks are being met, working closely with the operations team leader to ensure smooth handoffs between functions. The team leader resolves problems related to workflow, trains staff within the unit and in frontline services, hires and trains student workers, and looks at data generated from the resource sharing unit to determine affinities with reserves workflows. This staff member also works regular hours at the frontline service desks. Finally, the team leader is often the most experienced expert at resource sharing functions and may process more difficult borrowing or lending requests as triaged by other staff members.

Borrowing and Lending Specialists

Borrowing and lending specialists are responsible for processing borrowing and lending requests as directed by the team leader. While specialists may be more adept at borrowing or lending requests, all staff can process requests equally well for both functions. Staff are expected to assist in training frontline services staff and student workers and to work regular hours at the service points. Staff handle invoice work such as ILL fee management (IFM) and queries from both primary patrons and libraries requesting materials from the home library. Receiving, processing, shipping, and wrapping work is handled by the operations unit.

Borrowing and Lending Student Workers

Since most traditional Interlibrary Loan student assistant work such as checking in items and preparing for pick-up and shipping will be handled in operations, student workers in resource sharing would assist with the request triage operation and handling simpler borrowing, lending, and scan-and-deliver transactions.

Reserves and Scanning Team Leader

The reserves and scanning team leader is a high-level staff position responsible for the day-to-day operations of the reserves and scanning functions of the department's resource sharing and reserves unit. The staff member ensures that print and electronic reserve requests are being processed and benchmarks are being met. The team leader resolves problems related to workflow; trains staff within the unit and in frontline services; hires, trains and schedules student workers; and looks at data generated from the reserves unit to determine affinities with resource sharing workflows. This staff member also works regular hours at the frontline service desks. The team leader has a high level of expertise with scanning equipment and scanning software. The team leader also handles difficult requests and has a high level of communication and customer services skills in working closely with faculty.

Reserves and Scanning Specialists

Reserves and scanning specialists process print and electronic reserve requests and oversee the scanning output related to ILL lending, scan and deliver, and e-reserves. Specialists ensure that materials are checked for copyright compliance and work directly with faculty to resolve issues and offer solutions if e-reserves cannot be placed. They also communicate closely with staff in operations and resource sharing to ensure materials are processed in a timely manner and problems resolved. They will scan materials as needed and perform quality control checks on scans, and they are expected to have a high degree of understanding of scanning equipment and software. Staff work regular hours at the frontline service desks.

Reserves and Scanning Student Workers

Reserves and scanning student workers are responsible for scanning materials requested for ILL lending, scan and deliver, and e-reserves. They work with the team leader and specialists when citations are not clear. They need to be detail-oriented to ensure that scans are clear and legible.

Operations Positions

Operations Manager

While access services departments are essentially customer service operations, a tremendous amount of operational work occurs behind the scenes to support successful service efforts (see figure 8.5). Some of the responsibilities and skills necessary for running an effective operations unit are similar to those of librarians and managers in the service areas, but operations also requires certain unique skill sets that are suited to analyzing, problem solving, and continuous workflow improvement. Depending on the structure of a particular academic library, the head of operations may be a librarian, manager, or staff member with managerial responsibilities. It is important, however, that this position be structurally at the same level as the other middle manager librarians in the department.

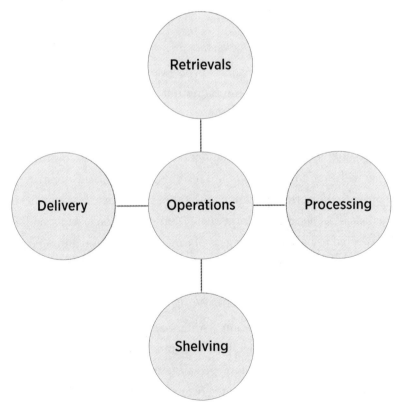

Figure 8.5
Functions of an operations unit

The operations manager oversees all retrieving, processing, shelving, and delivery functions of the access services operations unit. Responsibilities include working collaboratively with other librarians and managers in the unit and technical services, analyzing workflows to achieve maximum efficiency, participating in general planning for service enhancement and improvements, and managing the largest component of managers, staff, and student workers in the department. Successful operations managers should have at least three years of managerial experience and may or may not have a master's degree from an ALA-accredited library school. The operations manager should have demonstrated experience in analyzing workflows and business systems to achieve improvements, have excellent analytical and organization skills, and be able to work collaboratively with service providers and technical services librarians and staff. Depending on the size of the operation, there may also be a dedicated stacks supervisor.

The operations manager should be well versed in various kinds of enterprise software for managing requests for materials. Since all retrieving and processing work is centralized in this unit, the manager needs to have a deep understanding of the ILS software, document delivery software, and reserves management software. As more and more libraries are implementing next-generation discovery platforms that blend several types of catalogs to produce a wider range of available materials, it is equally important to develop solutions that enable better blending of the staff interfaces of these various types of enterprise software. The operations manager and business analyst should work closely with library IT to advocate for and develop these solutions that give staff in these units the best tools available for handling incoming requests.

Shelving and Delivery Supervisor

The shelving and delivery supervisor, or stacks supervisor, has overall responsibility for the management of the physical collection and reports to the operations manager. It is important to note that this position does not require a librarian, but it does require a tremendous amount of oversight for a management position. The stacks supervisor's responsibilities include oversight of all stacks maintenance and delivery service functions, which include shelving, discharging, shifting, deliveries, and hold-shelf maintenance. The supervisor oversees a mix of staff and a large student workforce to ensure that benchmarks are met and establishes and monitors performance indicators to assess and improve the shelving and delivery operation. The supervisor works closely with the team leaders to ensure smooth handoffs between the retrieval and processing operations and the shelving and delivery operations.

The stacks supervisor should have at least two years of managerial experience and be able to work collaboratively in a team environment with a large student workforce. While student workers are prevalent in access services departments, the stacks supervisor often has the largest student workforce, which is essential to materials being shelved and delivered in a timely way. Successful stacks supervisors should have good spatial knowledge and be able to create and manipulate data sets in order to successfully plan shifts and monitor work output. The supervisor should have demonstrated experience in managing a diverse workforce and be successful at motivating and directing student workers.

Retrievals and Processing Team Leader

The retrievals and processing team leader coordinates the work of the retrievals and processing unit in operations. Responsibilities include scheduling, directing and monitoring the day-to-day work of staff and student workers, resolving problems relating to workflow, ensuring benchmarks are met for unit functions, and hiring and training student workers. This is a high-level staff position that assists the operations manager in making improvements to the workflow, training, and documenting procedures. This team leader also works closely with the resource sharing, reserves, and shelving team leaders to ensure that handoffs between the units occur smoothly.

Retrievals and Processing Specialists

Retrievals and processing specialists assist the team leader in training student workers to perform retrieving and processing functions. They also troubleshoot problems with requests, correspond with patrons and technical services units, and modify item records as necessary to ensure requests can be fulfilled. They also forward requests that cannot be filled internally to other document delivery or interlibrary loan borrowing providers as is appropriate. These staff members also compile and report on productivity statistics and make recommendations for improvements to operations.

Retrievals and Processing Student Workers

Student workers in retrievals and processing perform the majority of transactional work as related to internal library retrieving and preparation of materials to be sent out for interlibrary loan. Students retrieve materials from the stacks, mark items found or returned, and prepare materials (e.g., wrap them) to be shipped for interlibrary loan. These students also perform simple processing tasks such as barcoding or simple item record changes. These student workers may also perform shelving and delivery work as needed.

Shelving and Delivery Team Leader

The shelving and delivery team leader coordinates the work of the shelving and delivery unit in operations. Responsibilities include scheduling, directing, and monitoring the day-to-day work of staff and student workers, resolving problems relating to workflow, ensuring benchmarks are met for unit functions, and hiring and training student workers. This is a high-level staff position that assists the shelving and delivery supervisor in making improvements to the shelving operation, conducts training, and documents procedures. This team leader also works closely with the retrievals and processing team leader to ensure close coordination of handoffs between the units.

Shelving and Delivery Specialists

Shelving and delivery specialists assist the team leader in the overall functions of the shelving and delivery unit. They assist in training and leading student workers who perform shelving and delivery functions, compile and report productivity statistics, and make recommendations for improvements as needed. Specialists also assist with shift planning and oversight, accuracy checking, and maintaining range signage as necessary in the stacks.

Shelving and Delivery Student Workers

Shelving and delivery student workers are often the largest student workforce in access services. These students shelve materials, shift, check for accuracy, and make deliveries to other library departments and hold shelves. These students may perform retrievals and processing work as needed. Highly effective student workers in this area may be good candidates for working at the service desks.

CONCLUSION

The work distribution and structure of a successful access services department involves a lot of complex pieces that must work in concert with each other in order to provide excellent services to library patrons. While Yale University Library's example illustrates one particular methodology for structuring an access services department, each library, while sharing similar tasks in the management and service provision to the physical collection, will have a structure that best meets the needs of its particular organization and the services it can support. The listing of positions in this chapter provides examples of the human resources necessary to provide frontline services in multiple locations that minimize unnecessary referrals and have the ability to answer the vast majority of questions posed at service desks in libraries. Staff are knowledgeable about their particular areas, but are exposed on a weekly basis to the work of other service providers in the department, which increases their effectiveness in answering questions about any of the services that are provided by the department. Because the high volume of physical book processing and preparation is separated from resource sharing and reserves, staff in those units can better focus on customer service activities and draw more upon their expertise in doing searches rather than their abilities to handle materials. Centralization of operations activities, although challenging because of the multiple types of software used to perform the work, focuses all of the expert work in retrieving, processing, and shelving materials with the staff who perform this function best. In this department structure, staff in all units are exposed on a daily basis to the whole of what an access services department does and are better able to provide excellent customer service. Staff are allowed to excel and move up to positions of greater responsibility because of their exposure to so many services and processes.

NOTES

1. Trevor A. Dawes, Kimberly Burke Sweetman, and Catherine Von Elm, *Access Services: SPEC Kit 290* (Washington D.C.: ARL, 2005).
2. Ross Housewright and Roger C. Schonfeld, *Ithaka's 2006 Studies of Key Stakeholders in the Digital Transformation in Higher Education* (New York: Ithaka, August 18, 2008), 31, http://lamar.colostate.edu/~pburns/IthakaReport.pdf.
3. Cathy De Rosa, *College Students' Perceptions of Libraries and Information Resources: A Report to the OCLC Membership* (Dublin, OH: OCLC, 2006), 4-7.

BIBLIOGRAPHY

Dawes, Trevor A., Kimberly Burke Sweetman, and Catherine Von Elm. *Access Services: SPEC Kit 290.* Washington, DC: Association of Research Libraries, 2005.

De Rosa, Cathy. *College Students' Perceptions of Libraries and Information Resources: A Report to the OCLC Membership.* Dublin, OH: OCLC, 2006.

Housewright, Ross, and Roger C. Schonfeld. *Ithaka's 2006 Studies of Key Stakeholders in the Digital Transformation in Higher Education.* New York: Ithaka, August 18, 2008, http://lamar.colostate.edu/~pburns/IthakaReport.pdf.

Access Services and the Success of the Academic Library

Nora Dethloff
Assistant Head of Information and Access Services, University of Houston

Paul Sharpe
Head of Access Services, University of Missouri–St. Louis

IN SPITE of valiant efforts to the contrary, academic librarians have a tendency to be poor marketers, likely due to a lack of formal training within library school curricula.[1] As experts in their field, librarians often believe they know how best to reach patrons, as well as how to fulfill the patrons' needs. Discovering that there is a breakdown between message delivery and receipt is cause for much consternation. Librarians and staff try a myriad of approaches to spread word of policies, special events, new enhancements and amenities, or sudden changes in service, often with very mixed results.

The concept of branding has become quite important in library marketing. Often such branding is crafted and viewed as an extension of the library's strategic plan. Within the context of access services, branding is how the department presents itself and its suite of services. It is the definition of who it is, what it does, and what its patrons can expect in the level of service provided. A well-established brand engenders loyalty. Users can rely on the fact that the services provided are identical to what has been promised. When established successfully, the brand is represented within each branch and at every service point throughout the library organization. For this reason, branding is a crucial first step in the marketing of services, including those provided by access services

MARKETING AND BRANDING

Signage

Once the message has been established, choosing the most effective delivery method for the library's patrons is necessary. This is achieved through a variety of standard and emerging methods. Arguably the most effective—and simultaneously least effective—method of conveying information in libraries has been through the use of signage. Its use as a quick and simple means of conveying information cannot be surpassed. Historically, access services has been the greatest stakeholder in the design and use of signage, as it receives the lion's share of directional questions. Consequently, poorly worded or ill-conceived signs can have unintended consequences. A bad sign can do as much damage as a good sign can fix, giving users the wrong message and increasing frustration. This brings the problem back to access services in the form of terse interactions and more questions. Clear, concise signage tends to result in fewer questions and a positive experience for the library user. Consistent fonts, images, and logos help to reinforce the library's brand. Electronic signage builds upon this simplicity through customizable graphics, scheduled messaging, and convenience for all parties involved.

Pamphlets and E-mails

Due to its simplicity, signage is unable to communicate all messages. Users are not willing to stand and peruse lists of rules and procedures or read a long-winded explanation for why an event isn't happening. For lengthier messages, patrons need to be able to digest the information at their leisure. E-mail is still one of the best options for sending links to online materials such as subject guides, policies, or video tutorials. The ease of including links to the library's website or other pertinent Internet resources is essential. Access services' use of e-mail has historically been a function of business operations: indicators of item availability, electronic delivery of documents, and overdue notices. Today, it's a vital method for informing users of new or changing services, scheduled downtimes for electronic resources, and upcoming or emergency facilities issues. The ability to take away a pamphlet still makes sense to a variety of users without Internet or wireless access. This provides library users with detailed information to read on their own time in a place of their choosing. The downside tends to be the likelihood of information overload; important information can be easily missed or overlooked among the barrage of personal e-mails, spam, and the like. Once highly effective, e-mail has experienced diminishing returns in usefulness.

Library Tours

Library tours provide many patrons with the chance to see—and gain a better understanding of the functionality of—the facilities. The access services staff often provide such tours, as they are often best equipped to point out and address the basic questions of new library users. For example, explanations of the Library of Congress system of classification are best when users can see the call number labels and the layout for themselves. Tours allow for a personalized experience, giving patrons the ability to ask questions and engage in face-to-face interactions. Making a personal connection with the librarian or staff member puts the patron at ease and makes the library a more comfortable environment. However, depending on the nature of the building, tours can also be distracting to users engaged in research or quiet study.

Library Workshops

A step beyond the library tour is creating a dedicated library course or workshop. Bibliographic instruction has been a hallmark of academic libraries for decades. Incorporating the core functions of access services, such as how to place holds or request interlibrary loan materials, is essential to student success. Patrons interested in gaining greater insight into the research process will be interested in taking notes and asking follow-up questions. The subject liaison, fully embedded in the classroom, either maintains a healthy working knowledge of basic access services tasks or coordinates efforts to bring access services into the classroom. Many access services professionals teach the course themselves, focused on a broad overview of reserves, interlibrary loan, circulation policies, and the layout of the building. This is especially beneficial to incoming freshmen and transfer students.

Courseware and Subject Guides

The advent of courseware for the promulgation of online learning has led to the integration of library services through the same methods. As more educational institutions provide courses via the Internet, users want all of the ancillary services to support their coursework in the same convenient space. Through the courseware package, libraries are able to create web-pages customized to the audience being served, often in conjunction with course instructors. Links are provided to specific library materials that support the course, reserve materials to supplement required texts, and databases within the disciplinary field. Additionally, useful information such as library hours, interlibrary loan links, and contact information for librarians in the subject area can all be incorporated into the virtual space. Many of these same services are also marketed through online library guides created by subject librarians and access services staff. These guides are used both as additional resources for coursework and as stand-alone aids to research within a specific discipline. Subject guides are generally most effective when provided online, but they can also be printed for low-tech research needs.

Social Media

Before the advent of social media, the library's virtual presence was generally confined to its own website. Today, a library's presence on social media is also a natural extension of its own branding initiatives. The aforementioned online tutorials and other links can now be pushed outward to interested parties who subscribe to a library's Twitter feed. By "liking" the library's Facebook page or "checking in" at the library on Foursquare, patrons are self-identifying as interested in the library. The best aspect of social media for libraries is the ability to engage in a direct and meaningful dialogue with their patrons. These platforms allow for real-time sharing of information, opinions, ideas, images, and videos— any of which have the ability to inform and enrich the library experience. Taken as part of the greater package, social media is capable of enriching what the library provides its users and what the users give back to the library. Access services, as the public face of the library, is best positioned to lead and manage these efforts in the library, disseminating information regarding everything from changes in service, hours, and special events to reminders to return books on time.

PUBLIC RELATIONS

In the traditional brick-and-mortar library, the access services department is the public face of the institution. This is also true from an operational standpoint. The circulation desk is often the first service point a patron finds upon walking into the building, providing directional assistance and a lay person's interpretation of basic library policies. In other organizational structures, a library security officer or library staff member stationed at a simplified service point can also provide this function. Even as many libraries move to technology-based solutions, such as touchscreen directories and electronic signage, the navigational information provided falls within the purview of access services.

From an organizational perspective, the processes housed in a typical access services department are mission-critical; they can be the initial, and sometimes the only, points of interaction a patron will have with the library. In an academic institution, this is certainly the case with adjunct faculty, some full-time faculty, and students in graduate/professional programs who already feel comfortable with research. This tendency can be attributed to self-sufficiency or confidence their ability to discover and use library resources. Their needs are often satisfied by interlibrary loan, reserves, and circulation. Conversely, reluctance on a patron's part to initiate contact with a reference librarian can be attributed to feelings of intellectual inferiority or intimidation. For this reason, frontline staff members are often the simplest access point for patron needs.

Access Services as Catchall

Access services has always defied easy definition. The makeup of the department, often comprised of "circulation and more," varies from library to library (see parts 1 and 2 of this book). The common thread tends to be its overall function as a catchall for the indefinable. In addition to the service units that occupy the department, access services can become a refuge for ancillary services and functions that do not fall under any other jurisdiction in a clearly defined manner. Often, this is a result of acknowledging that the department is ever-present during a library's full operating hours. It is important for the librarians and staff working in access services to embrace the notion of being all things to everyone. The ubiquitous nature of the department insures its role in the interdependency of the organization.

Explanation and Defense of Policies

Library policies vary greatly from one organization to another and are typically a reflection of the needs and idiosyncrasies of their constituencies. Regardless of why they have been created and by whom, it falls to access services to enforce and defend library policies as part of its role on the front lines. For that reason, it helps to be prepared for challenges to the rules. Invariably, policies are challenged due to changes in user needs, shifting institutional or societal values, and evolving technological capabilities. Also, people like to have things their way.

Access services serves as customer service for the library, weathering a barrage of complaints, sympathy pleas, and bargaining for exceptions to the rules. Customer service training is essential in dealing with the demands of library patrons. Providing excellent service to the library's users involves striking a balance between making users feel welcome and successful while still upholding the rules. Because of their unique role, all staff members who have direct contact with the public should be aware of the library's current policies and the arguments made against those policies. For example, if the library has a strict policy prohibiting food and drink, suggesting alternative locations for meals and snacks is in order. If staff members are ill prepared for these discussions, it is likely they will give in, allowing behaviors that contradict organizational policy.

SUPPORT FOR TEACHING AND LEARNING

In most libraries, the circulation desk occupies a prominent physical space in the library. Often, the circulation desk is the first thing patrons see when they arrive at the library and the last place they stop before leaving. The circulation desk and other service points in the library serve as touchstones for library patrons. Questions fielded at these service points are rarely limited to library-related subjects and range from simple directional inquiries to questions about the campus and the larger community. Service points set the tone for the library and for student success in the library. Service points are also the place where patrons are free to offer feedback, suggestions, and complaints. Because of this prominence and the access to patron feedback it affords, access services departments are well situated to receive and respond to patron feedback. This makes access services an ideal place for the development of new services. A focus on customer service and on responding to patron needs often results in a "give the people what they want" philosophy. With proper communication and an environment in which new ideas can be tried and vetted, this translates to the proliferation of services aimed directly at supporting patrons and their research.

Supplementing the Classroom Experience

Access services departments offer support for in-classroom and virtual teaching through a number of services. In today's educational landscape, these services and the department that supports them must be nimble, responsive, and adaptable as new situations and new needs arise.

Course Reserves and E-reserves

Course reserves are an example of a long-offered service that has seen rapid change in recent years. Although most libraries continue to offer traditional physical reserves services for circulating materials, as the amount of information available online and the demand for electronic access have increased, libraries have responded by offering electronic course reserves, or e-reserves.

Traditional course reserves provide guaranteed access to physical course materials by separating them from the circulating collection. Professors or instructors designate materials to be placed on reserve. Reserve materials are kept in a staff-only area. Patrons must inquire at a service point and have library staff retrieve the desired materials. Patrons can check out reserves materials for a limited amount of time, generally no more than a few hours, and usually reserves materials must be kept in the library building. Traditional course reserves allow for a high number of students to share access to course materials, although at the cost of some convenience.

Traditional course reserves require a substantial time investment for access services staff to set up and maintain. Items must be pulled from the collection or, if not enough copies are owned, purchased from a vendor. Catalog records must be modified to show that items are on course reserve or created in the case of new items. At the service point, reserves items must be retrieved for the patron, checked out and back in within a short amount of time, and rapidly reshelved. Certainly, course reserves are a labor-intensive service. Yet they are a particularly valuable service to both students and faculty. As textbooks and other course materials become more and more expensive, students appreciate not having to purchase additional course materials. Instructors can make assignments from a variety of sources without being concerned that the cost for students will be prohibitive. In addition, by limiting circulation periods, reserves services allow multiple students to share access to a single resource, saving money for the library and the institution. Course reserves allows for a broader, richer educational experience.

E-reserves allow for articles, chapters, and selections of other materials to be accessed in a secure online system. Again, instructors designate materials to be placed on e-reserve. Students can view the materials by logging in to the secure system. Unlike traditional course reserves services, e-reserves are available anywhere a student has access to the Internet.

As with traditional course reserves, setting up e-reserves can be a labor-intensive process for access services staff. Materials that are not available in an electronic format must be scanned and posted to the e-reserves system. The e-reserves software must be maintained and server space dedicated to e-reserves materials. Copyright and licensing concerns play a fundamental role in the management of e-reserves and must be monitored very closely to ensure compliance. As the nature of education evolves, however, e-reserves have become an increasingly important service. As educational content and learning experiences move into the online environment, the ability to access course materials electronically has become increasingly important. Students value round-the-clock access to information and the ability to access course materials when it is convenient to them. Students also value the ability to work away from campus without being tied to the physical classroom or the physical library. Some e-reserves systems allow multiple users to access the same item simultaneously, thus eliminating the need for multiple copies or long wait times for popular items often seen in traditional course reserves.

Streaming services are often offered as part of electronic course reserves. These services allow students to remotely access audio and video resources. While with traditional reserves services students must watch or listen to media items in the library on designated equipment, streaming services are a way to make audio and video works available at a distance and to a large number of patrons at once. Streaming involves mounting media files on a streaming server, where they can be accessed and viewed remotely without being downloaded or saved. Typically, libraries require patrons to authenticate or provide a password in order to access streaming materials.

Streaming can be a particularly costly service to provide. First, there is an up-front technological cost for a streaming server and the information technology department input to set up and maintain it. There is the work of converting the media (CDs, DVDs, or other formats) files into streaming media, and the work required to set up an authentication system to protect the files from unauthorized access. Streaming services, because they involve distributing audio and video files electronically, require strict attention to copyright and licensing considerations. However, streaming services provide enormous value to patrons. In particular, patrons who are unable to come to the library in person are still able to access media in order to complete class assignments or research. Even those patrons located near the library are well served by twenty-four-hour access and the ability to use media from their homes or wherever it is convenient for them. Streaming also allows for multiple patrons to access media files at the same time. Thus, one streamed file can take the place of multiple physical copies.

Textbooks Services

Many libraries offer textbook services in addition to, or as part of, their course reserves service. These services provide copies of commonly used or course-prescribed textbooks. Often these textbooks are available for shortened circulation periods or for use within the library. As the cost of textbooks continues to climb, these services are becoming both more expensive for libraries to maintain and more valuable to the students the libraries serve. Libraries offering textbook services must also keep up with the rapidly changing assigned textbooks and must work with the bookstore to guarantee assigned texts are available at the start of the term. Students appreciate the cost savings of not having to purchase a textbook, but these services are valuable in other ways as well. Students may use a library textbook during the first weeks of a class, purchasing a textbook only if they decide to remain enrolled in the class. Instructors, too, gain from a library textbook service. With textbooks available at the library, they may feel more able to assign multiple texts or very expensive texts that they might otherwise avoid. If a textbook collection is open to browsing, students can preview the textbook required by a certain instructor, and instructors can examine the textbooks being used by their colleagues.

With the increasing popularity of e-books in the marketplace, combined with the rising cost of print textbooks, electronic textbooks are beginning to gain a foothold in the student marketplace. At present, most electronic textbook services are tied to a specific e-reader or platform (Amazon's Kindle, Apple's iPad, and Barnes & Noble's Nook all offer e-textbook services) and require the purchase or rental of a particular title. As with other e-books, the dedicated platforms can make it difficult for libraries to offer e-textbooks. Many libraries offer e-textbooks through contracts with publishers, but ensuring compatibility with the wide variety of portable devices used by students is a difficult, and often impossible, proposition. As more and more of the textbook market moves into the electronic environment and student demand for electronic textbooks grows, libraries may see less need for print textbook services and a growing need to work with publishers and distributers to offer access to electronic textbooks across platforms.

Reciprocal Borrowing Programs

Many libraries are members of library consortia or networks. These cooperative groups may be small groups of libraries serving the same community, or they might be large networks spanning multiple states or regions. Many of these groups offer reciprocal borrowing privileges between libraries. This means that a patron of one library can be granted borrowing privileges at the library of another institution. Often, these borrowing privileges are scaled back or somewhat restricted when compared to those offered to an affiliated patron. Reciprocal borrowing services provide value to students and researchers whose work would otherwise be hampered by lack of proximity to a library or needed research materials. These services are often used by distance education students or by graduate students or faculty members doing research away from their home institution. These services allow students to pursue their studies regardless of geographic limitations. Reciprocal borrowing services can also allow researchers to gain access to items their home library may not own.

Interlibrary Loan

Interlibrary loan (ILL) supplies patrons with materials not readily available at their home library. Patrons place a request for a desired item. If the item is owned by another library, a request to borrow the item is sent; when the item is received, it is checked out to the patron for a loan period determined by the owning library.

Interlibrary loan can be a time-consuming service, with a considerable investment in both staff and monetary resources. Considerable research is often required to locate desired items, and the arranging, tracking, and managing of requests can be labor-intensive. Most large libraries invest in an ILL management system—specialized software designed for ILL services. This requires an additional financial investment. Shipping costs, fees to acquire items, and fees for lost or overdue items are also often absorbed by the library.

The primary benefit of interlibrary loan is the ability to supplement materials owned by the home library. Both student and faculty research is considerable enhanced by the ability to obtain items outside those in their local collections. ILL also allows scholars access to rare or primary-source materials that would otherwise require travel in order to access. The ability to access a variety of materials outside the local library's collection allows for broader, better, and more efficient scholarship and provides a benefit both for scholars and for the institution as a whole. Furthermore, borrowing these items from far away, rather than having to travel to them, frees up money and time resources.

Often, interlibrary loan also encompasses a range of services beyond traditional ILL. These services, which add value for patrons and simplify the research process, can include citation verification, research assistance, or connecting patrons with document suppliers, museums, or other libraries that may have collections relevant to patron research. When patrons place requests for items that are in the local collection, ILL often provides de facto library instruction, teaching the patron to properly search or navigate library systems in order to locate the desired materials. ILL services in many institutions also absorb the cost of obtaining difficult-to-find materials. These costs can range from shipping costs to borrowing charges and often to the purchase of materials not available for lending.

Increasingly, interlibrary loan services are also allowing patrons to request items that are owned in the local collection but are checked out by another patron, on course reserve, or otherwise unavailable. This allows multiple patrons to simultaneously utilize popular research materials or multiple students in a class to research the same topic without competition for resources.

Streamlining Library Research

Access services departments offer a variety of services designed not simply to provide patrons with access to library materials, but to make library research simpler, faster, and more easily accomplished. As technology becomes more complex, library systems have become increasingly difficult to navigate. Access services librarians offer services designed to simplify and streamline library research, getting the desired item into the hands of the patron as quickly and easily as possible. Taking the frustration out of library research to the extent possible allows more time for engagement with the research process and more effective learning overall.

Document Delivery

Document delivery services provide patrons with copies of locally held articles and book chapters. In many libraries, print journals cannot circulate or have very limited circulation periods. Patrons traditionally had to come to the library and make copies of the articles or chapters they needed. Document delivery services began as a way to save patrons the time and trouble of pulling and copying these materials. Most document delivery services now provide electronic copies of items, generally e-mailing scanned copies of documents to patrons. These services save a considerable amount of time for patrons, eliminating the need for them to come to the library and locate and pull the necessary items, as well as avoiding the monetary costs associated with photocopying. As patrons increasingly expect electronic content, document delivery services help to fill the gaps in electronic collections, providing convenience for the patron.

Local Holds and Delivery

Local holds services allow patrons to search the online catalog and place requests for desired materials. The materials are pulled by library staff and reserved for the patron. This service allows patrons access to print collections but eliminates the need for them to spend time searching the stacks themselves and the trouble of carrying a stack of books around the library. Researchers interested in multiple items can save a great deal of time by utilizing local holds services, but even patrons interested in only one book can gain value from having the desired item out and ready for them when they arrive at the library.

In addition to local holds, many access services departments offer delivery of physical materials as a convenience to faculty and students. This service allows requested items to be delivered directly to the patron's office or departmental mailbox. At many institutions, this service is available to both faculty and students. The costs of providing such a service are clear: staff time required to pull and deliver items, infrastructure for the timely delivery, and the possible cost of materials gone missing in their travels across campus. However, delivery services are very popular with both faculty and students, who enjoy the convenience of not having to come to the library or search the stacks. Both local holds and delivery services save valuable time for patrons.

Providing Resources for Student Success

In the traditional brick-and-mortar library, management of the physical space is often the provenance of access services departments. In recent years, libraries have undergone a transformation from stolid, quiet spaces for individual study and reflection to multifunction learning spaces that allow for a variety of learning styles and interactions. Sullivan provides an excellent overview of this shift in perspective and priorities and the need for ongoing assessment and continued change.[2] Although the need for quiet individual study space remains, libraries have also created areas for group study and collaborative learning. In addition, to keep pace with student demands and the changing nature of information and research, libraries have had to add spaces for the use of technology. Responsibility for these spaces typically rests in the access services department. Increasingly, access services departments are responding to the need for usable technology with the circulation of portable devices such as laptops, tablets, and other equipment. The management of both library space and technology plays a key role in fostering student success.

Physical Spaces: Study Spaces, Carrels, and Group Study Rooms

Libraries have traditionally offered spaces for quiet individual study. Most academic libraries were built with small, closet-sized carrels designed for an individual engaged in research and needing to spend a great deal of time near the resources housed at the library. The methods used to assign these carrels could vary by institution, but generally demand for carrels outpaced availability. Many institutions would charge a fee for carrel rental and would limit availability to doctoral students or undergraduate seniors. Other areas within the library were set aside for individual study, with furniture (also called carrels, confusingly) designed for isolation and the limiting of distractions. As the nature of the library and education has changed, libraries have seen an increase in the demand for group study areas and areas within the library set aside for socialization, group work, or other boisterous activities. Yet the demand for quiet individual study space has remained. Increasingly at issue for access services departments has been finding a way to appropriately balance space between quiet areas and areas where groups can work collaboratively. These group study areas can take the shape of large open areas with furniture designed for group use or larger study rooms designed for multiple people and available by reservation.

At most libraries, patron demand seems equally split between quiet spaces and areas for collaboration. This makes sense, as the same patron may use each kind of space depending on the nature of the work to be done. Yet libraries struggle to find the appropriate balance. Keeping quiet areas quiet and group study areas available for groups rather than individuals are common problems. Access services departments must find solutions to deal with these issues on a daily basis. Further, the cost of renovating existing spaces or purchasing new furniture can be problematic. Many libraries also struggle with finding enough space for both study areas and collections. Nonetheless, for many students the library remains the most important study space on campus. Students will be drawn to a library that can successfully offer both quiet and group study spaces, and students who spend more time in the library are far more likely to utilize library resources, perform more in-depth research, and gain more from their study time overall. Providing space for students to actively engage in learning is one of the most important day-to-day activities of an academic library.

Circulating Technology: Laptops, Tablets, and Other Equipment

Over the last two decades, technology has become more and more ubiquitous in higher education. Increasingly, research materials, course content, and even the courses themselves have moved into the online environment. Yet technology remains expensive and, when added to the already high costs of tuition and textbooks, may be out of reach for many. Libraries have long responded by offering on-site computer labs, but these are expensive to set up and maintain and require a great deal of space. Some libraries have sought solutions in portable technology, such as laptops or netbooks and, more recently, tablets. These items are generally offered for checkout at the circulation desk, and items are placed on a patron's library account, just like a book. Use of this equipment may be restricted to a few hours within the library, or the patron may be allowed several days of use.

At many libraries with these services, technology available for circulation has expanded beyond computing devices to include portable electronics, such as digital cameras, video cameras, portable scanners, microphones, or other small electronic devices, for checkout. These services provide support for scholars in a range of fields, allowing students access to and experience with expensive technology that may otherwise be out of their reach.

Obviously, these services come at a cost to the library. Laptops can be quite expensive and are subject to wear and tear beyond what a desktop computer might receive. Although netbooks and tablets are generally less expensive than desktop computers, they are still subject (and in the case of tablets, perhaps more subject) to being dropped, sat upon, cracked, or otherwise damaged in the course of student use. Cameras, scanners, and other tech items also run the risk of being damaged and often come with multiple small parts (data cards, cords, removable lenses, etc.) that may be lost or damaged while being circulated. Further costs come in the staff time required to circulate these items. Access services staff must be responsible not only for checkout and checkin, but for making sure equipment is properly charged and fully functioning and contains all of its parts. Yet the popularity of most technology circulation programs more than justifies the cost to libraries. Students have access to computers and other technology that will enhance their educational experience. Libraries get to provide access to computers without giving up precious space to a lab. Circulating technology is a win-win.

Extended Hours

College students are well known for their late hours. Libraries cannot provide study spaces during peak student study times if they are not open past traditional business hours. More and more college libraries are responding to student demand by increasing the number of hours they are open, with many libraries remaining open twenty-four hours for at least part of the week. This allows libraries to provide research support and study space for students when it is needed, but extended hours carry complications for libraries. Because access services departments typically manage library space, they are generally most impacted by extended hours. Of course, staying open longer carries the need for additional staff. Being open late into the night carries a need for additional security, in the form of both building design and security personnel. Yet students value the ability to use the library when it is convenient for them and value being able to have a place to study late into the night. Finding a balance between student demands, student safety, and fiscal reality often falls to access services librarians.

SUPPORT FOR DISTANCE EDUCATION

As education has increasingly moved online, many institutions of higher learning offer some kind of distance education program. This may take the form of a satellite campus with in-person classes, it may mean a class completely delivered through an online course management system, or it could be some combination of the two. In any case, access to library resources will be necessary for the students. However, library resources can be difficult to access when the student is physically separated from the campus. Although many resources are now available online, students must still have a means to access materials that are not available electronically. In order to keep pace with the growing demand for distance education, access services departments have developed a number of services to ensure resources are available to the distance user.

Document Delivery

Document delivery for distance education patrons works the same way as a document delivery service for those on campus. Patrons request articles or book chapters, usually via an online form. Access services staff pull the materials, scan the desired item, and deliver an electronic copy to the patron. Document delivery services are an important aspect of support for distance patrons. Without such a service, these patrons would be entirely unable to access print articles.

Paging Services

In order to provide distance education patrons with access to books, media, and other circulating materials, many libraries offer paging services that deliver books to patrons on satellite campuses. Patrons can request materials via the OPAC or an online request form, and library staff members pull the items and send them to the preferred location via a courier service or US mail. Patrons are then able to check out the requested items and, after use, return them to either the satellite location or the main library. This service allows students the opportunity to use library resources without travelling long distances or spending large amounts of time in order to get to the main campus library.

Shipping Physical Items

In lieu of delivery to a satellite location, many libraries offer distance patrons the option of having materials delivered directly to their home address. For schools that do not have satellite locations or patrons who are far from any campus, this service can provide valuable access to library materials. Some libraries also provide postage-paid packaging in which borrowed items can be returned to the library. This service provides valuable support to distance education students, who are given a connection to their home library and its resources. Obviously, the costs associated with shipping an item one way, let alone both ways, can be high. However, as long as much of the world's information remains available in print only, there will be a need for students to access books. Shipping items directly to distance education patrons allows libraries to support distance education and allows students equitable access to the library's collection.

E-reserves

Electronic reserves are a valuable service for all students but can be especially important for distance education students. Through e-reserves, instructors can make required and supplemental course materials available online in a safe, encrypted, and copyright-compliant system. Proactively communicating with instructors to set up e-reserves for distance education classes is an important task for access services staff. If course materials are made available online through the e-reserves system, there is likely to be a decrease in the number of distance education document delivery requests for those items. It is much more efficient to make these materials available through e-reserves rather than to pull and scan items multiple times in response to document delivery requests.

Streaming Services

Streaming services can provide distance education students with access to video or sound files remotely. While streaming services are convenient for local users, they are a necessity for distance education students. Streaming services are particularly important in support of distance classes in music, theater, film studies, or other disciplines that rely heavily upon the use of media. Again, streaming services ensure that students are provided access to these materials in a convenient and copyright-compliant manner.

CONCLUSION

Ultimately, the purpose of access services is to connect patrons with resources. As educational content is increasingly delivered online, access services departments must provide services that allow distance users access to all library materials without regard for format. Although technology provides tools for accessing library materials, it can also create barriers, particularly when it comes to older, print-only materials. Access services departments must strive to ensure that services for distance education students are the same as for in-person users. To accomplish this, access services librarians must be familiar with existing tools and services, but must also maintain awareness of the evolving educational landscape and be ready to create new solutions as new barriers arise.

NOTES

1. Kathy Dempsey, *The Accidental Library Marketer* (Medford, NJ: Information Today, 2009), 2.
2. Rebecca M. Sullivan, "Common Knowledge: Learning Spaces in Academic Libraries," *College and Undergraduate Libraries* 17, no. 2–3 (2010): 143.

BIBLIOGRAPHY

Dempsey, Kathy. *The Accidental Library Marketer*. Medford, NJ: Information Today, 2009.
Sullivan, Rebecca M. "Common Knowledge: Learning Spaces in Academic Libraries." *College and Undergraduate Libraries,* 17, no. 2–3 (2010): 130–148.

Assessing and Benchmarking Access Services

David K. Larsen
Head of Access Services and Assessment,
University of Chicago Library

EVOLUTION OF ASSESSMENT IN ACCESS SERVICES

Who uses libraries? Is that use changing over time? What hours should the circulation desk remain open? How much staffing is needed at service points? How quickly do library users expect to receive materials? What services do readers want from libraries? How well are libraries meeting user needs? What difference do my services make?

Answering these questions requires assessment and evaluation. As libraries become more user-centric, they are paying increasing attention to assessing user needs and designing services to meet those needs. The access services department is often at the center of these assessment efforts, since its services exist to meet user needs.

Early assessments of libraries in the United States focused on collection size rather than use.[1] When Charles Jewett of the Smithsonian Institution sought to obtain annual circulation figures for US libraries in

1849, few libraries were able to supply him with this information.[2] In the 1870s, the US Bureau of Education began collecting information about libraries that included some circulation statistics.[3] Circulation figures for public libraries in larger cities began appearing in the *ALA Bulletin* and *Library Journal* starting in the 1920s, but academic libraries lagged behind in sharing circulation information, though many likely tracked this information for internal use.[4] The Gerould Statistics on academic libraries, the earliest of which date from 1907 and which formed the basis for the Association of Research Libraries (ARL) *Statistics*, included only information about collection size, staffing, and expenditures.[5] The annual *ARL Statistics,* which have been collected since the 1960s, did not include information about interlibrary loan use until 1974 and did not include circulation statistics until 1991.[6] In a keynote address at the 2010 ARL Library Assessment Conference, Fred Heath traced the roots of library assessment to a late nineteenth- and early twentieth-century desire to prescriptively dictate standards for library collections and resources in order to attain consistent evaluation measures for accreditation or funding. He argued that this emphasis on common standards was succeeded in the middle decades of the twentieth century by quantitative measures like the ARL Index, which were designed to rank libraries according to collection size, staffing levels, and annual expenditures. However, during the last decades of the twentieth century, libraries began seeking "new measures" that sought to assess not just quantitative "inputs" (like acquisitions and expenditures) but also qualitative "outputs" (like service quality and effectiveness) and "outcomes" (like impact on readers and returns on investments).[7] The changes that Heath chronicles can be seen as part of a larger shift from a collection-centric to a user-centric model of libraries in which libraries are judged not just by what they contain but also by how well they meet the needs of those they are intended to serve. This new model aligns nicely with the goals of access services, which has always focused on meeting the needs of library users.

GOALS AND METHODS

There are numerous reasons to assess access services, and these varying motivations lead to differing modes of assessment. This chapter will highlight some of the more common incentives for evaluating services and provide examples of assessment methodologies that are appropriate for each, while highlighting examples relevant to access services.

Demonstrate and Document Use

The most basic motive for assessment is to assess how and to what extent libraries are being used. Generally, the methodology employed to demonstrate and document use comes down to some form of counting. Most libraries track statistics about use of libraries for annual or periodic library reports. There are numerous sources for information about use of libraries. Gate counters or card swipes are often employed to record entries and exits from spaces. Interlibrary loan processing systems provide reports on borrowing and lending requests, and course reserve management software can provide data on use of library materials for classes. Observational studies and head counts can provide additional information about how libraries are used. Reshelving data can show which materials are used in house but are never checked out. Commercial products like Compendium's Desk Tracker can be used to keep statistics on use of service points.

Statistics demonstrating and documenting use can be valuable in informing decisions about library collections, services, and spaces. Use statistics can inform collection development decisions by indicating the types of materials that library users are consulting. Heavy use of titles in a subject area may justify additional spending for collections in that area. Titles that have not circulated recently may be targeted for weeding. Identifying copies that are subject to frequent hold or recall requests may justify the purchase of additional copies. Information about material borrowed through interlibrary loan can help identify titles that should be purchased for library collections.

Data on library use can also be used to improve services. Knowing when users come to libraries can be helpful in determining how much staffing is needed for specific shifts or certain days of the week. This data can also be useful in setting appropriate service hours. For example, knowing how many library users are asked to leave the library at closing can help indicate whether a library should stay open longer. Services that are underused may need to be promoted more heavily or may be abandoned in favor of newer (and hopefully more popular) services.

Use data can also shed light on space needs. Observational studies on library spaces can show whether there is sufficient seating for those working together and those working alone. Seating preferences can be inferred if certain types of furniture fill up before others. Room or computer reservation software can provide additional information about how spaces are used.

Understand How Use Changes over Time

In addition to examining current use patterns, it is also important to examine how library use has changed and is changing. The source data and methodologies are often the same as those listed above, but the goal is identifying and understanding patterns of change. Has annual circulation been increasing or decreasing? Has the size of the population eligible for library services also changed? Are more or fewer people entering library buildings? How has remote use of library services and collections changed? Are library users asking more questions of library staff about technology?

Libraries typically track changes to key statistics in annual reports, often analyzing data over a five-year period. National datasets of library statistics also aid the tracking of trends in use patterns and can be used to trace changes over longer periods of time. These include the *ARL Statistics,* Association of College and Research Libraries (ACRL) statistics, the Public Libraries in the United States Survey produced by the Institute of Museum and Library Services (IMLS), the Academic Libraries Survey and School Library Media Center Survey produced by the National Center for Education Statistics (NCES), and the *Annual Statistics of Medical School Libraries in the United States and Canada* produced by the Association of Academic Health Sciences Libraries (AAHSL).

Although analyses of longitudinal use data can identify areas where use of libraries is changing, this information can shed little light on why use is changing. In order to understand the impetus for change, additional assessments focused on determining causes will likely be necessary. For example, one could conduct a focus group with library users asking how their use of the library has changed and why.

Gauge User Satisfaction

Although understanding the extent to which libraries are used and how that use changes over time can be very helpful, this information does nothing to indicate whether library users are pleased with library services or whether those services are meeting their expectations. User satisfaction studies are intended to answer these questions. The most common method for assessing user satisfaction is through a survey.

Although libraries often develop their own surveys to evaluate user satisfaction, increasing use is being made of standardized surveys that have been heavily tested and designed to improve their reliability. One of the more popular is the LibQUAL+ survey designed by the ARL and based on the SERVQUAL measure of service quality. This instrument asks respondents to rate twenty-two aspects of libraries, which fall into three broad categories: (1) affect of service (which includes staff empathy, professionalism, and competence); (2) information control (including adequacy of collections, ease of access to information, and ability to self-navigate information resources); and (3) library as place (including adequacy of buildings and facilities). For each aspect, respondents are asked to indicate the minimum level of service they would accept, the level of service they expect or would like to see, and the level of service they feel they actually receive. These three ratings allow libraries to identify areas where they are not meeting minimum expectations, to see areas where they are surpassing even desired levels of service, and to find areas where they can improve to meet expectations. However, libraries sometimes struggle to understand how to interpret the ratings they receive and how to know what changes to make to improve performance. One factor that helps shed light on responses is the inclusion in the survey of a final text box that respondents can use to supply comments about their answers or about other topics not included on the survey. The comments can be a rich source of information about areas where libraries can improve, and specific access services areas are sometimes singled out. The LibQUAL+ survey is very easy to conduct since ARL administers the survey and provides initial analysis. In order to reduce the effort required to complete the survey, ARL also offers a LibQUAL+ Lite version, which asks respondents to answer only a subset of the questions but provides the surveying library with responses to all the questions by changing which questions are asked of individual respondents.

Another approach to assessing user satisfaction is the LibSat survey marketed by Counting Opinions, a company focused on helping libraries conduct assessment. This satisfaction survey was developed for public libraries but now includes versions for academic libraries. It differs from LibQUAL+ in that is intended to be made available as a permanent link on library websites so that libraries can obtain ongoing, "continuous" feedback from library users. It includes measures of satisfaction, quality, use, importance, willingness to recommend or refer, and expectations, which together are combined into what the company calls a SQUIRE index.

In the United Kingdom, many public libraries use the PLUS survey developed by the Chartered Institute of Public Finance and Accountancy (CIPFA). Since its introduction in 1995, CIPFA has also created a version for children (1997), an ePlus version focused on information and communication technology (2001), and a Home Delivery survey (2005).[8]

User satisfaction is a key measure of performance, but it should not be taken as the sole measure of effectiveness. Sometimes users will report being satisfied even when their needs were not objectively met. For example, someone may report high satisfaction levels even if she could not find needed library resources because her interactions with library staff were pleasant and everyone who tried to help her seemed competent. Or a person may find that his needs were mostly met, so he will report being "satisfied" without providing information about how the library could improve the service. Sometimes users may not be in a position to judge the effectiveness of a service. For example, a user might be satisfied with course reserves services because she has no experience with reserves services at other libraries and thus has no real point of comparison when making judgments about her satisfaction. A person who is told incorrect information by a library staff member may report being satisfied on a survey and only later find out the information he was given was wrong. These limitations should not detract from the need to assess user satisfaction (and work to improve satisfaction), but they should prevent one from equating satisfaction with effective performance.

Compare Oneself to Others (Benchmark)

Library administrators often seek to compare their institutions to those they regard as peer institutions or to those whose peers they aspire to become. The ARL Investment Index is an "input" measure that ranks research libraries based on how much they spend on staffing and materials. Libraries can use this index to compare their own spending to those they would like to emulate and perhaps use this information to seek additional resources for collection or staffing that will allow them to improve their ranking on the index.

Creating change based on comparisons to other institutions or processes is called *benchmarking*. Benchmarking is "an organized process for measuring products, services, and practices against external partners to achieve improved performance."[9] It often involves identifying effective practices and seeking to implement those practices to gain the benefits associated with those practices. Using the ARL Index to make changes is a form of *data benchmarking*, which looks at "inputs, outputs and outcomes, and often focuses on quantitative data analysis."[10] Another example of data benchmarking would be using the LibQUAL+ survey to establish specific goals for improvement in relation to other libraries that have taken the survey. The other type of benchmarking is *process benchmarking*, which examines similar processes or functions across organizations and seeks to improve local performance by implementing what are perceived to be best effective practices elsewhere. An example of process benchmarking would be identifying interlibrary loan departments with excellent turnaround times and then examining their workflows to find the best practices that allow them to excel.

Assess Usability

Libraries may contain needed information, but this information is of no value if library users cannot find it or make use of it. Library usability assessments attempt to determine how well library users are able make use of resources and services. Usability testing is commonly employed when testing new computer interfaces or web designs, and it reflects a desire to create user-centered designs based on data about how individuals actually interact with systems. Usability tests typically ask subjects to do predefined tasks while being carefully observed to see how efficiently the subject is able to perform the activity, the approaches taken, and the stumbling blocks the subject encountered. Often the subject is asked to "think aloud" while performing the tasks so that the observer can better understand what the subject is doing. Software such as Morae, developed by TechSmith, can assist usability testing by recording all aspects of the testing, including audio and video recording the subject, capture of the subject's workstation desktop information, and logging all keystrokes and mouse movements made when completing tasks. Usability testing can be useful in determining whether library users can find information about access services on library websites. Can library users find out policies for overdue fines, locate building hours, or figure out how to access course reserve readings? Usability testing can provide these answers.

Although usability testing is most commonly applied to computer testing, its techniques can also be used to assess the usability of physical spaces. For examples, staff members at the University of Chicago have conducted "wayfinding" studies using usability techniques to determine how well library users were able to locate books in the library collections.[11]

Improve Quality or Efficiency

An important reason for conducting assessments in access services is to improve quality control or processing efficiency. Numerous methods or approaches can be applied depending on the service or process being evaluated.

Employees can be tested to ensure that they understand key concepts or policies. For example, some libraries use the LC Easy and Dewey Easy software produced by LibraryTools.com to test whether staff members understand how to place books in correct call number order. Staff can be quizzed to see if they remember protocols for handling emergencies or dealing with security issues.

Another method is periodic quality control testing. Bookstacks managers may spot-check a certain percentage of books that were reshelved recently to see if they were shelved in the correct locations. Staff at Miami University developed a mobile app that can take a photograph of a bookshelf and determine if the books on the shelf are in the proper order.[12] Inventory control programs can help locate missing books or books that have not been checked in properly.

Process mapping can be used to assess and improve the efficiency of access services operations. Process mapping involves creating a flowchart that documents each step and decision involved in performing a task. This flowchart can be used to identify bottlenecks, duplicative or unnecessary steps, and areas of unclear responsibility. Staff at the University of Chicago used process mapping techniques to make their interlibrary loan lending department more efficient.[13] Harvard University library staff have engaged in process mapping exercises to improve access services operations in four areas: (1) materials transportation, (2) local collection management, (3) student coordination, and (4) fine management.[14]

Some libraries have tested the quality of their customer service by using the "secret shopper" method frequently employed in retail operations. The library variant of this method makes use of specially recruited library "users" who are sent to service points specifically so that they can evaluate and report on the service they received. For example, staff at the Arapahoe Library District in Englewood, Colorado used secret shoppers to evaluate the quality of circulation checkout and checkin procedures as well as other aspects of library service.[15] The University of Central Florida has also applied these techniques to evaluate circulation services in an academic setting.[16]

Meet Performance Standards

Assessment is frequently used to determine whether libraries are meeting performance standards. Sometimes standards are set by accrediting bodies or professional associations, such as ACRL's *Standards for Libraries in Higher Education* or the Medical Library Association's "Standards for Hospitals Libraries 2007."[17] The ACRL standards specify that libraries develop performance indicators that focus on outcomes for users and then "conduct assessments that may be quantitative and/or qualitative," "collect evidence from assessments that demonstrate degree of success," and "use assessment data for continuous improvement of library operations."[18] Some of these performance indictors may touch on access services. For example, a performance indicator specifying that students will make increasing use of library resources for their class assignments might draw on circulation data to demonstrate this outcome.

Sometimes consortial agreements include performance standards. One example is the OCLC Research Library Partnership SHARES program, which specifies standards for turnaround times, loan periods, loan policies, delivery methods, and lending fees, among other things.[19] Working groups in SHARES use assessment to determine which libraries in the partnership are "high-performing lenders" and to determine what kinds of materials are not being lent.[20]

Standards internal to a library organization may also be assessed. For example, the Mansueto Library at the University of Chicago promises that materials requested through its automated storage and retrieval system will be available for use within fifteen minutes. Staff at this library use daily performance reports to evaluate how well that performance standard is met.

Determine User Needs

The previous reasons for conducting assessment have focused on evaluating existing services and operations. However, libraries need to not just evaluate how well they are doing but also determine what they should be doing that they are not. To accomplish this, one must assess user needs.

Surveys can be constructed to provide information about user needs. For example, a survey conducted by the University of Washington Libraries listed potential "library services, programs, and initiatives" and asked faculty to indicate which "would be most useful."[21] A 2011 survey conducted by the MIT Libraries asked respondents to suggest "other library services that . . . the MIT Libraries should be offering" and asked them to assign weights to ten potential new services.[22] While surveys can gather feedback from large numbers of people, they do not facilitate the nuanced sharing of ideas, and they do not allow for "back and forth" between the survey administrator and the respondents.

Some libraries create advisory groups composed of representative library users that they can consult when planning changes or new services. The Duke University Libraries have an Undergraduate Advisory

Board, a First-Year Advisory Board, and a Graduate and Professional Advisory Board.[23] The Ohio State University Libraries have a Faculty Advisory Council that "serves as a vehicle through which the Library Director and the Associate and Assistant Directors consult the faculty on matters of planning, policy, and other items of general interest."[24] These groups can be rich sources of information about the needs of library users, but care should be taken not to rely too heavily on these groups since standing groups can become so well informed about the libraries they serve that they cease to be representative of typical library users.

A potentially useful way to gain information about user needs is through individual interviews or by conducting focus groups. Interviews with individuals or groups allow trained facilitators to obtain detailed information about areas of interest, and the format allows the researcher to ask follow-up questions to be sure she understands what is being said. However, care must be taken that the person conducting the interview or focus group is not invested in the issue in order to avoid potentially influencing the outcome. It is also important to recognize that information obtained from a small number of individuals may not be generalizable to the entire population of users. Even so, the surest way to learn about what library users need is to talk with them about those needs.

Improve Work Environment

Although assessment in access services generally should be user-focused, it is also important to understand the needs of staff and improve their work environment. These issues are not unrelated, as satisfied and productive staff members are more likely to provide excellent customer service. The same tools that are used to learn about user needs can also be used with staff, but special care must be taken to ensure that staff members are able to share information without fear of repercussion or job loss. Assessment methods that allow for anonymous feedback are typically best when assessing the organizational climate.

While numerous tools exist to evaluate job satisfaction and organizational climate, the Association of Research Libraries (ARL) markets an organizational climate survey that is specifically designed for libraries. This ClimateQUAL survey was developed from a survey created by the University of Maryland Libraries in partnership with the University of Maryland Industrial and Organizational Psychology program. Among the organizational climate issues addressed by the survey are "diversity, teamwork, learning, and fairness, as well as current managerial practices, and staff attitudes and beliefs."[25] ClimateQUAL is a web-based survey consisting of approximately 150 questions plus a comments box that allows respondents to submit additional free-text information. Because of the sensitivity of the information asked, ARL promises to report information back to institutions "in a way that will not compromise respondent identity."[26] Like LibQUAL+, ClimateQUAL provides opportunities to benchmark results against other institutions that have completed the survey. ARL also asks institutions using ClimateQUAL to commit to "repeat the survey periodically to measure the impact of improvement strategies over time."[27]

Demonstrate Value and Impact

Although libraries have long tracked inputs (like library expenditures and staffing) and outputs (such as use of libraries), only very recently have libraries made significant and sustained efforts to determine the impact or effect that libraries have on those they serve. Libraries are seeking to document outcomes and demonstrate the value of libraries in a context where the continuing relevance of libraries is being questioned as never before.

Two major initiatives seek to assist academic libraries in demonstrating their value: the Association of College and Research Libraries (ACRL) has undertaken a Value of Academic Libraries initiative, and the Association of Research Libraries (ARL) is sponsoring a LibValue project. These efforts have similar goals, but they differ in their approaches and methods.

The ARL LibValue project aims to develop a toolkit for (primarily large research) libraries to use in demonstrating their value to their administrations and donors. In seeking to document value, ARL has gravitated toward return on investment (ROI) measures that aim to quantify the sometimes intangible "good" provided by libraries into economic terms and to compare the calculated economic value of libraries to the actual amount invested in library collections and operations. One way to determine the economic value of libraries is to determine their "contingent value," i.e., the amount that users say they would pay for library services if the library were to no longer provide them. Other measures of value include the actual assessed value of library collections and facilities, the use of libraries as an indicator of value, subjective reports of the value of libraries by users, and the value of libraries in securing research grants for universities. The original genesis of the project was a 2006 study at the University of Illinois at Urbana-Champaign (UIUC) in partnership with Elsevier, which showed a relationship between institutional grant monies received and faculty members' use of library materials. This study was later expanded to include eight institutions in eight different countries. The final phase of the LibValue project was conducted 2009–2012 with funding from the Institute for Museum and Library Services (IMLS) and includes researchers from the University of Tennessee (Knoxville), Syracuse University, Bryant University, UIUC, and ARL. This phase moved beyond grant funding as a measure of value and looked at the economic, environmental, and social good provided by libraries.[28] Ultimately, the LibValue project is meant to provide libraries with models for determining ROI, to give academic libraries a Web-based toolkit for determining their own ROI, and to provide data on ROI studies at three institutions. The LibValue project also maintains an extensive online bibliography of studies related to library return on investment and value. Although the ARL LibValue project has done much to provide libraries with approaches to demonstrating value, some prominent librarians have criticized ROI studies for being reductionist, since they tend to characterize value primarily in economic terms. Stephen Town at the University of York has argued that libraries should seek to find their value in their transcendent values rather than in their mere economic worth, and James G. Neal at Columbia University has sharply criticized simplistic approaches to ROI (while praising the ARL and ACRL efforts for their greater sophistication).[29]

The ACRL Value of Academic Libraries initiative (http://www.acrl. ala.org/value/) differs from the ARL LibValue project by its emphasis on demonstrating the value and impact of libraries on student learning, achievement, and outcomes as well as on faculty teaching and research and institutional quality. The Value of Academic Libraries initiative also focuses on a broader range of academic libraries than the ARL project. The program originated in 2009, when ACRL pointed out the need to investigate library outcomes.[30] In 2010, ACRL produced *The Value of Academic Libraries: A Comprehensive Research Review and Report* prepared by Megan Oakleaf at Syracuse University.[31] This document not only analyzed the professional literature on value and outcomes research, but it also charted a research agenda for library value and outcomes research. It is essentially a manifesto appealing to academic libraries to take seriously their need to show in academically credible ways how they are tangibly and substantially advancing the learning, teaching, and research missions of the universities they serve. ACRL responded to Oakleaf's call to action by holding two national summits on the Value of Academic Libraries in 2011 with representatives from twenty-two institutions of higher learning and fifteen representatives from higher education organizations and accreditation bodies. The resulting white paper from these summits underscored the need for libraries to undertake serious assessment efforts to show how they are contributing to positive outcomes for those they serve.[32] In January 2013, ACRL launched an IMLS-funded effort to recruit seventy-five libraries to participate in a project called Assessment in Action: Academic Libraries and Student Success (AiA).[33] This study, which is intended to run from April 2013 to June 2014, represents ACRL's initial effort to conduct the research it has identified as necessary for demonstrating library outcomes.

Public libraries also have a strong need to demonstrate their value, since they are often subject to budget reductions when communities face tough economic times. There are numerous studies that have been published showing the economic and social value of public libraries, including reports from such diverse libraries as those in New South Wales (Australia), UK public libraries, the St. Louis Public Library, and the Norwegian Public Libraries.[34]

Assessments of library value sometimes have as their goal to document and quantify worth that is intuitively perceived or assumed. The ARL description of the LibValue project asserts that "the value of academic libraries is greater than ever before" and that "return on investment (ROI) measures are a concrete means of demonstrating to institution administrators and public audiences the vital role academic libraries hold within both their respective communities and on a global scale."[35] Such statements risk politicizing assessment by making the goal of assessment to advance a particular agenda. Although ARL has brought academic rigor to its studies, less careful researchers seeking to prove the worth of their libraries might be tempted to suppress or ignore data that does not reinforce perceptions of value. Rather than simply seeking to show value, libraries would do better to honestly evaluate their value and impact on users, determine whether that value is increasing or decreasing, and assess what factors are most successful in improving library outcomes.

Access services can further the efforts to assess library outcomes by studying the value and impact of specific services on library users. What difference does keeping library spaces open twenty-four hours have on student learning and success? To what extent does having a free document delivery service make faculty more effective researchers? Does the expanded access to research materials provided by a consortial borrowing service help graduate students to complete their dissertations more quickly? Do public computers and free Wi-Fi programs in public libraries help low-income library users obtain jobs? Answering these questions will take considerable effort, but they are answerable. Having the answers to these and similar questions will help document the contribution that access services makes to furthering the mission of libraries and help libraries know how to expand their impact on those they serve.

USER INFORMATION, SERVICE, AND PRIVACY

Assessments in access services can provide valuable information about library users. However, in conducting assessments that collect or use information about specific individuals, care must be taken to honor the privacy and confidentiality rights of those studied. The *Code of Ethics of the American Library Association* (ALA) affirms, "We protect each library user's right to privacy and confidentiality with respect to information sought or received and resources consulted, borrowed, acquired or transmitted."[36] ALA calls protecting user privacy and confidentiality a "core value of librarianship."[37] Many states and municipalities have laws protecting the confidentiality of library records, and some user information in academic settings may be protected under the Family Educational Rights and Privacy Act (FERPA).[38]

Most academic institutions have an institutional review board (IRB) that oversees research involving human subjects and seeks to protect those studied from harm. Institutions with an IRB likely require that any assessments involving human subjects be submitted to the IRB for approval. While library assessment activities usually involve minimal risk, the IRB will ensure that effective measures are taken to protect the confidentially of data collected.

Because librarians are serious about protecting user privacy and confidentiality, most libraries choose to not keep detailed information about how individuals use libraries. Given that the government has the power to search library records under the USA PATRIOT Act, it is understandable that libraries are reluctant to keep records that document what individual library users consult.[39] However, not keeping this information prevents libraries from being able to offer the highly tailored and individualized recommendations that companies like Amazon and Barnes & Noble routinely provide their customers by basing suggestions on their previous searches and sales history. Libraries may be throwing away the very information they need to better serve their users. Moreover, Megan Oakleaf has pointed out how important this information can be in researching and documenting the impact libraries have on users. In *The Value of Academic Libraries*, she argued,

> Currently, most libraries do not maintain records on individual users' behavior; consequently, they cannot easily correlate behaviors with the outcomes of those behaviors. For example, they do not track data that would provide evidence that students who engage in more library instruction are more likely to graduate on time, that faculty who use library services are more likely to be tenured, or that student affairs professionals that integrate library services into their work activities are more likely to be promoted.[40]

Oakleaf recommended that libraries "develop systems to collect data on individual library user behavior, while maintaining privacy."[41] Hopefully, as libraries work to document user behaviors and outcomes, best practices will emerge for protecting the confidentiality of user information while still providing librarians with the information they need to improve service to users and document libraries contribute to positive user outcomes.

THE ASSESSMENT CYCLE AND CONTINUOUS IMPROVEMENT

It has become commonplace to speak of assessment as occurring in cycles. While there is no set formula for describing the steps in the assessment cycle, activities generally break down into the following steps:

1. formulating a research question or issue to be studied
2. examining existing data on the topic (e.g., similar studies in the professional literature, locally gathered statistics, and data from previous assessments)
3. determining what new data is needed
4. choosing an appropriate methodology to obtain needed information
5. conducting the assessment
6. analyzing the results
7. reporting the results and making recommendations for changes
8. acting on the results by implementing changes identified
9. testing the effect and effectiveness of changes

The point of speaking of assessment in cycles is to underscore that each assessment should result in specific actions or changes and that these changes should also be assessed to determine their effectiveness, which essentially restarts the assessment cycle. Thus assessments drive further assessments, with the goal being continuous improvement (or more accurately, continual improvement). Seeking to continually improve is a worthy goal for access services, which after all exists to meet the continually changing and evolving needs of library users.

NOTES

1. Robert V. Williams, Kristina McLean, Elizabeth Brinley, and Kristin Rowan, "A Bibliographical Guide to a Chronological Record of Statistics of National Scope on Libraries in the United States," University of South Carolina, School of Library and Information Science website, 2009, http://faculty.libsci.sc.edu/bob/LibraryStatistics/LIBSTAT1829-1899.pdf (Part 1: 1829–1899); http://faculty.libsci.sc.edu/bob/LibraryStatistics/LIBSTAT1900-1999.pdf (Part 2: 1900–1999).

2. C. C. Jewett, "Second Report of the Assistant Secretary of the Smithsonian Institution, Relative to the Library," in *Fourth Annual Report of the Board of Regents of the Smithsonian Institution, to the Senate and House of Representatives, Showing the Operations, Expenditures, and Condition of the Institution during the*

Year 1849, 31st Congress, 1st session, Senate Miscellaneous No. 120 (Washington, DC: 1850), 32–43. http://books.google.com/books?id=pMArAQAAIAAJ&dq=Fo urth+Annual+Report+of+Board+of+Regents+of+Smithsonian+Institution,+to+ the+Senate+and+House+of+Representatives,+Showing+the+Operations,+Expen ditures,+and+Condition+of+the+Institution+during+the+Year+1849

3. Williams et al., "A Bibliographical Guide."

4. Walter, H. Kaiser, "Statistical Trends of Large Public Libraries, 1900-1946," *The Library Quarterly* 18, no. 4 (October 1948): 275-281.

5. Robert E. Molyneux, *The Gerould Statistics, 1907/08–1961/62* (Washington, DC: ARL, 1986).

6. Association of Research Libraries, "Timeline," *ARL Statistics*, accessed February 1, 2013, http://arlstatistics.org/about/timeline.

7. Fred Heath, "Library Assessment: The Way We Have Grown," *Library Quarterly* 81, no. 1 (January 2011): 7-25.

8. CIPFA, "Libraries," *CIPFA Social Search*, accessed February 1, 2013, http://www .cipfasocialresearch.net/libraries/.

9. Joseph R. Matthews, *Measuring for Results: The Dimensions of Public Library Effectiveness* (Westport, CT: Libraries Unlimited, 2004), 80.

10. Peter Brophy, *Measuring Library Performance: Principles and Techniques* (London: Facet, 2006), 150.

11. Nancy Kress, David Larsen, Tod Olson, and Agnes Tatarka, "Wayfinding in the Library: Usability Testing of Physical Spaces," in *Proceedings of the Library Assessment Conference: Building Effective, Sustainable, Practical Assessment (September 25–27, 2006; Charlottesville, Virginia)*, ed. Francine DeFranco, Steve Hiller, Lisa Janicke Hinchliffe, Kristina Justh, Martha Kyrillidou, Jim Self, and Joan Stein (Washington, DC: ARL, 2007), 33–41; David Larsen, and Agnes Tatarka, "Wayfinding Revisited: Improved Techniques for Assessing and Solving Usability Problems in Physical Spaces," in *Proceedings of the 2008 Library Assessment Conference: Building Effective, Sustainable, Practical Assessment (August 4–7, 2008; Seattle, Washington)*, ed. Steve Hiller, Kristina Justh, Martha Kyrillidou, and Jim Self (Washington, DC: ARL, 2009), 65–73.

12. Jennifer Howard, "Shelving Made Easy (or Easier)" *The Wired Campus* (blog), *Chronicle of Higher Education*, April 6, 2011, http://chronicle.com/blogs/ wiredcampus/shelving-made-easy-or-easier/30792.

13. Gretel Stock-Kupperman, "Process Mapping for Organizational Improvement," *MLS E-nnounce* 1, no. 5 (March 21, 2007), Metropolitan Library System, http:// www.mls.lib.il.us/ennounce/2007/01_05/processimprovement.asp.

14. "Call for Participation—Access Services Process Mapping," Harvard Library, May 15, 2012, http://isites.harvard.edu/icb/icb.do?keyword=k77982&pageid=icb.page501475.

15. Marlu Burkamp and Diane E. Virbick, "Through the Eyes of a Secret Shopper: Enhance Service by Borrowing a Popular Business Technique," *American Libraries* 33, no. 10 (November 1, 2002): 56–57.

16. Cynthia M. Kisby and Marcus D. Kilman, "Improving Circulation Services through Staff Involvement," *Journal of Access Services* 5, no. 1–2 (2008): 103–112, doi:10.1080/15367960802198390.

17. *Standards for Libraries in Higher Education* (Chicago: ACRL, October 2011), http://www.ala.org/acrl/standards/standardslibraries; Hospital Libraries Section Standards Committee, "Standards for Hospital Libraries 2007," *Journal of the Medical Library Association* 96, no. 2 (April 2008): 162–169, doi:10.3163/1536-5050.96.2.162.

18. *Standards for Libraries in Higher Education*, 6.

19. "SHARES Interlending, Document Supply and On-Site Procedures," OCLC Research, August 28, 2012, http://www.oclc.org/research/activities/shares/procedures.html.

20. "SHARES Working Groups," OCLC Research, August 28, 2012, http://www.oclc.org/research/activities/shares/workgroups.html.

21. "Triennial Survey," 2010, University of Washington Libraries, https://digital.lib.washington.edu/dspace/bitstream/handle/1773/19828/2010TriFacultyFinalVersionSurveyPRINT.pdf?sequence=1

22. Lisa Horowitz, "MIT Libraries' Assessment Program: MIT Library Surveys," accessed January 21, 2013, http://libguides.mit.edu/loader.php?type=d&id=362810.

23. Aaron Welborn, "Join Our Student Library Advisory Boards," Duke University Libraries blogs, August 27, 2012, http://blogs.library.duke.edu/blog/2012/08/27/join-our-student-library-advisory-boards/.

24. "Faculty Advisory Council," Ohio State University Libraries, November 27, 2012, http://library.osu.edu/about/committees/faculty-advisory-council/.

25. "About ClimateQUAL," ARL, accessed February 1, 2013, http://www.climatequal.org/about.

26. Ibid.

27. "Association of Research Libraries (ARL): Call for Participation in ClimateQUAL: Organizational Climate and Diversity Assessment (OCDA) 2012," June 17, 2010, accessed February 1, 2013, www.arl.org/news/pr/climatequal-17jun10.

shtml (Page now discontinued but available via the Internet Archive at http://web.archive.org/web/20130125234837/http://www.arl.org/news/pr/climatequal-17jun10.shtml).

28. LibValue, "The Lib-Value Project," *LibValue*, accessed February 2, 2013, http://libvalue.cci.utk.edu/content/lib-value-project.

29. J. Stephen Town, "Value, Impact, and the Transcendent Library: Progress and Pressures in Performance Measurement and Evaluation," *Library Quarterly* 81, no. 1 (January 2011): 111–125.; James G. Neal, "Stop the Madness: The Insanity of ROI and the Need for New Qualitative Measures of Academic Library Success" (presentation, ACRL National Conference, Philadelphia, PA, April 2, 2011), http://hdl.handle.net/10022/AC:P:10126.

30. Mary Ellen K. Davis and Lisa Janicke Hincliffe, "Foreword." In *The Value of Academic Libraries: A Comprehensive Research Review and Report*. Chicago: Association of College and Research Libraries, 2010, p.8 .

31. Megan Oakleaf, *The Value of Academic Libraries: A Comprehensive Research Review and Report* (Chicago: ACRL, September 2010), http://www.acrl.ala.org/value/?page_id=21.

32. Karen Brown and Kara J. Malenfant, *Connect, Collaborate, and Communicate: A Report from the Value of Academic Libraries Summits* (Chicago: ACRL, 2012), http://www.ala.org/acrl/sites/ala.org.acrl/files/content/issues/value/val_summit.pdf.

33. Kara Malenfant, "Apply to Be Part of New ACRL 'Assessment in Action' Learning Community," *ACRL Value of Academic Libraries* (blog), January 15, 2013, http://www.acrl.ala.org/value/?p=505.

34. For a discussion of ROI studies in public libraries, see Oakleaf, *Value of Academic Libraries*, 72–82.

35. "The Lib-Value Project," ARL, accessed February 1, 2013, http://libvalue.cci.utk.edu/content/lib-value-project.

36. *Code of Ethics of the American Library Association* (Chicago: ALA, 1939; last amended January 22, 2008), accessed February 2, 2013, http://www.ala.org/advocacy/proethics/codeofethics/codeethics.

37. *Core Values of Librarianship* (Chicago: American Library Association, June 29, 2004), http://www.ala.org/offices/oif/statementspols/corevaluesstatement/corevalues.

38. "State Privacy Laws Regarding Library Records," ALA, accessed February 2, 2013, http://www.ala.org/offices/oif/ifgroups/stateifcchairs/stateifcinaction/stateprivacy; "Family Educational Rights and Privacy Act (FERPA)," US

Department of Education, October 4, 2012, http://www2.ed.gov/policy/gen/guid/fpco/ferpa/index.html.

39. Uniting and Strengthening America by Providing Appropriate Tools Required to Intercept and Obstruct Terrorism (USA PATRIOT ACT) Act of 2001, Pub. L. No. 107-56, 115 Stat. 272 (2001), http://www.gpo.gov/fdsys/pkg/PLAW-107publ56/pdf/PLAW-107publ56.pdf; "The USA Patriot Act in the Library," ALA, accessed February 2, 2013, http://www.ala.org/offices/oif/ifissues/usapatriotactlibrary.

40. Oakleaf, *Value of Academic Libraries*, 12–13.

41. Ibid.

BIBLIOGRAPHY

American Library Association. *Code of Ethics of the American Library Association.* Chicago: American Library Association, 1939; last amended January 22, 2008, accessed February 2, 2013, http://www.ala.org/advocacy/proethics/codeofethics/codeethics.

———. *Core Values of Librarianship.* Chicago: American Library Association, June 29, 2004, accessed February 2, 2013, http://www.ala.org/offices/oif/statementspols/corevaluesstatement/corevalues.

———. "State Privacy Laws Regarding Library Records." American Library Association, accessed February 2, 2013, http://www.ala.org/offices/oif/ifgroups/stateifcchairs/stateifcinaction/stateprivacy.

———. "The USA Patriot Act in the Library." American Library Association, accessed February 2, 2013, http://www.ala.org/offices/oif/ifissues/usapatriotactlibrary.

Association of College and Research Libraries. *Standards for Libraries in Higher Education.* Chicago: Association of College and Research Libraries, October 2011, http://www.ala.org/acrl/standards/standardslibraries.

Association of Research Libraries. "About ClimateQUAL." Accessed February 1, 2013, http://www.climatequal.org/about.

———. "Association of Research Libraries (ARL): Call for Participation in ClimateQUAL: Organizational Climate and Diversity Assessment (OCDA) 2012." Association of Research Libraries, June 17, 2010, accessed February 1, 2013, http://www.arl.org/news/pr/ClimateQual1june11.shtml (Page now discontinued but available via the Internet Archive at http://web.archive.org/web/20130125232225/http://www.arl.org/news/pr/ClimateQual1june11.shtml.).

———. "Timeline." Association of Research Libraries. Accessed February 1, 2013, http://arlstatistics.org/about/timeline.

———. "The Lib-Value Project." Association of Research Libraries, accessed February 1, 2013, http://libvalue.cci.utk.edu/content/lib-value-project.

Brophy, Peter. Measuring *Library Performance: Principles and Techniques*. London: Facet, 2006.

Brown, Karen, and Kara J. Malenfant. *Connect, Collaborate, and Communicate: A Report from the Value of Academic Libraries Summits*. Chicago: Association of College and Research Libraries, 2012, http://www.ala.org/acrl/sites/ala.org.acrl/files/content/issues/value/val_summit.pdf.

Burkamp, Marlu, and Diane E. Virbick. "Through the Eyes of a Secret Shopper: Enhance Service by Borrowing a Popular Business Technique." *American Libraries* 33, no. 10 (November 1, 2002): 56–57.

CIPFA, "Libraries." *CIPFA Social Search*. Accessed February 1, 2013, http://www.cipfasocialresearch.net/libraries/.

Davis, Mary Ellen K., and Lisa Janicke Hinchliffe. "Foreword." In *The Value of Academic Libraries: A Comprehensive Research Review and Report*. Chicago: Association of College and Research Libraries, 2010, 6-9.

Harvard Library. "Call for Participation—Access Services Process Mapping." Harvard Library, May 15, 2012, http://isites.harvard.edu/icb/icb.do?keyword=k77982&pageid=icb.page501475.

Heath, Fred. "Library Assessment: The Way We Have Grown." *Library Quarterly* 81, no. 1 (January 2011): 7–25.

Horowitz, Lisa. "MIT Libraries' Assessment Program: MIT Library Surveys." Accessed January 21, 2013. http://libguides.mit.edu/loader.php?type=d&id=362810. http://libguides.mit.edu/content.php?pid=286364&sid=2355782.

Hospital Libraries Section Standards Committee. "Standards for Hospital Libraries 2007." *Journal of the Medical Library Association* 96, no. 2 (April 2008): 162–169.

Howard, Jennifer. "Shelving Made Easy (or Easier)." *The Wired Campus* (blog), *Chronicle of Higher Education*, April 6, 2011, http://chronicle.com/blogs/wiredcampus/shelving-made-easy-or-easier/30792.

Jewett, C. C. "Second Report of the Assistant Secretary of the Smithsonian Institution, Relative to the Library." In *Fourth Annual Report of Board of Regents of Smithsonian Institution, to the Senate and House of Representatives, Showing the Operations, Expenditures, and Condition of the Institution during the Year 1849*, 32–43. 31st Congress, 1st session, Senate Miscellaneous No. 120, Washington, DC: 1850. Google Books URL: http://books.google.com/books?id=pMArAQAAIAAJ&dq=Fourth+Annual+Report+of+Board+of+Regents+of+Smithsonian+Institution,+to+the+Senate+and+House+of+Representatives,+Showing+the+O

perations,+Expenditures,+and+Condition+of+the+Institution+during+the+Ye
ar+1849.

LibValue. "The Lib-Value Project," *LibValue*. Accessed February 2, 2013, http://libvalue
.cci.utk.edu/content/lib-value-project.

Kaiser, Walter H. "Statistical Trends of Large Public Libraries, 1900-1946." *The Library
Quarterly* 18, no. 4 (October 1948): 275–281.

Kisby, Cynthia M., and Marcus D. Kilman. "Improving Circulation Services through
Staff Involvement." *Journal of Access Services* 5, no. 1–2 (2008): 103–112.

Kress, Nancy, David Larsen, Tod Olson, and Agnes Tatarka. "Wayfinding in the
Library: Usability Testing of Physical Spaces." In *Proceedings of the Library
Assessment Conference: Building Effective, Sustainable, Practical Assessment
(September 25–27, 2006; Charlottesville, Virginia),* edited by Francine DeFranco,
Steve Hiller, Lisa Janicke Hinchliffe, Kristina Justh, Martha Kyrillidou, Jim Self,
and Joan Stein, 33–41. Washington, DC: Association of Research Libraries, 2007.

Larsen, David, and Agnes Tatarka. "Wayfinding Revisited: Improved Techniques for
Assessing and Solving Usability Problems in Physical Spaces." In *Proceedings
of the 2008 Library Assessment Conference: Building Effective, Sustainable,
Practical Assessment (August 4–7, 2008; Seattle, Washington),* edited by Steve
Hiller, Kristina Justh, Martha Kyrillidou, and Jim Self, 65–73. Washington, DC:
Association of Research Libraries, 2009.

Malenfant, Kara. "Apply to Be Part of New ACRL 'Assessment in Action' Learning
Community." *ACRL Value of Academic Libraries* (blog), January 15, 2013, http://
www.acrl.ala.org/value/?p=505.

Matthews, Joseph R. *Measuring for Results: The Dimensions of Public Library
Effectiveness.* Westport, CT: Libraries Unlimited, 2004.

Molyneux, Robert E. *The Gerould Statistics, 1907/08–1961/62.* Washington, DC:
Association of Research Libraries, 1986.

Neal, James G. "Stop the Madness: The Insanity of ROI and the Need for New
Qualitative Measures of Academic Library Success." Presentation, ACRL National
Conference, Philadelphia, PA, April 2, 2011, http://hdl.handle.net/10022/
AC:P:10126.

Oakleaf, Megan. *The Value of Academic Libraries: A Comprehensive Research Review
and Report.* Chicago: Association of College and Research Libraries, September
2010, http://www.acrl.ala.org/value/?page_id=21.

OCLC Research. "SHARES Interlending, Document Supply and On-Site Procedures."
OCLC Research, August 28, 2012, http://www.oclc.org/research/activities/shares/
procedures.html.

OCLC Research. "SHARES Working Groups." OCLC Research, August 28, 2012, http://www.oclc.org/research/activities/shares/workgroups.html.

Ohio State University Libraries. "Faculty Advisory Council." Ohio State University Libraries, November 27, 2012, http://library.osu.edu/about/committees/faculty -advisory-council/.

Stock-Kupperman, Gretel. "Process Mapping for Organizational Improvement." *MLS E-nnounce* 1, no. 5 (March 21, 2007), Metropolitan Library System, http://www .mls.lib.il.us/ennounce/2007/01_05/processimprovement.asp.

Town, J. Stephen. "Value, Impact, and the Transcendent Library: Progress and Pressures in Performance Measurement and Evaluation." *Library Quarterly* 81, no. 1 (January 2011): 111–125.

University of Washington Libraries. "Triennial Survey." University of Washington Libraries, 2010, https://digital.lib.washington.edu/dspace/bitstream/handle/1773/ 19828/2010TriFacultyFinalVersionSurveyPRINT.pdf?sequence=1.

Welborn, Aaron. "Join Our Student Library Advisory Boards." Duke University Libraries blogs, August 27, 2012, http://blogs.library.duke.edu/blog/2012/08/27/ join-our-student-library-advisory-boards/.

Williams, Robert V., Kristina McLean, Elizabeth Brinley, and Kristin Rowan. "A Bibliographical Guide to a Chronological Record of Statistics of National Scope on Libraries in the United States." University of South Carolina, School of Library and Information Science website, 2009. http://faculty.libsci.sc.edu/bob/ LibraryStatistics/LIBSTAT1829-1899.pdf (Part 1: 1829-1899); http://faculty.libsci .sc.edu/bob/LibraryStatistics/LIBSTAT1900-1999.pdf (Part 2: 1900-1999).

The Kept-Up Access Services Professional

Michael J. Krasulski

Assistant Professor of Information Science and Coordinator of Access Services, University of the Sciences, Philadelphia, PA

ACCESS SERVICES is in a continual state of flux, as demonstrated by the various challenges and opportunities presented in this book. As access services departments assume new responsibilities and move into sometimes unfamiliar and exciting territory, it is up to practitioners to prepare themselves and their departments to meet these challenges and to seize these opportunities by monitoring relevant trends and developments. One must think holistically—larger trends in academic librarianship and higher education can have as great an impact as any access services trend. In other words, one must "keep up."[1]

The thought of keeping up with trends and new developments in access services (let alone academic librarianship and higher education) may seem overwhelming. With time constraints and pressing departmental issues, keeping up may seem like an extra burden. Further, every access services department is unique, right? Hardly! Access services departments of all sizes and types confront similar challenges and face similar pressures to solve them. And it is here where keeping up becomes so important. Keeping up enables access services practitioners to tap the collective wisdom of the "invisible college." Academic librarians like to share. Seize upon this expertise, learn from the successes and mistakes of others, and ask questions. This chapter serves as a guide for the access services professional in navigating the professional associations (table 11.1), conferences (table 11.2), journals (table 11.3), e-mail discussion lists (table 11.4), and social media (table 11.5) to remain current with the ever-shifting front lines of access services, academic librarianship, and higher education landscapes.

PROFESSIONAL ASSOCIATIONS

The American Library Association (ALA), founded in 1876, is *the* library association in the United States. No other library association can compare to ALA's scope, resources, and membership. ALA's activities are profoundly influential on the activities of the profession. ALA, encompassing every aspect of American librarianship, is organized into divisions, subdivisions, committees, and roundtables, and it is through these suborganizations that the real work of ALA is accomplished. Three of ALA's divisions—Association of College and Research Libraries (ACRL), the Library Leadership and Management Association (LLAMA), and the Reference and User Services Association (RUSA)—work on issues and concerns relevant to access services practitioners in academic libraries. In a perfect world, one without professional membership dues, the access services practitioner would be best served by joining all three ALA divisions. Joining all three would be an expensive proposition, however, since each division charges an annual membership fee in addition to the requisite ALA membership fee. Not many will have the luxury of time and funding to stay active in each division. Therefore, the access services practitioner must be judicious in choosing to allocate limited resources.

ACRL is the largest division within ALA, with about 12,000 members, which accounts for about 20 percent of the total membership of ALA. ACRL is also the oldest division within ALA, formed in 1938, and the only division with a singular focus on academic librarianship. ACRL is organized into various special interest sections. Members are encouraged, but not required, to join sections. Further, since the early 1950s, ACRL has attempted to bridge the divide between the national association and those in the proverbial trenches through various state and regional chapters. Chapter dues are often separate from dues to the national organization. Each chapter's activities will vary depending on the needs and interests of chapter members. Yet ACRL's influence upon academic libraries is so important that access services practitioners in academic libraries are strongly encouraged to participate in the organization.[2]

LLAMA was established in 1957 to help foster and develop current and future library leaders and administrators as well as to promote effective management practices in all libraries, regardless of type. This ALA division is interested in areas that are central to access services, including library facilities, human resource management, and assessment. LLAMA's System and Services Section (SASS) is concerned primarily with the intersection of technology and library services. SASS, through its Circulation/Access Services Committee and Cooperative/Remote Circulation Committee, as well as related discussion groups, provides the most coverage of all access services topics of any group within the entire ALA organization. For example, the Circulation/Access Services Committee sponsors a forum titled Future and Emerging Access Services Trends (FEAST) at the annual ALA conference, and the Cooperative/Remote Circulation Committee works collaboratively with the RUSA/STARS (see next section). Access services practitioners looking to become involved professionally are encouraged to consider participating in LLAMA.[3]

RUSA is the ALA division concerned with excellence in the delivery of library services. As denoted by the section's name, excellence in reference is central to its work. However, RUSA takes an active interest in the area of resource sharing as evidenced by the recent formation of the Sharing and Transforming Access to Resources Section (STARS). STARS is composed of sixteen committees and task forces devoted to interlibrary loan/document delivery. STARS's power and influence within the document delivery/interlibrary loan areas of access services cannot be overstated. Therefore, STARS is the premier professional organization for anyone interested in the interlibrary loan side of access services. Among the sixteen committees and task forces that compose STARS, the Codes, Guidelines, and Technical Standards Committee is responsible for the maintenance and distribution of the National Interlibrary Loan Code, while the Boucher Award Committee is responsible for naming the Interlibrary Loan Librarian of the Year. Further, STARS is currently collaborating with LLAMA/SASS to promote and enhance resource-sharing methods. STARS even sponsors two interlibrary loan discussion groups.[4]

The International Federation of Library Associations and Institutions (IFLA) was organized in 1927 at an international library conference. Since then, IFLA has provided a global voice to the interests of libraries and librarians while promoting both the delivery of high-quality library services and the value of said library services. Since 1971, IFLA has been based in The Hague, Netherlands, and the National Library of the Netherlands serves as its base of operations. IFLA's activities may seem far removed from the day-to-day operations of the average North American access services department. IFLA's membership is primarily national libraries and professional associations. However, in terms of interlibrary loan and document delivery, the workings of IFLA are worthy of note. IFLA's Section on Document Delivery and Resource Sharing maintains the Model National Interlibrary Loan Code, which serves as a template to codify interlibrary loan best practices at the national level. IFLA also administers an interlibrary loan voucher program, which helps streamline the payment process, especially for international interlibrary loan transactions.[5]

Organization	Circulation/ Reserves	Interlibrary Loan	Academic Librarianship	Higher Education	URL
ALA			✓		http://www.ala.org
ACRL			✓	✓	http://www.acrl.org
LLAMA	✓		✓		http://www.ala.org/llama/
RUSA		✓			http://www.ala.org/rusa/
STARS		✓			http://www.ala.org/rusa/sections/stars
IFLA		✓			http://www.ifla.org

Table 11.1
Professional organizations

CONFERENCES AND MEETINGS

ALA, by virtue of being the oldest and largest librarian professional association in the United States, can rightfully claim that its annual meeting is the largest singular gathering of librarians in the United States. ALA holds two meetings annually. The annual conference is held in the early summer and is a combination programming and meeting conference, while the midwinter meeting is primarily focused on the running of the organization and has traditionally had little to no programming, although this has been changing in recent years. Because of the broad attendance at the ALA annual conference, the programming attempts to have something for everyone. Each division and section hosts some sort of annual program aimed at the needs of that constituency. Programming at the national meeting has been subject to some criticism. For example, one reason the ACRL conference was organized in 1978 was due to the lack of academic library programming at the ALA annual conference.[6]

ACRL has a biennial conference, which is almost entirely programming. The bulk of ACRL's business is conducted at the ALA meetings and online. Programs concerning access services–related issues were slow to appear at the biennial conference. A review of the conference proceedings shows that a limited number of access services issues are covered at the conference and will most likely take the form of poster sessions or roundtable discussions. For this to change, those in access services must make a concerted effort to submit access services–related proposals for consideration. The more access services proposals submitted, the more likely content of interest to access services will appear at the ACRL conferences.

Since access services lacked a singular professional organization, it also lacked a singular access services conference. Karen Glover and Stella Richardson, Georgia Tech University in Atlanta, began the process to organize an access services conference. Frustrated with the lack of coverage of access services issues at both local and national conferences, they surveyed their colleagues and found that the access services community overwhelmingly supported the idea of having a dedicated conference. Thanks to their efforts and the work of others, the inaugural Access Services Conference was held in Atlanta in 2009. The conference was a success, and it was decided the conference should continue annually. Several contributors to this volume, including Karen Glover, are instrumental in the continued success of this conference.[7]

The Owens Library at Northwest Missouri State University in Maryville, Missouri, hosts the annual Brick and Click Symposium. The Brick and Click Symposium started as a one-day regional meeting for Midwestern academic librarians to discuss the convergence of academic libraries as both a physical place (bricks) and an online space (clicks). The first symposium, in 2001, was such a success that the conference has now grown into a national venue for academic librarians.[8]

The interlibrary loan segment of the access services community has an abundance of conference opportunities at the regional level. For example, the Northwest Interlibrary Loan Conference, Colorado Interlibrary Loan Conference, Midwest Interlibrary Loan Conference, and Minitex Interlibrary Loan Conference are all held annually and consider interlibrary loan and document delivery issues for their specific geographic localities. Unfortunately, no such regional meetings exist specifically for those interested in the circulation, stacks, or reserves side of access services. However, in 2001 the access services staff at Columbia University Libraries held the inaugural Ivies+ Access Services Symposium. This annual event brings together access services practitioners from the Ivies+ and invited institutions to discuss common areas of access services and ways to continually improve services. The Access Services Symposium is open only to access services practitioners at Ivies+ institutions.[9]

Vendor user group meetings provide important national and international forums for staying current on the latest trends of the various information management systems, which are vital to running an access services department. These forums also provide users to share, commiserate, or otherwise kvetch about their experiences with the vendor's products. Users will present new and innovative ways their libraries are using the vendor's products. Vendors will announce new products and enhancements through the user group first. Additionally, the user group is the mechanism through which users can petition for suggested enhancements or upgrades. Although it is not practical to mention every access services–related user group, four major vendor user groups are mentioned here. Atlas Systems holds an annual ILLiad user group meeting in Virginia Beach, Virginia. Ex Libris, III (Triple I), Sirsi-Dynix, and any other ILS vendor each has an annual user group meeting, though the meetings will vary in size and scope. For example, Ex Libris's user group, Ex Libris Users of North America (ELUNA), is very active and sponsors regional groups, which also have their own annual meetings, as well as various special interest groups that meet at the national level.[10]

Conference organizers do an excellent job getting the word out about their upcoming events. Calls for proposals appear in the journals, across the various e-mail discussion lists, and sometimes on the blogs. Keeping track of the relevant academic librarianship and access services conferences and meetings can seem dizzying. Douglas Hasty, Head of Access Services and University Librarian, Florida International University, has created the Library Conference Planner (LCP), online at http://lcp .douglashasty.com/, which is a central list of almost every library-related conference worldwide. Hasty has attempted to make the LCP a one-stop for conference planning. Not only are links provided to the various conferences, links are also provided to airlines, hotels, and other relevant sites travelers would find helpful.

Conference/Meeting	Circulation/Reserves	Interlibrary Loan	Academic Librarianship	Higher Education	URL
ALA			✓		http://www.ala.org
ACRL			✓	✓	http://www.acrl.org
Access Services Conference	✓		✓	✓	http://accessservicesconference.org
Brick and Click			✓	✓	http://brickandclick.org
Northwest Interlibrary Loan Conference		✓			http://www.nwill.org
Colorado Interlibrary Loan Conference		✓			http://coill.cvlsites.org/
Midwest Interlibrary Loan Conference		✓			http://www.dalinc.org/midwestill/
Minitex Interlibrary Loan Conference		✓			http://www.minitex.umn.edu/Events/Conferences/
Ex Libris User Group	✓	✓			http://el-una.org
III (Triple I) User Group	✓	✓			http://innovativeusers.org
Sirsi-Dynix User Group	✓	✓			http://www.sirsidynix.com/user-groups
Access Services Symposium	✓	✓			http://www.lib.uchicago.edu/e/iviesplus/

Table 11.2
Conferences and meetings

JOURNALS

The *Journal of Access Services* (*JAS*), founded by Haworth Press in 2002, is the first and only peer-reviewed quarterly journal singularly focused on publishing pure and applied research, as well as effective practices in all areas of access services. The journal features book reviews as well as Fred Smith's digest of interesting or unique discussions from the various access services–related e-mail discussion lists (see below). The early years of *JAS* were a struggle in both content and reliability, as its publication schedule was woefully behind. *JAS* improved greatly after Taylor & Francis acquired the publication in 2007. Under the current editorial direction of Paul Sharpe, Head of Access Services, University of Missouri–St. Louis, *JAS* continues to fulfill its vital role as the only journal dedicated to the exploration and distribution of the latest research in all aspects of access services. Several contributors to this volume currently serve on the *JAS* editorial board.[11]

The *Journal of Interlibrary Loan, Document Delivery, and Electronic Reserve* (*JILL*) is a peer-reviewed quarterly journal focused upon presenting original and applied research as well as effective practices in the areas of interlibrary loan and electronic reserves. *JILL*, under the title of *Journal of Interlibrary Loan and Information Supply,* was established by Haworth Press in 1990. An emphasis on electronic reserves was added in 2005. *JILL* also incorporated the much older *Resource Sharing and Information Networks* in 2009. From the beginning, *JILL* and its antecedent titles published articles of high quality; however, the publication was hampered by a chronically delayed publication schedule. *JILL* was acquired by Taylor & Francis in 2009, and its publication schedule improved greatly. At present, *JILL*, is under the editorial direction of Rebecca Dolan, Gulf Coast University, Fort Myers, Florida.[12]

Interlending and Document Supply (*IDS*) is a peer-reviewed quarterly journal that publishes research on topics of international interest ranging from traditional interlibrary loan to electronic delivery and remote access. Once dubbed "one of the dreariest English serials," *IDS* is now an international powerhouse thanks to a steady stream of manuscript submissions from IFLA's Interlending and Document Supply International Conference. Since the conference's conception in 1987, *IDS* has the right of first refusal to publish any paper accepted for the conference. Access services practitioners looking to globalize their perspective are encouraged to consider *IDS*.[13]

College and Research Libraries (*CRL*) is the peer-reviewed bimonthly journal published by ACRL. Founded in 1939, *CRL* was the first journal dedicated to the needs and interests to librarians in an academic setting and helped create a unique professional identity for academic librarians. *CRL* specializes in publishing empirical research of interest to academic librarians on such topics as open access, information literacy, and citation analysis. Access services practitioners must monitor *CRL* to stay abreast of the latest trends within academic librarianship. *CRL* recently became an open-access publication, and the entire publication run is available on the *CRL* website (historical content added thanks to the University of Illinois–Urbana-Champaign).[14]

Journal of Academic Librarianship (*JAL*) is a peer-reviewed bimonthly journal published by Elsevier. The early to mid-1970s was a time when many academic librarians wanted ACRL to secede from ALA in response to ALA's perceived unresponsiveness to the needs to academic librarians. During this period of flux, in 1975, Richard Dougherty and William Webb founded *JAL* as an independent voice for academic librarians. As the only nonaffiliated journal aimed toward academic librarians, *JAL* enjoyed a privileged place. Up-and-coming leaders in academic librarianship published their research here. In 1999, Elsevier acquired *JAL*, and many in the profession recoiled. Early in its publication history, occasional articles related to access services were printed. However at present the frequency of access services–related articles gracing *JAL*'s pages is low. In a similar fashion to *CRL*, *JAL* is recommended as a place to stay current with academic librarianship trends.[15]

portal: Libraries and the Academy (*Portal*) is a quarterly peer-reviewed journal published by Johns Hopkins University Press. In response to

Elsevier's acquisition of *JAL, Portal* was organized in 2001. *Portal's* early editorial goals were to provide a journal that was affordable (in response to Elsevier's extreme pricing) and to have an editorial board that would mentor promising authors (in response to *CRL's* low acceptance rate). *Portal* has continued to live up to its founding ideals and in the process has become an important vessel for research in academic librarianship during a relatively short period of time.[16]

Chronicle of Higher Education (*CHE*) and *Inside Higher Ed* are two venerable news and information services for the American higher education community. *CHE*, which is available in print and online, and *Inside Higher Ed,* which is a free Web-based site, enables all associated with the academic world to stay better informed of the ever-changing higher education landscape. Library-related issues frequently appear in the *CHE* and *Inside Higher Ed*. Since their inception, *CHE* and *Inside Higher Ed* have proved essential to academic librarians. For example, Steven Bell, ACRL president from 2012 to 2013, suggests that monitoring *CHE* is a daily essential, just "like brushing your teeth or taking a shower before work."[17] Even though *CHE* and *Inside Higher Ed* rarely touch upon the issues directly applicable to access services librarians, monitoring *CHE* and *Inside Higher Ed* is a must to any keeping-up regimen since the issues and ideas discussed in these sources will invariably arise in discussions across campus.

Monitoring these recommended access services– and academic librarianship–related journals can seem daunting. The most efficient way to monitor for new journal content is to utilize a table of contents (TOC) alerting service. At its most basic, a TOC alerting service notifies the user when new journal content is available. Publishers often provide an alerting service that allows users to either sign up for TOC alerts to be e-mailed directly to them or create their own alerts utilizing RSS (Rich Site Summary) technology—and sometimes publishers utilize both. RSS technology makes TOC alerts a "feed" that can be automatically deliverable to a news aggregator such as Feedly or Reeder (Mac users only). When one subscribes to a TOC feed with his or her preferred news aggregator, the moment the new TOC is available; it is delivered to the news aggregator. Therefore, unlike e-mail alerts, which can clutter one's inbox, utilizing RSS technology is ultimately more convenient since it allows all of the alerts to be stored in one central place and can be cloud-based to provide anytime, anywhere access.

Title	Circulation/Reserves	Interlibrary Loan	Academic Librarianship	Higher Education	TOC Alert	RSS Feed	URL
Journal of Access Services	✓	✓			✓	✓	http://www.tandfonline.com/toc/wjas20/current
Journal of Interlibrary Loan, Document Delivery, and Electronic Reserve	✓	✓			✓	✓	http://www.tandfonline.com/toc/wild20/current
Interlending and Document Supply	✓	✓				✓	http://www.emeraldinsight.com/journals.htm?issn=0264-1615
College and Research Libraries			✓		✓	✓	http://crl.acrl.org
Journal of Academic Librarianship			✓		✓	✓	http://www.journals.elsevier.com/the-journal-of-academic-librarianship/
portal: Libraries and the Academy			✓		✓	✓	http://muse.jhu.edu/journals/pla/
Chronicle of Higher Education				✓			http://chronicle.com
Inside Higher Ed				✓	✓		http://www.insidehighered.com

Table 11.3
Journals

E-MAIL DISCUSSION LISTS

E-mail discussion lists have been a part of the academic library landscape since the early 1990s and could be thought of as the first social networks for academic librarians. An e-mail discussion list, or distribution list, (sometimes called by the trademarked term Listserv) is generally dedicated to a specific topic, and those interested in the topic will subscribe. These are places were a user posts a question or idea and the community of subscribers discuss, tackle, and debate the issue at hand. E-mail lists also provide forums for posting conference news and job openings. In the early 2000s, Steve Cohen, librarian blogger, and others began to question the need for e-mail lists in a Web 2.0 environment. Cohen went as far as to suggest, in 2004, that "listservs are dead."[18] Cohen's comments were a tad premature. For example, a 2012 report on attitudes of academic library staff found that over 68 percent of academic librarians relied on e-mail lists as their primary way to keep up with new trends in the field.[19] For the foreseeable future, e-mail discussion lists will continue to be a key source for information exchange in access services and academic librarianship.

The e-mail lists covered in this section represent a broad variety of areas relevant to access services professionals. Be judicious when subscribing to e-mail lists; otherwise, your inbox can become cluttered quickly with e-mail. Unlike RSS technology to manage TOC alerts, technology does not exist to manage or control e-mail list content. Instead, users may want to choose the "digest" option when subscribing to the various lists. The digest option allows users to receive groups of messages in one e-mail at regular intervals, for example once per day or once per week. Alternatively, list subscribers who use e-mail management programs, like MS Outlook, could utilize functions to route e-mail list content into their own folders for later review.Here are some of the most popular:

- Lib-circplus, hosted by Princeton University since 2007, is the only e-mail discussion list dedicated to all aspects of access services. With over 1,200 subscribers, Lib-circplus is a microcosm of the entire access services community. The list provides support and advice to those new to access services as well as the most seasoned access services practitioners. Lib-circplus serves as the default list for LLAMA's SASS Circulation/Access Services Discussion Group.

- ILL-L is the central list to monitor issues related to interlibrary loan, document delivery, and resource sharing. Experienced practitioners and interlibrary loan newbies trade questions, offer advice, and debate best practices in a collegial environment. Over 2,000 interlibrary loan practitioners subscribe to ILL-L, giving participants access to a diverse cross-section of the interlibrary loan community. ILL-L serves two fundamental purposes. First, the list is a place to seek assistance with difficult requests. Daily practitioners seek assistance with deciphering incomplete journal citations or seeking rush-loan requests. Second, the list serves as a default training ground for those new to interlibrary loan. Help is there for the asking, and many new to the interlibrary loan community tap this source to improve their interlibrary loan skills. Any access services practitioner who has any connection to interlibrary loan, document delivery, or resource sharing is advised to subscribe to this list.

- Lib-Ereserves, hosted by Princeton University since 2007, is the only e-mail discussion list dedicated to issues related to e-reserves. Over 700 e-reserves practitioners subscribe to Lib-Ereserves. Because of its unique focus, Lib-Ereserves is among the least active list mentioned here, but it is invaluable to anyone who works in e-reserves or manages those who do.

- COLLIB-L, the official list of ACRL's College Libraries Section (CLS), is among the most active academic librarianship lists. With over 2,700 subscribers, COLLIB-L serves a dual purpose as the official communication method for CLS and as a broad forum for all ideas that would interest the entire academic librarianship community. CLS membership is not required to participate on this list. Besides being the source for current thinking in academic librarianship, COLLIB-L is an excellent source for job postings. Even though access services topics barely register in the discussions (save copyright concerns), COLLIB-L is vital to staying current with the trends in academic librarianship.

- STARS-L is the official e-mail discussion list for the RUSA section of the same name. The over 570 subscribers make this list a rather active information-sharing resource for STARS news and programming as well as the activities of the various committees of the section itself. Participation on STARS-L is recommended for those whose primary responsibility is interlibrary loan.

- OCLC-Sharing-L is the best source for news, information, and updates concerning OCLC's resource-sharing products and services, which are the backbone of most interlibrary loan operations. Although the list is not particularly active, staying current with OCLC news is vital to any interlibrary loan operation. For example, if there is a disruption to OCLC's services, OCLC-Sharing-L and its subscribers will know first.

- DOCDEL-L is an international interlibrary loan and document delivery list hosted by IFLA. DODEL-L serves as a dual purpose as the official list for IFLA's Document Deliver and Resource Sharing Standing Committee and as an open forum for discussing issues involving international document delivery and interlibrary loan. DOCDEL-L is the go-to list for seeking assistance when trying to fill requests for rare or hard-to-find international materials.

Too numerous to mention here specifically are the various e-mail discussion lists sponsored by the individual integrated library system (ILS) user groups. Since the ILS, in many ways, serves as the backbone of any access services department, staying current on the system and having assistance at hand are vital. These lists serve the dual purpose of reporting new product enhancements or updates and being a place to turn when troubleshooting vendor-related problems. These types of lists are the most useful for access services professionals. If your site is having technical issues, it is likely that another site has already solved that problem. Help is shared freely and collegially given. Refer to the user group information from the various vendors to learn more about the discussion lists they have available.

E-mail Discussion List	Circulation/ Reserves	Interlibrary Loan	Academic Librarianship	Higher Education	URL
Lib-Circplus	✓				http://www.lsoft.com/scripts/wl.exe?SL1=lib-circplus&H=princeton.edu
ILL-L		✓			http://listserv.oclc.org/archives/ill-l.html
Lib-Ereserves		✓			http://www.lsoft.com/scripts/wl.exe?SL1=lib-ereserves&H=princeton.edu
Collib-L			✓	✓	http://lists.ala.org/wws/info/collib-l
Stars-L		✓			http://lists.ala.org/wws/info/stars-l
OCLC-Sharing-L		✓			https://www3.oclc.org/app/listserv/sharing/
Docdel-L		✓			http://infoserv.inist.fr/wwsympa.fcgi/info/docdel-l

Table 11.4
E-mail discussion lists

SOCIAL MEDIA

Social media, such as blogs, Twitter, and Facebook, are all important communication modes in our social lives yet have overall made sporadic impact on our professional lives. And this is especially true for access services practitioners. Access services practitioners looking to utilize social media in their keeping-up regimen will be hard pressed to find current outlets for such endeavors. Blogs have made significant inroads to complement, and in some cases even supplement, traditional channels of information sharing among academic librarians. Yet, while there were several interesting and insightful access services blogs in the past, these blogs have gone dormant as their authors move or advance into other areas.

Facebook and Twitter as keeping-up outlets are practically nonexistent. For example, a recent OCLC report found that 83 percent of academic librarians do not use Twitter, and a similar number don't use Facebook to stay abreast of library trends.[20] Facebook and Twitter have the potential to become significant venues for professional discourse. At the moment, however, academic librarianship looks toward traditional venues as well as blogs to keep up with the changing academic librarianship landscape.

Bloggers, generally speaking, can be thought of as information filters. They look for the newest and most interesting, and perhaps controversial, content to digest, contemplate, and analyze. Commentary happens in real time, without any editorial lag time. Further—and this is especially true of librarianship-related blogs—bloggers will experiment with new technologies and provide insights to its usefulness. Readers may already have their favorite library blogs. (*Annoyed Librarian, Free Range Librarian, In the Library with the Lead Pipe,* and *The Ubiquitous Librarian* are rather popular and have a wide following.) Unfortunately, there are a limited number of blogs with a singular focus toward academic librarianship. *ACRLog Information Wants to Be Free,* and *Library Babel Fish* are three excellent academic librarianship blogs that should be monitored regularly. Keeping up with new blog content is easy since blogs utilize

RSS technology (see the Journals section above to learn more about RSS technology and how to utilize it).

ACRLog is the work of various thinkers in academic librarianship including Steven Bell, Temple University, Philadelphia, Pennsylvania, and Barbara Fister, Gustavus Adolphus College, Saint Peter, Minnesota. The blog began in 2005 in response to a perceived void in the blogosphere for one central and all-encompassing voice for academic librarians through a higher education lens. Since then, *ACRLog* has grown into a key source for academic news and information and has attempted to serve as the bridge between academic librarianship and higher education. It should also be noted that both Steven Bell and Barbara Fister have their own academic library blogs. Bell's *From the Bell Tower* is an academic library blog sponsored by *Library Journal*. Fister's *Library Babel Fish* is an academic library technology blog sponsored by *Inside Higher Ed*. One may be inclined to conclude that since both blog for *ACRLog* both authors have little left to say. This is certainly not the case since their work on their own respective blogs complements their work at *ACRLog*.

Information Wants to Be Free (*IWTBF*) is written by Meredith Farkas, Portland State University. *IWTBF* began as a blog focused on intellectual property issues but has grown to address all aspects of academic librarianship, including information literacy instruction, collection development, and technology applications. Since its inception, *IWTBF* has been highly regarded and often cited. It is easy to see why, since Farkas provides erudite postings on whatever topic she chooses to address.

Title	Author/Sponsor	Academic Librarianship	Higher Education	URL
Annoyed Librarian	*Library Journal*	✓		http://lj.libraryjournal.com/blogs/annoyedlibrarian/
Free Range Librarian	K. G. Schneider	✓		http://freerangelibrarian.com
The Ubiquitous Librarian	Brian Mathews	✓	✓	http://chronicle.com/blognetwork/theubiquitouslibrarian/
In the Library with the Lead Pipe	Various	✓		http://www.inthelibrarywiththeleadpipe.org
ACRLog	ACRL	✓	✓	http://acrlog.org
From the Bell Tower	Steven Bell	✓	✓	http://lj.libraryjournal.com/category/opinion/steven-bell/
Library Babel Fish	Barbara Fister	✓	✓	http://www.insidehighered.com/blogs/library-babel-fish
Information Wants to Be Free	Meredith Farkas	✓	✓	http://meredith.wolfwater.com/wordpress/

Table 11.5
Social media

NOTES

1. Steven J. Bell, "To Keep Up, Go Beyond," *College and Research Libraries News* 61, no. 7 (2000): 581–584.

2. American Library Association, "ACRL History," *ACRL*, accessed February 3, 2013, http://www.ala.org/acrl/aboutacrl/history/history.

3. American Library Association, "LLAMA and its History," *LLAMA,* accessed February 3, 2013, http://www.ala.org/llama/about/history/lamaitshistory.

4. American Library Association, "STARS Committees," *RUSA,* accessed February 3, 2013, http://www.ala.org/rusa/sections/stars/section/starscomcharges.

5. International Federation of Library Associations and Institutions, "IFLA's History," accessed February 3, 2013, http://www.ifla.org/history.

6. Michael J. Krasulski and Steven J. Bell, "ACRL's Hall of Fame: An Analysis of Academic/Research Librarian of the Year Award," *portal: Libraries and the Academy* 10, no. 3, 284.

7. Access Services Conference, "The Birth of a New Conference," *Access Services Conference*, accessed February 3, 2013, https://conferences.library.gatech.edu/access/index.php/access/access09/about/editorialPolicies#custom0.

8. Brick and Click, "About Us," *Brick and Click: An Academic Library Symposium*, accessed February 3, 2013, http://www.nwmissouri.edu/library/brickandclick/aboutus.htm.

9. Ivies +, "Ivies Plus Access Services Symposium," *Ivies + Access Services Symposium*, accessed February 3, 2013, http://www.lib.uchicago.edu/e/iviesplus/.

10. Atlas Systems,"2013 ILLiad International Conference," *Atlas Systems Conference*, accessed February 3, 2013, http://www.atlas-sys.com/conference/.

11. Eric Schnell, "Journal of Access Services Jumps the Shark," *The Medium is the Message* (blog), accessed February 3, 2013, http://ericschnell.blogspot.com/2008/11/journal-of-access-services-jumps-shark.html; Paul Sharpe, "Making a Difference: A New Editor Ponders the Road Ahead," *Journal of Access Services* 8, no. 4 (2011), 148.

12. Journal of Interlibrary Loan, Document Delivery, & Electronic Reserve, "Publication History," *Taylor and Francis Online*, accessed February 3, 2013, http://www.tandfonline.com/action/aboutThisJournal?journalCode=wild20#.UZaJFEp8hGM.

13. Graham P. Cornish, "Many Titles, One Editor: a history of Interlending an Document Supply," *Interlending and Document Supply* 29 no. 2 (2001), 88.

14. Association of College and Research Libraries, "Homepage," *College & Research Libraries*, accessed February 3, 2013, http://crl.acrl.org/.

15. Richard M. Dougherty and William H. Webb, "Uncertain Times," *Journal of Academic Librarianship* 1, no. 1, 3. ; Gloriana St. Clair, "Editorial: Consonant Actions," *Journal of Academic Librarianship* 25, no. 1, 170.

16. Gloriana St. Clair, "Through Portal," portal: Libraries and the Academy, 1, no. 1 (2001), v.

17. Steven J. Bell, "Hey, New Academic Librarian: You Need to Keep Up, Too," From The Bell Tower, *Library Journal Academic Newswire*, June 16, 2011, http://www .libraryjournal.com/lj/communityacademiclibraries/891021-419/hey_new_ academic__librarian.html.csp.

18. Steven M. Cohen, "Are Listservs Dead?" *Library Stuff* (blog), accessed February 3, 2013, http://www.librarystuff.net/2005/02/03/are-listservs-dead/.

19. *A Snapshot of Priorities and Perspectives: US Academic Libraries* (Dublin, OH: OCLC, 2012), 4, https://www.oclc.org/content/dam/oclc/reports/us -libraries/214758usb-a-A-Snapshot-of-Priorities-and-Perspectives.pdf.

20. Ibid.

BIBLIOGRAPHY

A Snapshot of Priorities and Perspectives: US Academic Libraries (Dublin, OH: OCLC, 2012), 4, https://www.oclc.org/content/dam/oclc/reports/us-libraries/214758usb -a-A-Snapshot-of-Priorities-and-Perspectives.pdf.

Access Services Conference. "The Birth of a New Conference," *Access Services Conference*, accessed February 3, 2013, https://conferences.library.gatech.edu/ access/index.php/access/access09/about/editorialPolicies#custom0.

American Library Association. "ACRL History," *ACRL*, accessed February 3, 2013, http://www.ala.org/acrl/aboutacrl/history/history.

———. "LLAMA and its History," *LLAMA,* accessed February 3, 2013, http://www.ala .org/llama/about/history/lamaitshistory.

———. "STARS Committees," *RUSA*, accessed February 3, 2013, http://www.ala.org/ rusa/sections/stars/section/starscomcharges.

Association of College and Research Libraries. "Homepage," *College & Research Libraries*, accessed February 3, 2013, http://crl.acrl.org/.

Atlas Systems."2013 ILLiad International Conference," *Atlas Systems Conference*, accessed February 3, 2013, http://www.atlas-sys.com/conference/.

Bell, Steven J. "To Keep Up, Go Beyond," *College and Research Libraries News* 61, no. 7 (2000): 581–584.

———. "Hey, New Academic Librarian: You Need to Keep Up, Too," From The Bell Tower, *Library Journal Academic Newswire,* June 16, 2011, http://www

.libraryjournal.com/lj/communityacademiclibraries/891021-419/hey_new_
academic__librarian.html.csp.

Brick and Click. "About Us," *Brick and Click: An Academic Library Symposium*,
accessed February 3, 2013, http://www.nwmissouri.edu/library/brickandclick/
aboutus.htm.

Cohen, Steven M. "Are Listservs Dead?" *Library Stuff* (blog), accessed February 3,
2013, http://www.librarystuff.net/2005/02/03/are-listservs-dead/.

Graham P. Cornish. "Many Titles, One Editor: a history of Interlending an Document
Supply," *Interlending and Document Supply* 29 no. 2 (2001), 86-92.

Dougherty, Richard M. and Webb, William H. "Uncertain Times," *Journal of Academic
Librarianship* 1, no. 1, 3.

International Federation of Library Associations and Institutions. "IFLA's History,"
accessed February 3, 2013, http://www.ifla.org/history.

Ivies +. "Ivies Plus Access Services Symposium," *Ivies + Access Services Symposium*,
accessed February 3, 2013, http://www.lib.uchicago.edu/e/iviesplus/.

Journal of Interlibrary Loan, Document Delivery, & Electronic Reserve. "Publication
History," *Taylor and Francis Online*, accessed February 3, 2013.

Krasulski, Michael J. and Bell, Steven J. "ACRL's Hall of Fame: An Analysis of
Academic/Research Librarian of the Year Award," *portal: Libraries and the
Academy* 10, no. 3, 283-308.

Schnell, Eric. "Journal of Access Services Jumps the Shark," *The Medium is the Message*
(blog), accessed February 3, 2013, http://ericschnell.blogspot.com/2008/11/
journal-of-access-services-jumps-shark.html.

Sharpe, Paul. "Making a Difference: A New Editor Ponders the Road Ahead," *Journal of
Access Services* 8, no. 4 (2011), 147-149.

St. Clair, Gloriana. "Editorial: Consonant Actions," *Journal of Academic Librarianship*
25, no. 1, 169-170.

———. "Through Portal," portal: Libraries and the Academy, 1, no. 1 (2001), v-vii.

CONCLUSION

Trevor A. Dawes
Associate University Librarian, Washington University in St. Louis

Michael J. Krasulski
Assistant Professor of Information Science and Coordinator of Access Services, University of the Sciences, Philadelphia, PA

THIS VOLUME has brought together, over eleven chapters, a variety of access services practitioners to examine the state of access services in academic libraries at the beginning of the twenty-first century. Each chapter demonstrates the tangible and intangible contributions access services makes daily to the functioning of the academic library. Even experienced academic librarians may be surprised by how much access services operations contribute to the overall success of the academic library and to the college or university. Why? To the uninitiated, access services is *just* circulation desk functions. As this volume has demonstrated, access services has expanded its reach beyond the circulation desk and plays an integral role in connecting students and faculty members to resources and to the spaces in which these resources can be used effectively and efficiently.

As evidenced by the chapters of this volume, the state of access services can be best described as "Like always, like never before," the short-lived tag line to a mid-2000s Saturn automobile commercial. "Like always" because at its very core, access services retains traditional functions such as staffing the circulation desk and shelving books. Concurrently, access services is "like never before" as new service functions are assumed in response to technological and institutional changes. As we have seen in this volume, the introduction of automated shelving and retrieval systems, access to 3-D printers, and self-service laptop kiosks have the potential to enhance the delivery of access services.

As positive as these technological changes are, the literature of academic librarianship seems to suggest we have entered a period of uncertainty. Although this sense of uncertainty predated the great recession of 2008, the recession has only exacerbated fears as the financial markets have had a significantly negative impact on institutional endowments and, therefore, their spending. In our libraries, the effects of the economy have sometimes meant freezing vacant positions, eliminating resources, or the general expectation of doing more with less or, if we dare, even less with less. Despite this climate, we editors are bold to declare that the future of access services in academic libraries is strong. The editors would like to offer up a several directions we see access services in academic libraries moving toward in the next five to ten years.

- **Coupling of circulation and reference desks.** The combination of service desks has already been realized in several libraries as described elsewhere in this volume. We believe libraries will, as they continue to streamline operations and services, have more single service points, which will more than likely be managed by the staff in access services.
- **Increasing importance of interlibrary loan.** The economic recession of 2008 and its effects in the years following led more libraries to actively consider and implement shared-service models. Libraries have always cooperated with each other, but shared services now have a different meaning, and libraries are not only cooperatively purchasing materials, but also sharing staff, though at this point mostly in processing areas. As shared collections become more the norm, resource sharing (ILL) operations will play an even more important role in getting material not physically on site to library users.

- **Decreasing importance of print reserves.** Electronic reserve services have already gained prominence in providing access to course readings. With the advent of massive open online courses (MOOCs) and the continued desire of many library users to access content online, the decline in print reserves is inevitable.

- **Blurring of access services staff duties.** Our contributors have noted the varied duties of access services staff in different organizations. They have also highlighted the need for access services staff—indeed all library staff—to be more collaborative, not only within the library, but with other student support and educational service centers on campus. As access services staff reach out to these other colleagues, it will be increasingly difficult to determine where their "defined" role ends and that of another person begins. This blurring will have serious implications for the skills, knowledge, and abilities of access services staff, as also discussed in this volume.

- **Increasing importance of customer service skills.** It should go without saying that the changing and increasingly important role of access services staff—at the front line of library services— requires excellent customer service skills. Libraries are the universities in which they are located, are being asked for more accountability. Although the library patron is, in some ways, a captive audience, providing excellent customer service will help ensure that he or she will hold the library in high regard and may think of the library as the place to begin future research processes. There have not been studies of the effect of excellent customer services in libraries, but there is well-documented evidence in the business world[1] to suggest the same would be true in libraries.

The greatest risk in predicting the future is predicting the future. Although we are confident these trends will continue, irrespective of the directions in which access services moves over the next five to ten years, it is incumbent upon access services practitioners to stay abreast of the latest trends. As demonstrated in chapter 11, there are numerous ways to stay current. We recommended a combination of e-mail discussion lists, journals, conferences, and blogs and encourage active participation in the profession—post on discussion lists and blogs, publish in journals, and present at conferences. Access services has made great strides since the days of Brown and Bousfield, and it is up to us to continue this tradition.

NOTE

1. Robert Spector and Patrick McCarthy, The Nordstrom Way to Customer Service Excellence: The Handbook for Becoming the "Nordstrom" of Your Industry, 2nd ed. (Hoboken, NJ: John Wiley and Sons, 2012).